BERNARD SHAW

Playwright and Preacher

LEON HUGO

Methuen & Co Ltd
11 New Fetter Lane London EC4

First published in Great Britain in 1971
by Methuen & Co. Ltd
11 New Fetter Lane London EC4
Copyright © 1971 Leon Hugo
Printed in Great Britain
by Cox & Wyman Ltd.,
Fakenham Norfolk

SBN 416 07820 6

CONTENTS

AUTHOR'S ACKNOWLEDGEMENTS

I should like to thank the Society of Authors and the Trustees of the Bernard Shaw Estate for permission to quote from Shaw's writings. I should also like to thank the University of South Africa for, first, monetary assistance, without which this book could not have been written, and, second, permission to publish a work which in its original form was presented as a doctoral thesis at that University under the title of *Didacticism and Drama*.

PREFACE

'What a man. Is he a man !'[1]

Bernard Shaw's career as a writer spanned seventy years.

It was a long stretch and he had a lot to say. He wrote art criticism, music criticism, and drama criticism; essays on Fabian Socialism, Ibsenism, and Wagnerism; to the newspapers constantly and to people incessantly.[2] He wrote scores of articles and reviews on scores of topics, a 500-page guide to Socialism and Capitalism, a 350-page analysis of the Political What's What. He wrote a good deal more than is gathered into the thirty-seven volumes of the Standard Edition of his works, more than bibliographies have yet been able to determine. And he delivered thousands of public speeches. All this may not be a record, but it is prodigious.

Apart from the mass of his writings – and in itself mass is barely a consideration – there is the many-sidedness of his thought. Shaw was probably the most versatile man of ideas of his age, an encyclopaedia of opinion. Was there a matter of moment he did not express an opinion on? One doubts it. Is it possible to define him? Again one doubts it. There really does not seem to be an end to him.

It is, however, a fact that the endlessness of great men provokes in ordinary men an irresistible desire to find an end to them. Ever since the eighteen-nineties ordinary men (and some extraordinary ones) have been pursuing Shaw, determined to cut him down to a size and shape that would fit into their particular scheme of things. The result has been

[1] *Arms and the Man*, Act III, p. 71. (Unless otherwise stated, all references to Shaw's work are to the Standard Edition, London, Constable, 1931 continuing to 1950. My practice throughout is to cite only the title and page in this edition.)

[2] Dan H. Laurence, the editor of *Bernard Shaw: Collected Letters*, estimates conservatively that Shaw must have written some 225,000 letters and post-cards in his life-time. See Introduction to the first volume of the above (1874–1897), London, Reinhardt, 1965, p. xi.

a body of literature on him which may, for all one knows, exceed in size the body of literature by him – a body of literature on Shaw which, whether good, bad, or indifferent, has certainly cut him up, down, across, and slantwise.

And the best that can be said of all this snipping and slicing is that the zealous surgeons have probably found only an end to themselves. They have not found an end to Shaw.

Naturally I must say this. How else am I to justify my joining the throng at Shaw's heels? He has instructed and delighted and fascinated me for several years and the ensuing pages are an acknowledgement of my sense of indebtedness to him. They would have had to be written sooner or later. I would have had to find my end in Shaw.

There is a more far-reaching, though no less personal, justification. One is either for Shaw or against him. I am for him. I know before beginning my appraisal that he is a great man of letters.[1] This is back-to-front logic perhaps, but not necessarily inadmissible, and anyway it is the correct method for propaganda.

The ensuing work *is* propaganda. Let me hasten to add that the trumpet calls are muted and I do not believe myself to be altogether blind to Shaw's faults and shortcomings. It may be asked whether propaganda for the great propagandist is still necessary in the 1970's. I I think it is, partly because I am a South African and hopeful enough to believe that Shavian thought and art could beneficially influence the economic, social, political *and* cultural situation in my country, and partly because in the English-speaking world at large there still seems to be a good deal of antagonism to and ignorance about Shaw.

This second claim may raise eyebrows. Shaw's plays are, after all, more often produced throughout the world than are those of any other twentieth-century playwright. They are possibly more often produced than those of any playwright in any period, except those of Shakespeare. There can surely be no more emphatic an indication of acceptance than this. Yes – as far as the world of the active theatre is concerned.

But not as far as certain elements in the world of academic and jour-

[1] Though not quite as huge as Colin Wilson would have him. 'Shaw . . . seems to me the greatest figure in European literature since Dante,' Wilson says. See his *Religion and the Rebel*, London, Gollancz, 1957, p. 20.

nalistic criticism are concerned. I have two articles before me, reviews of the first volume of Shaw's collected letters, one from *The New York Review of Books*, the other from *The Times Literary Supplement*. Without wishing to press the claims of these papers inordinately, I think we can say that they represent educated opinion to a fair degree on their respective sides of the Atlantic, and both articles, though obviously not establishing a general misconception, make it clear that there is still work to be done in the world. A case for Shaw is still to be made.

In *The New York Review*, Denis Donoghue stylishly instructs his readers on Shaw's style without, it seems, ever having paid his subject the compliment of reading what he himself had to say about the matter. According to Mr Donoghue, Shaw is nearly all style: 'Indeed, one often has the impression that Shaw's conduct was dictated by the immediate requirements of that style: once he had acquired it, it acquired him.' Later he says this about the plays written in the 1890's: 'They don't ring many bells in the age of Beckett.'[1] No one would in all charity wish to deny Mr Donoghue as much cotton wool in his ears as he likes, but what irritates is that he is stuffing cotton wool into the ears of people who could and should derive benefit and pleasure from Shaw's bells, Beckett or no Beckett.

The writer of the article for the *T.L.S.* is a writer racked by high moral seriousness, which at least has the virtue of compelling him to admit that his remarks about Shaw are contentious. They are:

> A certain coarseness of mind will have been observable in some of the quotations already given – a coarseness not necessarily in the sense of vulgarity but in the evident inability to comprehend the nature, or even perhaps the existence, of qualities of feeling beyond Shaw's own notably narrow range.

It is this 'notably narrow range' of perception which makes

> . . . his 'solutions' insufferable, his plays clever but empty, and his philosophy a charade.[2]

Why is there such palpable incomprehension of Shaw, why such

[1] 'Man of Letters', *The New York Review of Books*, New York, 3 February 1966.
[2] 'Life and Letters', *The Times Literary Supplement*, 16 June 1966.

antagonism to him? I try to answer these questions, as they touch on ideational and literary considerations, in the last chapter. Here, by way of a general introduction, I may mention a few other aspects of the matter.

The first thing to mention is that there *are* difficulties about Shaw, and the first difficulty is Shaw himself. At times one may very nearly be forgiven for concluding that Shaw did his utmost to disqualify himself as a man of wisdom. He was his own best publicist and also his worst. He created a public image of himself which was as unlike the real Shaw as Barnum is unlike Bunyan. He created it and he was almost undone by it, simply because a Barnum is more spectacular than a Bunyan. The consequence was that in the eyes of many of his contemporaries he was no more than a kind of literary stunt man, an intellectual acrobat, a clown done up in a motley of nineteenth-century philosophy. The image, visible and distracting, lingers on, and to many people still it is impossible to conceive of Shaw for what he really was: an extraordinarily kindly, modest, and disinterested person; a wholly committed reformer and artist.

Besides this, Shaw wrote too much. Had he not written, say, *Major Barbara* or the Preface to *Back to Methuselah*, the world of art and ideas would be distinctly poorer; had he not written a good deal else the world would have lost nothing. He consumed too many words; he weakened his campaigns by over-emphasis and exhausted them at times with his prolixity. In arguments where clarity of exposition and wit ceaselessly cascaded, he would sometimes achieve obscurity and vitiation of the subject. The super-abundance of his genius glutted the literary market, and as Shaw's favourite economist, Jevons, could have told him, the exchange value of his gifts was fixed by the least useful part of the supply.

Paradoxically, to many people the 'least useful' part of Shaw was the mainspring of his genius, his sense of fun, or as they would probably say, his levity. Although I, at the moment of writing, can recall very few instances in his considered work where his tact and good taste lapse, and although, as I try to show, the laughter of his comedy is never mindless or heartless, the fact is that many people find high spirits and high seriousness totally incompatible. The writer of the article in the *T.L.S.* may be taken as a contemporary case in point, and Florence Farr – a high-minded lady, if there ever was one – earned the following rebuke from Shaw. 'You are wrong' – he told her – 'to scorn farcical comedy. It is by jingling the bell of the jester's cap that I, like Heine, have made people listen to me. All genuinely intellectual work is humorous.'[1] Not all intellectual work is humorous, of course (although some of us may well wish it were), but the issue here is that intellectual work may and can be humorous, humorous work may and can be intellectual. Failure to see this in Shaw is failure to enter into the spirit of his kind of humour.

Another difficulty about Shaw is that he is, partly of historical necessity, his own touchstone. We do not gain a great deal by trying to compare him with Ibsen or Chekhov, because Shaw was too much like Shaw and not sufficiently like the two Continental masters for anything particularly illuminating to emerge; and there is no immediate tradition of good English drama by which to measure him. He stands virtually alone, or so it seems; his drama suddenly emerged, to all appearances *sui generis,* and criticism fell back bewildered by the declamatory accents of the Shavian stage figures, by the dramatic as well as the moral conventions by which these figures behaved. The idiom was not poetic, it was not naturalistic. The convention was not that of sentimental comedy, or of drawing-room comedy, or – strictly speaking of comedy of manners, although there was a little of all this, and more, in the plays. The idiom and convention were those of an original dramatic genius who was consummating a fugitive tradition, that of the nineteenth-century theatre, in a style of play one may best sum up as modern rhetorical comedy of morals.

It was Shavian morality which, fifty years ago, completed the picture of critical incomprehension. What, to Shaw, was morality? Anything that is in accord with established manners and customs. Immorality was the obverse: 'Whatever is contrary to established manners and customs. . . .'[2] By this definition private ownership, inequality of incomes,

---

[1] *Florence Farr, Bernard Shaw, W. B. Yeats: Letters,* ed. Clifford Bax, London, Home and Van Thal, 1946, p. 7.
[2] 'The Rejected Statement', Part I, the Preface to *The Shewing-Up of Blanco Posnet,* p. 375.

Capitalism, were moral; state ownership, equality of incomes, Socialism, were immoral. Crosstianity was moral; Shavian Christianity was immoral. Natural selection was moral; Creative Evolution was immoral. The womanly woman, the heroic soldier, romantic love, were moral; the unwomanly woman, the un-heroic soldier, unromantic love, were immoral. Max Beerbohm's drawing of the 'dear fellow' standing on his head summed up the general attitude to Shaw's projection of 'morality' and 'immorality', and the Prince of Wales's well-known verdict that the fellow was mad 'of course' gave, so to speak, royal consent to public perplexity.

Today we may be much less disposed to see Shaw upside-down – his 'immoralities' have largely become our 'moralities' – and yet one may be forgiven for wondering if *every* Shavian immorality has yet been accepted even in theory. Private wealth and public poverty are still very moral, so moral that they are the cornerstones of existence in the 'free world'. Liberal democracy (manipulated by private wealth) muddles through from one crisis to the next, sustaining itself by catchphrases, demagogy, opinion polls – by that whopping morality, 'the will of the people'. At least, had Shaw been alive today he would certainly have observed the economic and governmental scenes in this light. And not only these scenes: had he been alive today, he would have observed how half-baked literacy, Hollywood, and sheer human incompetence had baffled his campaigns – and he would have felt compelled to write at least a dozen more 'immoral' plays.

On balance, it is not Shaw's fault but ours that he has not yet fully won his way. What then should be done to correct our fault? The answer is obvious: get to know Shaw better, get to know him as an economist, a politician, a theologian, of course, but more important, as that by which his name is becoming increasingly known – a dramatist.

This book is an attempt at getting to know, understand, and appreciate him in this way, which is to say that it is an attempt at relating Shaw the teacher to Shaw the dramatist. The implication in this is the crux of the subject, for he claimed that his plays were nothing if not didactic. Accordingly, the first part of the appraisal is devoted to following up what seems the mainstream of Shaw's philosophy. The discovery of a mainstream, let alone following it, is no easy task in a man whose thought has been described as a 'chaos of clear ideas'.[1] There is no articulated system, but there is cohesion and a progression of ideas. This I try to indicate – at the cost of a good deal of important Shavian doctrine, especially Shaw's thoughts on the family and the professional scoundrelism of science. But omissions such as these are dictated by the plays selected for discussion, and both the family and science are highlighted in comparatively minor plays, which do not fit into my scheme.

A discussion of Shaw's theory of drama bridges the section on the philosopher and the section on the playwright.

The second and major part of the book is primarily an assessment of Shaw the dramatist. What is his convention, how may we define his idiom? What is Shavian comedy, what is Shavian tragedy? What is his method of characterization, how does he present conflict? Above all, what cumulative impact is there in the plays, what imaginative response do they call on us to give? These are among my general considerations.

Fifty-two plays are too many to discuss without running the risk of wearisome repetition; thirty plays are also too many. Consequently I discuss comparatively few at length, and even these are by no means exhaustively analysed. Rather, I approach each selected play from what strikes me as an interesting side and, whilst evaluating each play on its own merits, try as well in the work as a whole to create (with as little repetition as possible) a cumulative portrait of Shaw's drama.

[1] Desmond MacCarthy, *Shaw*, London, MacGibbon and Kee, 1951, p. vii.

PART I: PHILOSOPHER

Chapter One

SOCIAL AND POLITICAL ECONOMY

*I 'Property, said Proudhon, is theft. This
is the only perfect truism that has been
uttered on the subject.'*[1]

1

Shaw's life – as far as we need at present be concerned – began on an
evening in 1884. Quite by chance he attended a meeting at which an
American economist, Henry George, spoke. The revival of Socialism
in England was already under way, but Shaw had not yet been affected.
He listened to George and was awakened; he read Karl Marx and was
inspired. He joined the newly formed Fabian Society and persuaded
his friend, Sidney Webb, to join as well. As he tells us, he found his
purpose in life, his faith.[2]

He also (in 1885) began writing his first play – but this was inci-
dental to his Socialist activities: meetings, debates, discussion, study,
took up most of his time. Facts were what the Fabians wanted and
Shaw pursued facts with the single-mindedness and diligence that were
to characterize his whole career. Economics was his subject, not politics. The Fabians were laggard in turning their attention to politics,
and it was not until the Anglo-Boer War that they perceived the
national scene to contain elements which a more thorough knowledge
of government would have made comprehensible. But in the beginning
it was economics, and the more fully to teach this to himself Shaw
lectured every Sunday. He relates: '. . . it was not until I could deliver
separate lectures, without notes, on Rent, Interest, Profits, Wages,
Toryism, Liberalism, Socialism, Communism, Anarchism, Trade
Unionism, Co-operation, Democracy, the Division of Society into

---

[1] 'Maxims for Revolutionists', *Man and Superman*, p. 216.
[2] See 'Biographers' Blunders Corrected', *Sixteen Self Sketches*, p. 109.

Classes, and the Suitability of Human Nature to Systems of Just Distribution, that I was able to handle Social Democracy as it must be handled before it can be preached in such a way as to present it to every sort of man from his own particular point of view.'[1]

The list extends well beyond economics, to realms on which the casual may doubt that any one, and not only Shaw, can speak with certainty. But the Marxist certainty – the Fabian certainty – was that economics was the basis of all social, and individual, life: thus not merely the Suitability of Human Nature to Systems of Just Distribution, but politics, ethics, religion – everything was formed and informed by the distribution of money.[2] Even, as Shaw was to claim, his own drama. 'Indeed', he wrote to his authorized biographer, Henderson, 'in all the plays my economic studies have played as important a part as a knowledge of anatomy does in the works of Michael Angelo.'[3]

When asked to pay tribute to Shaw, economists, both practising and academic, do not seem inclined to regard their subject as a great name in their fraternity.[4] This does not matter at all, for Shaw never tried to be, and in view of his eclecticism never could have been, a serious economist pure and simple. This or that theory was not important in itself, so long as it served the reformatory aims of Socialism, and the fact that the Fabians repudiated Marx in several respects and supported Ricardo in one or two respects and clove to Jevons in other respects is fortuitous; for as Shaw wrote to Henderson, '. . . if you steal a turnip the theory of the turnip's value does not affect the social and political

---

[1] 'The Fabian Society: What it has done and how it has done it', *Essays in Fabian Socialism*, p. 144.

[2] Characteristically, however, Shaw insisted that 'the materialistic basis of history can be over done'. See 'Modern Religion I', *The Religious Speeches of Bernard Shaw*, ed. Warren Sylvester Smith, Pennsylvania, Pennsylvania State University Press, 1963, p. 43.

[3] The letter dated June 30, 1904. Quoted in Archibald Henderson's *George Bernard Shaw: Man of the Century*. New York, Appleton-Century-Crofts, 1956, p. xvii. (This volume hereafter referred to as *G.B.S.: Man of the Century*.)

[4] See, for example, Maurice Dobb's 'Bernard Shaw and Economics', *G.B.S. 90: Aspects of Bernard Shaw's Life and Work*, ed. S. Winsten, London, Hutchinson, 1946, pp. 131–139. Also Hugh Dalton's 'Shaw as Economist and Politician', *Shaw and Society: an Anthology and a Symposium*, ed. C. E. M. Joad, London, Odhams, n.d., p. 252.

aspect of the transaction.'[1] It was the social and political aspect of the national theft of turnips that interested the Fabians.

For all this, they were the sons of nineteenth-century scientism, and were determined to give their Socialism the basis of a respectable economic theory. This Shaw did for the Society in 1889, in his treatise 'The Economic Basis of Socialism'. 'Let us, in the manner of Political Economics', he says, 'trace the effects of settling a country by private property with undisturbed law and order . . .';[2] which he does, in the form of a parable. It may be remarked in passing that his method is distinctly not in the manner of Political Economists, if by the term we understand the verbal obscurity which disfigures so much modern work on the subject. Shaw's prose is here not as supple and elastic as it will become, but it is as lucid as it will ever be.

His parable of the settlers proceeds. Soon the original settlers discover that some later settlers are willing to work their land for them, which enables them (the original settlers) to retire on unearned incomes. Immediately three things are established: Ricardo's principle of economic rent, the county family – and the opportunity for Shaw to give vent to moral indignation.

Eventually all land is taken, a lot of it is paying rent to as many as three landlords, people still come, the population grows. Economic rent gives way to 'rent' which is controlled by – is in fact subject to – 'the landholder's eagerness to be idle on the one hand, and the proletarian's need of subsistence on the other.'[3] Further moral indignation, for Socialism was and always had been an attack on idleness,[4] and the propertied class was being very idle while its land and other possessions did its work for it.

Finally there are people who are utterly propertyless – except that they own their bodies; and since generally speaking it is preferable, if not better, to be a bondsman and eat than a free man and starve, they 'rent' out their bodies to the highest bidder. 'The economic

---

[1] Henderson, *G.B.S.: Man of the Century*, p. 276.
[2] In *Fabian Essays (1889)*; from *Essays in Fabian Socialism*, p. 4.
[3] Ibid. p. 10.
[4] Shaw's Preface to the 1908 edition of *Fabian Essays*: 'Fabian Essays Twenty Years Later', *Essays in Fabian Socialism*, p. 292.

change is merely formal: the moral change is enormous',[1] is Shaw's summing-up.

The parable ends at this point, having come abreast of Victorian England. What follows in the essay is an analysis of the forces that determine the nature of such phenomena as Exchange Value, Wages, and so on. I do not propose to go into these theories because – as theories – they are not strictly germane to the argument and also because they no longer carry much weight in economics. It will be enough to say that from Ricardo's theory of economic rent Shaw develops Jevons's theory of value, which is in essence that the value of a commodity is fixed, not by the amount of labour put into it, but by its utility; further, that the 'exchange value of the least useful part of the supply fixes the exchange value of all the rest.'[2] This is the theory, and people are able to work within its terms to odious ends:

> Individuals are constantly trying to decrease supply for their own advantage. Gigantic conspiracies have been entered into to forestall the world's wheat and cotton harvests, so as to force their value to the highest possible point. Cargoes of East Indian spices have been destroyed by the Dutch, as cargoes of fish are now destroyed in the Thames, to maintain prices by limiting supply. All rings, trusts, corners, combinations, monopolies, and trade secrets have the same object. Production and the development of the social instincts are alike hindered by each man's consciousness that the more he stints the community the more he benefits himself. . . .[3]

The products of society as a whole – for the Dutch spice trade, the British fishing fleets, and anything and everything else on such scales are demonstrably the results of communal effort – are regarded as the 'rent' of the 'man of property', who may be as wasteful as he likes. Small wonder then that Tanner, that ill-fated Don Juan, repeated Proudhon's dictum with such emphasis: 'Property is theft';[4] and no wonder the Fabians were convinced that a system which encouraged

---

[1] 'The Economic Basis of Socialism', *Essays in Fabian Socialism*, p. 12.
[2] Ibid. p. 14.
[3] Ibid. pp. 17–18.
[4] 'Maxims for Revolutionists', *Man and Superman*, p. 216.

practices so inimical to general welfare should be changed. Common-sense, to say nothing of a sense of justice, cried out for a more equitable system of distribution; and what the community produced should be distributed among the community. This was Socialism.

The beauty of Jevons's principle to the Fabians was that it gave them the rationale they wanted whilst it allowed for the play of human resourcefulness among several possibilities. Shaw soon perceived this. As we shall note, he came to invoke the 'Jevonian spirit', if not the Jevonian letter, with great readiness.

*   *   *

Technically 'The Economic Basis of Socialism' has dated, yet the essay remains interesting, partly because of its historical importance, mainly because it is imbued with a strong moral tone, which formed an essential part of the Fabian campaign. Moral indignation is of course a potent weapon of propaganda, always provided the indignation emanates from popular predispositions. Of this the Fabians were fully aware. They were certainly not less aware that no scientific principle ever began or maintained a revolution, whereas the moral sense could topple a dynasty in a fortnight with barely a cue from scientific principle. They had their science – their Ricardian and Jevonian laws; they had their facts, gathered, annotated, stored by that monumentally industrious couple, Sidney and Beatrice Webb. They had enough and more to satisfy the rational mind that Capitalism induced inefficiency, waste, and qualitative bankruptcy. And this was not enough. Even although by definition of their method of work 'scientific theory (was) ruthlessly indifferent to the moral sense',[1] they had equally to present an ethic. So, in a manner which echoes Marx, we have their appeal to the sense of injustice (for the benefit of the under-privileged), to the sense of justice (for the shaming of the privileged), to democratic sentiment; and so their avowal through Shaw that the cause of Socialism was 'not only unobjectionable, but sacredly imperative':[2] a

[1] Shaw, *The Illusions of Socialism*. Reprinted by the Shaw Society, London, as Shavian Tract No. 4, November 1956, p. 17.
[2] 'The Transition to Social Democracy', *Essays in Fabian Socialism*, p. 40.

statement which genuflects almost simultaneously to 'maximum utility' and a more popular deity.

This is only a fraction of the picture: no one with the slightest knowledge of the Webbs, Shaw, and other Fabians could imagine that they used morality as a tap to be turned on whenever the occasion seemed to call for an emotional drenching. They were not sufficiently cynical; anyway, they fully believed in their moral rightness. In his essay *The Illusions of Socialism*, which is a brilliant rationalist diagnosis of the 'necessary illusions' required to bring people to act as one would want them to act, Shaw states a case that in the end leaves the essential irrationalism of illusions and their underlying morality none the worse for having been aired; for Shaw shows himself to be standing firmly in both camps, in one a hard-headed rationalist to whom the only truth is in the notebooks of the Webbs, in the other camp the supremely illusioned reformer. He has, one might say, no illusions about illusions, but he has his illusions, and he has the intellect to perceive that no one – not the Webbs, not even Bernard Shaw – will do anything worthwhile without these.

> Take from the activity of mankind (he says) that part of it which consists in the pursuit of illusions, and you take out the world's mainspring. Do not suppose, either, that the pursuit of illusions is the vain pursuit of nothing: on the contrary there can no more be an illusion without a reality than a shadow without an object.[1]

I shall inquire no further into the Fabian (and Shavian) 'mainspring': to do so would be merely to embark on unhelpful speculation. That Shaw could see his illusions rather more clearly than most people can see theirs is no reduction of their validity; it is in fact indicative of that quality of his which, if it is paradoxical, most definitely stamps him as a great humanitarian and artist: that quality of mind which synthesized apparently irreconcilable opposites.

Shaw's moral convictions inform and affirm all his writing. Whether they were illusions or not, whether they were relative or absolute, hardly seems to matter when, fifteen years after 'The Economic Basis of

[1] *The Illusions of Socialism*, p. 1.

Socialism', he elevates his role as a reformer to an unchallengeably noble mystique:

> This is the true joy in life, the being used for a purpose recognized by yourself as a mighty one; the being thoroughly worn out before you are thrown on the scrap heap; the being a force of Nature instead of a feverish selfish little clod of ailments and grievances complaining that the world will not devote itself to making you happy. And also the only real tragedy in life is the being used by personally minded men for purposes which you recognize to be base. All the rest is at worst mere misfortune or mortality: this alone is misery, slavery, hell on earth. . . .'[1]

But was Shaw always used for a 'mighty' purpose? Was his ethic always in tune with 'Nature'? We shall have to keep these questions before us, and since Shaw spent his life attacking 'respectability', 'morality', and 'religion', it is clear that intriguing prospects lie ahead.

*   *   *

'Responsibility and Revolution' was not a Fabian slogan but it could well have been. Their programme of reform was extraordinarily sober. Less temperate Socialist associates, whose thirst for change had to be satisfied with stronger stuff than the communization of gas and water, were driven to despair. Gas and water were not the only examples of Fabian moderation. They did not pretend that Socialism would be a panacea of all ills, and they believed in compromise, in the permeation of their ideas among all organizations, in the 'inevitability of gradual-ness', an unfortunately woolly phrase which entered the lists fairly late in the day. What Sidney Webb (who coined the phrase) meant was simply that social and political change would have to come slowly because social and political institutions could not be radically changed before the people who lived by them were themselves taught to desire a change. This, the Fabians were optimistic enough to believe, would happen in a generation or two.

But 'the inevitability of gradualness' has somewhat different

[1] 'Epistle Dedicatory': the Preface to *Man and Superman*, p. xxxi.

connotations, which is probably why Beatrice Webb repudiated it eventually. It suggests that the Fabians, like the Marxists, saw themselves as the elected instruments of an inexorable historical process. This is not so. Apocalyptic visions are minimal in Fabian writing. It is very much to be doubted if they ever sang the Internationale. They certainly never exhorted the workers of the world to unite. For one thing, they knew that the workers of the world were highly unlikely to unite, because many of them did well under the prevailing system: Capitalism corrupted all strata of society. And for another, they opposed the catastrophic change which is implicit in the 'class-war' concept. Their reason was purely practical: assuming a sanguinary revolution on Monday afternoon they saw that the country would not be ready for Socialism on Tuesday morning.[1]

According to Henderson, Shaw had at first to be dissuaded by his fellow Fabians from aligning himself with the bloodbath school of revolutionist thought,[2] although once he had been brought to realize that Socialism could not be put into working order in a fortnight (his original modest estimate), he supported the policy of gradual, constitutional change with every appearance of personal conviction. He confidently asserted the Fabian view that the 'consummation of Democracy', that is of Social Democracy, would be automatically achieved with 'manhood suffrage, abolition of all property disqualifications, abolition of the House of Lords, public payment of candidature expenses, public payment of representatives, and annual elections'.[3] This list of anticipated changes was and still is not entirely realistic, and the suspicion that Shaw perceived it to be occasionally divorced from reality – in one eminent respect especially – is not groundless. He concludes his paper, 'The Transition to Social Democracy', with this paragraph:

> Let me, in conclusion, disavow all admiration for this inevitable, but sordid, slow, reluctant, cowardly path to justice. I venture to claim your respect for those enthusiasts who still refuse to believe

[1] See 'The Transition to Social Democracy', *Essays in Fabian Socialism*, p. 42.
[2] Henderson, *G.B.S.: Man of the Century*, p. 231.
[3] 'The Transition to Social Democracy', *Essays in Fabian Socialism*, p. 47.

that millions of their fellow creatures must be left to sweat and
suffer in hopeless toil and degradation, whilst parliaments and
vestries grudgingly muddle and grope towards paltry instalments of
betterment. The right is so clear, the wrong so intolerable, the gospel
so convincing, that it seems to them that it *must* be possible to enlist
the whole body of workers – soldiers, policemen, and all – under the
banner of brotherhood and equality; and at one great stroke to set
Justice on her rightful throne. Unfortunately, such an army of light
is no more to be gathered from the human product of nineteenth-
century civilization than grapes are to be gathered from thistles. But
if we feel glad of that impossibility; if we feel relieved that the change
is to be slow enough to avert personal risk to ourselves; if we feel
anything less than acute disappointment and bitter humiliation at the
discovery that there is yet between us and the promised land a wilder-
ness in which many must perish miserably of want and despair: then I
submit to you that our institutions have corrupted us to the most
dastardly degree of selfishness. The Socialists need not be ashamed
of beginning as they did by proposing militant organization of the
working classes and general insurrection. The proposal proved
impracticable; and it has now been abandoned – not without some
outspoken regrets – by English Socialists. But it still remains as the
only finally possible alternative to the Social Democratic program
which I have sketched today.[1]

One should normally be careful about separating Shaw's thought from
Fabian thought; nevertheless, these words have a militancy more in
keeping with Shaw's pronouncements in the nineteen-thirties and
'forties than with the temperament of the Webbs. Not that the Webbs,
or other Fabians, were irrevocably committed against catastrophic
revolution: one has merely to remember the final article of the Fabian
Manifesto to know that they would have been prepared to think
otherwise.[2] Nor was it only that Shaw was naturally more pugnacious.

[1] Ibid. pp. 60–1.
[2] 'That we had rather face a Civil War than such another century of suffering as
the present one has been.' The whole Manifesto quoted by Henderson, *G.B.S.:
Man of the Century*, p. 221. (See, however, Pease's comments on this: *The History
of the Fabian Society*, London, Cass, 1963, p. 43.)

But he maintains his reservations on the effectualness of gradual change because he has his reservations on the teachability of people and because (this is where 'the true Jevonian spirit'[1] becomes evident) he always looked for the most useful way of getting things done and accordingly foreswore principles, even the principle of gradual change, on principle.

He was, as he cheerfully declared, an unprincipled Socialist; so unprincipled that Socialism meant only certain definite economic measures which he wished to see taken,[2] so unprincipled, moreover, that he could say:

> I myself am firmly persuaded that Socialism will not prove worth carrying out in its integrity – that long before it has reached every corner of the political and industrial organization, it will have so completely relieved the pressure to which it owes its force that it will recede before the next great movement in social development, leaving relics of untouched Individualist Liberalism in all directions among the relics of feudalism which Liberalism itself has left.[3]

This attitude is acutely sensible, of course; consequently it tended to disconcert (and still disconcerts) a lot of people who see it as inconsistency, contrariness, or mere indecisiveness playing the clown with the time-hallowed absolutes of 'firmness', 'principle', and 'honour' – with those attitudes which, according to Shaw, had made English morality the preposterous thing it was. It was hardly surprising therefore that stage characters like Bluntschli and Caesar were incomprehensible at first, and occasionally still are. For if it is not the whole explanation it is a substantial part of it that Jevons's theory of economic utility ends on the stage in men whose flexibility of outlook makes them the new heroes in a world still paying homage to the old, inflexible heroes.

This journey of the theory of 'maximum utility' from the pages of abstract economics to the theatre, is a curious and, on the face of it, an implausible one. All the same, it is the journey Shaw took.

---

[1] *The Illusions of Socialism*, p. 22.
[2] See 'The Impossibilities of Anarchism', *Essays in Fabian Socialism*, p. 65.
[3] *The Illusions of Socialism*, p. 19.

Was he therefore – are his Bluntschlis and his Caesars therefore – pragmatists? The answer is yes, but a heavily qualified yes. The golden rule that there are no golden rules,[1] not even for Socialism, had finally to concede a golden rule. In an address delivered in 1919, Shaw said of 'pragmatic religion':

> ... it is not any use when you come to governing a great state. There it is no use saying that the thing that works is right, because things that you know to be abominably wrong, and that you cannot pretend to be made right by any sort of working, can nevertheless be made to work politically if only you will put sufficient brute force into making them work. ... Accordingly, when you come to governing a country, then there is no use in talking pragmatism. You have to come back to your old Platonic ideals. ... In governing a country you have to arrive at the best conclusion you can, the conclusion that certain institutions are in harmony with what we call the Platonic ideal of right and truth, and trust your instinct more or less to guide you. ...[2]

Pragmatic Platonism is hardly an accredited philosophic system; yet it is Shaw's.

2

Shaw resigned from the Executive of the Fabian Society in 1911. The ostensible reason for his resignation was to make way for younger men, the apparent reason was that the Fabians were being pushed into the background and sedulously ignored by the child of their endeavours, the Labour Party. The real reason may have been that Shaw's thinking had progressed well beyond the mechanics of reform and the strict probabilities which were the business of Fabianism to maintain. He remained a Fabian Socialist, needless to say, but a Fabian with independent views; and almost immediately he announced that equal incomes for all was the logical and necessary conclusion of socialistic enterprise.

[1] 'Maxims for Revolutionists', *Man and Superman*, p. 211.
[2] 'Modern Religion II', *The Religious Speeches of Bernard Shaw*, pp. 64, 65.

The idea is not original. An American novelist, Bellamy, had propounded it in 1894,[1] and it is to be questioned whether Bellamy had originated the idea or transposed some early Utopian system such as More's into dollars and cents. The scheme for equal incomes is evolutionary rather than revolutionary, a fact which makes Shaw's contribution to it no less remarkable. His first public utterance on the matter was in 1913 in an address, *The Case for Equality;*[2] then some fifteen years later, in *The Intelligent Woman's Guide to Socialism and Capitalism*, he re-proclaimed the idea, with such eloquence and expository mastery that one person at least was moved to describe the book as 'the world's most valuable next to the Bible'.[3]

A summary trial of six possible methods of distribution begins the argument – not the most convincing section. But once Shaw has cleared the way for the seventh method – Socialism – he soon develops his theme to take in most facets of modern life. There are fallacies in the argument, no doubt; there is a tendency to oversimplify; there will always be debate on the soundness of the central theme. And yet the verdict must be allowed that *The Intelligent Woman's Guide* is a remarkably sagacious work and possibly unrivalled in this century as a diagnostic of society.

We are all sufficiently indoctrinated in the faith that unequal incomes are right, proper, and inevitable, to be arrested by the plan for equal incomes. And not the least arresting aspect is the skill with which Shaw anticipates possible objections to his plan, discusses them, and demolishes them with an air of irrefutable finality. A doubter may say: Some jobs are surely less meritorious than others – compare a labourer's work to a king's, for example. Shaw answers: It is impossible to determine merit – or achievement, or dignity, or individual quality of any sort – as it is impossible to determine the difference between the work done by a labourer and by a king in terms of so much money a week; and the labourer and the king need exactly the same allowance of food to keep

[1] See Henderson, *G.B.S.: Man of the Century*, pp. 239–40.
[2] Delivered before the National Liberal Club: Political and Economic Circle, 1 May 1913.
[3] The person was Ramsay MacDonald. His opinion is not perhaps authoritative.

them in health.[1] But what, says the doubter, about man's grasping nature? Shaw answers: '. . . covetousness is not the whole of human nature: it is only a part, and one that vanishes when it is satisfied, like hunger after a meal.'[2] What about idleness then – the Weary Willies of society who are quite willing to take less and be poor and dirty and ragged or even naked for the sake of getting off with less work? Shaw's firm answer: '. . . voluntary poverty is just as mischievous socially as involuntary poverty: decent nations must insist on their citizens leading decent lives, doing their full share of its income. . . . poverty and social irresponsibility will be forbidden luxuries. Poor Willie will have to submit, not to compulsory poverty as at present, but to the compulsory well-being which he dreads still more.'[3]

Presented as it is by one of the most committed and persuasive propagandists in English letters, the case for equal incomes looks well on paper, and the mother of six hungry children, each one clamouring for the largest slice of cake, will see its necessity and virtue: six equal portions of cake is the only solution in a home that values peace. But what if the youngest child sings sweetly for his supper? Should he be allowed an extra large portion? The answer, for the sake of consistency, is apparently no; and in saying yes, Shaw appears to have weakened his argument considerably.[4] The 'rent of ability', specifically the rent of a 'lucrative talent' which pleases all and harms no one, should be allowed to stand. So little Tommy Tucker will always be slightly better fed; or to be more pointed, a world-famous dramatist will always be a little bit richer than ordinary people.

But this is not the end of the matter, and if I labour something which is unimportant in the context of the book as a whole, I do so to put a typical example of popular misunderstanding of Shaw to rights. Speaking to a reporter about T. E. Lawrence, he once wryly said: 'With the single doubtful exception of myself, no man of our time has had such a power of setting journalists and even diplomats to tell lies

[1] *The Intelligent Woman's Guide to Socialism, Capitalism, Sovietism, and Fascism*, pp. 27–9, etc.
[2] Ibid. **p.** 160.
[3] Ibid. p. 72.
[4] Ibid. p. 332.

about him.'[1] This is no idle claim, as the present issue proves. Even Shaw's Boswell, Henderson, who is nothing if not a panegyrist of his subject, pauses to click his tongue. But in fact Shaw is not saying that mother should give her Tommy an extra portion; he is saying that the enchanted brothers and sisters could well reward him with pieces of their cake. And since the distinction is between privilege and gratitude, Shaw is not being inconsistent. The 'rent' of a 'lucrative talent' is after all dependent entirely on popular goodwill and liable to fail at any time.

Shaw made Parliament, or rather his adapted legislature, responsible for placing the scheme for equal incomes on the statute books and putting it into effect. Nothing less than this would make it work, he said. We might justifiably doubt if even this would make it work, because the provision of equal portions of the national cake to everyone simply does not fall within the bounds of present-day practical politics. The national income per head, in even the most prosperous states, is not high enough. The history of Communist Russia, despite everything Shaw says to the contrary, amply proves this.

Yet Shaw will not let the matter rest. He cannot let the matter rest, for his theme is nothing more nor less than the preservation of civilization. It is the conditional of the entire book: present-day practical politics must make equal incomes a reality, else mankind will continue its Gadarene rush to the abyss. And if man is unable to divide wealth equally even for the sake of his survival, well then, a new being will have to be created to succeed where man has failed. The Life Force will not be denied.

*　　　*　　　*

Shaw never abandoned his ideal of equal distribution, although, as his past career shows was likely to happen, he came to adjust his plan, not to the realities of the contemporary world, since to have done that would have implied the defeat of an ideal by mere baseness, but to certain inescapable exigencies of twentieth-century economics. In an open letter to Joad in the *New Statesman* of July, 1943, he declares:

[1] *Natal Advertiser*, Durban, 22 May 1935.

... to give everybody an equal share of the national income to-day would reduce us all to such overcrowded poverty that science, art, and philosophy would be impossible. Civilization would perish, and with it most of the people. .... It is the business of the favoured ones to work up production until there is enough to afford the ten-fold figure for everybody.[1]

And a year later he asserted that 'mathematical equality is not an end in itself', that 'even in capitalist society there is a level at which it ceases to matter', and that when 'democratic Socialism has achieved sufficiency of means ... its work will be done'.[2] This in his eighty-eighth year. Plainly the 'Jevonian spirit' still obtained.

3

We may now inquire what good it would do if everyone had, if not an equal income, 'sufficiency of means' at least. The inverse could be put, since this was Shaw's more usual way. Thus: what evil would sufficiency of means undo? And the answer lies in several prefaces and essays, as well as in *The Intelligent Woman's Guide*. The evil that would be undone is Capitalism: the evil is the poverty of 90 per cent of the population.

In modern civilized societies the need for money came before every other need. Money meant a decent life, no money meant degradation. Money gave meaning to our noblest aspirations, no money gave the cynical lie to them. Money was not happiness, it was not virtue, but it made both seem attainable.[3] Poverty, on the other hand, brought hopelessness and despair:

Nothing but a very narrow mind can save you from despair if you look at all the poverty and misery around you and can see no way out of it all. And if you had a narrow mind you would never have dreamt of buying this book and reading it. Fortunately, you need not be afraid to face the truth about our Capitalism. Once you

---

[1] Quoted by C. E. M. Joad in his *Shaw*, London, Gollancz, 1949, pp. 143–4.
[2] *Everybody's Political What's What?*, pp. 56–7.
[3] See, for example, the Preface to *Major Barbara*, p. 215.

understand it, you will see that it is neither eternal nor even very old-established, neither incurable nor even very hard to cure when you have diagnosed it scientifically. I use the word cure because the civilization produced by Capitalism is a disease due to shortsightedness and bad morals; and we should all have died of it long ago if it were not that happily our society has been built up on the ten commandments and the gospels and the reasonings of jurists and philosophers, all of which are flatly opposed to the principles of Capitalism. Capitalism, though it has destroyed many ancient civilizations and may destroy ours if we are not careful, is with us quite a recent heresy, hardly two hundred years old at its worst, though the sins it has let loose and glorified are the seven deadly ones, which are as old as human nature.[1]

The words point to both the cause of Shaw's revolt against society and the traditional standards he set himself to restore – not simply by being an economist, or a statesman, or a scientist, or by being any single one of the seven-odd celebrities he claimed were him,[2] but by being the whole man. Capitalism with its attendant evils was the adversary of all the Shaws.

But what specific evils? Not (and in this we see afresh Shaw's sane way of looking at the world) – not inequality of opportunity and not human suffering. Inequality of opportunity was a fact of Capitalism, but it would be a fact of any economic or political system. It was a fact of human nature, and in frequent emphasis of his contention Shaw would genially invite his audiences to compete with him in writing a play. The fact of human suffering brought forth no geniality, however; it brought instead an argument that is startling perhaps, but true. There is no sum of human suffering; there is only the individual, who in his extremity suffers the utmost that can be suffered on this earth. It is fanciful to think of the accumulated sufferings of mankind, wrong

---

[1] *The Intelligent Woman's Guide*, pp. 127–8.
[2] Frank Harris cites seven 'international reputations' of Shaw. See *Frank Harris on Bernard Shaw: An Unauthorised Biography*, London, Gollancz, 1931, p. 136. For what the information is worth, Hesketh Pearson reports 'fifteen reputations'.

to despair about the fancy, and fallacious to suppose that sufficiency of means could remove an inexorable truth.

What *was* cumulative was waste: and this monstrous aspect of Capitalism could be studied under three headings. First, the political heading,[1] under which Shaw argued that no true democracy could prevail when money in the hands of the few made for class government, for plutocracy, and for newspapers which moulded public opinion by saying exactly what the newspaper owners wanted to have said – which was that plutocracy created the best of all possible governments. This was waste: the waste of potential leaders, a waste through reactionary legislation, a waste of time. Then, the economic heading, under which one had a state of affairs in England that made it compulsory for the country to spend 'very large sums on perfuming its handkerchief while it (was) starving and while it (was) rotting'.[2] In other words, a very rich man would put his surplus money into the market and make very poor men work to produce luxuries for him. More waste: the poor men should be producing necessities. The poor men should be richer. And then, the third heading, the most important, under which Shaw had a great deal to say: the biological heading.

Shaw was an evolutionist, and eugenics became an important part of his belief. Eugenics is a very old theme, of course. Plato suggested a programme of race hygiene and improvement. Thomas More's *Utopia* had a similar scheme. Darwin thought that selective breeding was important. Malthus sounded a warning which made it seem that preventive eugenics would be not merely expedient but imperative.[3] Shaw added his quota of words to the literature, beginning by consigning most men to the scrap-heap – or worse:

> The majority of men at present in Europe have no business to be alive; and no serious progress will be made until we address ourselves

[1] The ensuing remarks are abstracted chiefly from *The Case for Equality*, in which Shaw speaks mildly of 'objections'; but his more plainspoken moments show these objections to be central to his concept of the evil of Capitalism.

[2] *The Case for Equality*, reprinted by the Shaw Society, London, as Shavian Tract No. 6, December 1958, p. 12.

[3] See Georg Roppen, *Evolution and Poetic Belief: A Study in Some Victorian and Modern Writers*, Oslo, University Press, 1956, pp. 350–1.

C

earnestly and scientifically to the task of producing trustworthy human material for society.[1]

An uncompromising picture, which he frequently touched up:

> You see measure after measure brought out, accompanied by extensions of the franchise; but all the time we are going more deeply into the mire, and increasing the evils I have been fighting all my life. Although people are constantly assuming that these evils are being got rid of, I assure you they are not being got rid of at all; and the reason of that, it seems to me, is that we are not capable of getting rid of them. We are a stupid people; and we are a bad-looking people. We are ugly; we have narrow minds; and we have bad manners. A great deal of that is due to the effect of being brought up in a society of inequality.[2]

And his conclusion once again: '. . . you need a new sort of human being.'[3]

If this was so, the next problem was what sort of human being? Part of the answer is the Superman, whose place in the Shavian system will be discussed in the next chapter. The other part of the answer is that there is and can be no answer. We do not know what new sort of human being the world needs, beyond that he should be able to fix the world. But whether he should be healthy, or virtuous, we cannot say, because our concepts of health and virtue may be completely at variance with the qualities the world-fixer requires for his mission. He may, for all we know, need to be a self-contained epileptic whose exclusive diet is ten gallons of proof spirit a day.[4] Science then, no matter how earnestly it be studied, cannot provide the whole answer.

Only Nature, that mysterious entity of Shaw's thinking, can be expected, although not absolutely relied on, to set about the problem in the right way. And Nature's method is for a man and a woman to 'feel that curious physiological attraction which we all recognize as the sex

---

[1] 'The Perfect Wagnerite', *Major Critical Essays*, p. 215.
[2] *The Case for Equality*, pp. 13–14.
[3] Ibid. p. 15.
[4] Ibid.

attraction. . . . It is what you call the Voice of Nature. You fall in love, as the saying is.'[1] But more often than not in a Capitalist society you are obliged to fall out of love; you are obliged to turn your back on your possible first choice and find your partner in your own limited class.

> The result is that you have, instead of a natural evolutionary sexual selection, a class selection which is really a money selection. Is it to be wondered at that you have an inferior and miserable breed under such circumstances?[2]

This was the greatest single cause of waste, the greatest evil, for a nation was dissipating its birthright of vigorous life and denying the godhead in each and every individual. Implement equality of income and this evil would be routed. The duke would marry his charlady's daughter, the debutante would accept the dustman; the nation would surge forward and upward. The gentleman would come into his own.

Shaw's definition of a 'gentleman' is worth quoting at length because it incorporates so fully the ideal of service which he set for himself. First enunciated in reply to discussion on his address *The Case for Equality*, it is re-echoed (in the feminine gender) in the Peroration of *The Intelligent Woman's Guide*. Both passages enable one to see the rightness of Chesterton's judgement, that whatever the crude new names Shaw stitched to his banner (and Social Democracy is only the first of several 'crude new names'), he is on the side of 'the good old cause . . . the cause of creation against destruction . . . of yes against no'.[3]

> What is the ideal of the gentleman? The gentleman makes a certain claim on his country to begin with. He makes a claim for a handsome and dignified existence and subsistence; and he makes that as a primary thing, not to be dependent on his work in any way; not to be doled out according to the thing he has done or according to the

[1] Ibid. p. 16.
[2] Ibid. p. 17.
[3] G. K. Chesterton, *George Bernard Shaw*, London, Guild Books, Bodley Head, 1949, p. 46.

talents that he has displayed. He says, in effect: 'I want to be a cultured human being; I want to live in the fullest sense; I require a generous subsistence for that; and I expect my country to organise itself in such a way as to secure me that.' Also the real gentleman says – and here is where the real gentleman parts company from the sham gentleman, of whom we have so many – 'In return for that I am willing to give my country the best service of which I am capable, absolutely the best. My ideal shall be also that, no matter how much I have demanded from my country, or how much my country has given me, I hope and I shall strive to give to my country in return more than it has given to me; so that when I die my country shall be the richer for my life.' When you have a man of that type, you never find that he asks for more than any other man. Such a man never says 'I want a handsome and dignified existence; but a less handsome and dignified existence is good enough for other people.' He never says it, or thinks it. It is part of his conception of a handsome and dignified existence that it should be an existence shared with other men enjoying the same grace and dignity. If any man wants a better life, he should not seek for that life for himself alone, but should attain it by raising of the general level of life. The real constructive scheme you want is the practical inculcation into everybody that what the country needs, and should seek through its social education, its social sense and religious feeling, is to create gentlemen; and when you create them all other things shall be added unto you.[1]

II 'Nothing can be unconditional: consequently nothing can be free.'[2]

2

Shaw's career in politics began with *Fabianism and the Empire*[3] and

[1] *The Case for Equality*, p. 24.
[2] 'Maxims for Revolutionists', *Man and Superman*, p. 212.
[3] This is not strictly Shaw's work. He drafted it for the approval of the entire Fabian Society and incorporated many suggestions in the final copy.

ended with *Everybody's Political What's What?* It was a spectacular career but hardly successful, in many respects wrongheaded,
and characterized almost throughout by an apparently ambivalent
attitude to that cause of the whole problem of government – man
himself.

What was man? As we have noted, Shaw began by subscribing to
the Fabian belief that man was a teachable being whose redemption lay
in his quietly absorbing the truth that Social Democracy was good for
him and in altering his habits to live accordingly. But as we have also
noted, Shaw soon began to entertain doubts about this, until by about
1905 he appears to have given up all hope in education and progress.
'Any pamphleteer can show the way to better things,' he wrote; 'but
when there is no will there is no way.'[1] At which point he set out to
show that the only way was the will – a mystical way, which failed,
unfortunately, to solve any immediate problems. These still came
thick and fast, and these he continued to solve as a pamphleteer and a
propagandist. So we have the bizarre image of two Shaws, the first a
frankly diabolonian one taking man by the shoulder and marching him
off the face of the earth, the second a furiously pedagogical one taking
man by the other shoulder and bombarding him with instruction on
any and every thing on the face of the earth and off the face of the earth,
as well.

Discouragement was Shaw's mortal foe.[2] To give way to discouragement was to die; and although the non-realization of effective Socialism, the two World Wars, the failure of full adult suffrage – in short,
the entire history of twentieth-century Europe – caused him to append
a huge question mark to his original hopeful thesis, he never gave up
hope. Poverty did not at times seem the only evil; man seemed determined to destroy himself, whether he was poor or not: but to have
admitted that man was unregenerate would have been to admit a mis-
directed life, and this Shaw could never bring himself to do. Is Human
Nature Incurably Depraved? he asks in his eighty-eighth year, and he
answers as he has constantly answered, that the pessimistic 'Yes' with
which men of past ages and beliefs debased themselves before their

[1] 'Epistle Dedicatory': the Preface to *Man and Superman*, p. xxiv.
[2] This is, of course, a central theme of *Back to Methuselah*.

gods is a 'delusion caused, not only by ignorance of contemporary facts but, in so far as they are known, by drawing wrong conclusions from them'.[1]

It cannot be said that Shaw was generally ignorant of contemporary political facts. What can be said is that he tended to draw wrong conclusions from them. Not always. His (or more correctly the Fabian) reading of Kruger and the Boer republics was (some will think) detached and sane: these republics were anomalies in the twentieth century and had to give way to progress.[2] His anticipation of Wilson's 'Fourteen Points' and the League of Nations shows deep thought and practical humanitarianism.[3] His warnings against savage peace-terms with Germany were prophetic.[4] He could, and did, speak like a statesman at times. But he could, and did, sound like a charlatan at other times. There is his *Common Sense About the War*, misread to a large extent by the public, if read at all, and denounced only a trifle less hysterically than the author himself. Even so, in this essay Shaw fails signally to draw the right conclusion from the paramount fact. This fact was that England had already gone to war. Sheer buffleheadedness in high places *may* have been the cause; the propaganda that accompanied the human sacrifices to the trenches was monstrously distorted; the war itself was terrible. But cries of 'I told you so!' and 'If you had only listened to me!' did no good. Common sense then became uncommon silliness and indicated an incomplete understanding of men when the frenzy of war is upon them.

After the war Shaw enters on the major political phase of his career. Then his abandonment of trust in the proletariat seems complete. His denunciation of Liberal Democracy grows progressively more vehement; Mussolini is praised for describing democracy as a 'putrescent corpse' and for burying it as soon as possible;[5] Hitler receives a pat on

[1] *Everybody's Political What's What?*, pp. 1–2. See Chapter Nine of this work for further comments.
[2] See *Fabianism and the Empire*.
[3] See Henderson, *G.B.S.: Man of the Century*, p. 295.
[4] See 'Peace Conference Hints', in *What I Really Wrote about the War*.
[5] See, for example, the Preface to *The Apple Cart*, p. 184.

the back for having 'settled everything in Europe';[1] and Communist Russia offers Shaw an increasingly joyous prospect as first Lenin then Stalin get bloodier. The deeper implications of what was happening in Europe seemed to pass him by, perhaps because he was growing old or because he was constitutionally incapable of conceiving of the evil revealed by Stalin's purges or Hitler's concentration camps. Perhaps because he did not realize that the comparatively stable society which he had known before 1914 and on which he based his political diagnostic had passed away. Whatever the cause, he presents a chilling picture of himself at first glance – of a sprightly seventy-year old discoursing at large on affairs from which he seems too readily to have excluded elementary human rights. Neither is one's impression made more favourable when he turns to England and wonders whether the Fabians might not have been wrong after all to have repudiated catastrophic revolution.[2] There seems to be only one thing in his favour and that is, as he himself sadly admitted, that he had been a failure as a politician.[3]

The issues here raised obviously have an important bearing on an estimation of Shaw the artist–philosopher, and we may pause to see what we can make of his sympathies for the dictators of the 'twenties and 'thirties.

The first thing to make of them is that the Shaw of the picture outlined above is to a large extent the result of his inveterate play-acting before the public and his conscious – his habitual and deliberate – way of overstating a case: 'to make people sit up and listen to it, and to frighten them into acting on it',[4] as he explains. Also, as a second look at his writings will show, he is really much more responsible, much less impromptu in disposing of the world's problems, than the popular, newspaper notion allows. He came to realize that Fascism, so far from

[1] Quoted by H. M. Geduld in 'Bernard Shaw and Adolph Hitler', *The Shaw Review*, New York, Vol. IV, No. 1, Jan. 1961, p. 15.

[2] 'Fabian Essays Forty Years Later', *Essays in Fabian Socialism*, p. 305.

[3] 'In Praise of Guy Fawkes', *Platform and Pulpit: Bernard Shaw*, ed. Dan H. Laurence, London, Hart-Davis, p. 235: 'So far as I can make out, those speeches have not produced any effect whatever', Shaw says of his forty-eight years as a campaigner.

[4] *Everybody's Political What's What?*, p. 49.

being 'national socialism', was merely State Capitalism; and he was one of few to sense that unless Mussolini and Hitler were kept within the bounds of sanity by some constitutional check, the good work both were doing in their countries would be disastrously undone. Lord Acton's maxim that absolute power corrupts absolutely was a cornerstone in Shaw's political philosophy – at least, as far as every country but Russia was concerned. Russia was a special case to him. For twenty years this slowly awakening nation stood as his model of what a nation should be. It had embraced Communism, and if it made mistakes that a pinch of Fabian revisionism would have prevented, the very nature of Communism and its sainted leader guaranteed a prosperous future for its happy though necessarily diminished citizenry. In spite of which, even Communism, specifically, it seems to me, Stalin's absolutism, receives its warning: '. . . a totally Catholic Church or Communist State is an impossible simplification of social organization. It is contrary to natural history.'[1] The sentiment is characteristic; the terms are notable.

We have the advantage of hindsight to help us know that Shaw was wrong about the dictators; but he was not damnably wrong. Rather, he persisted in hoping (probably in believing) in the face of numerous signs to the contrary that Mussolini, Hitler, and Stalin were the sort of men western civilization needed. Strong men, Supermen, men whose wills might well have found a way to good, stable government. Two of them failed catastrophically, tragically, but Shaw has no need to eat his words or hedge when he pronounces his final judgement on them:

> The moral for conquerors of empires is that if they substitute savagery for civilization they are doomed. If they substitute civilization for savagery they make good and establish a legitimate title to the territories they invade.[2]

The inference to be drawn from Shaw's misadventures among the despots of his time is that his ideal of civilization made strong leadership a prerequisite of government. Efficiency, order, progress would be otherwise unattainable. He knew that he was treading on treacherous

[1] Preface to *Farfetched Fables*, p. 74.
[2] Preface to *Geneva*, p. 21.

ground; that the central problem of good government was this problem of leadership and the leader's proneness to abuse his powers in his
own interests or those of his class.[1] Yet the risk had to be taken.
Liberal Democracy had failed and England was in a mess. There was a
masquerade of civilized government – a noisy pretence that votes for
all adults and the Party System made for the consummation of efficiency
and justice whilst it actually made for the consummation of inefficiency
and injustice. Something had to be done. Some way out of the mess had
to be found.

So, Shaw believed, a first step would be to admit that the Gettysburg
axioms were nonsense. They postulated a physical impossibility.
Government of the people was of course both necessary and unavoid-
able; government for the people was no less necessary, if frequently
avoided; but government by the people was resounding humbug. It was
little better than a cry by which demagogues fooled us into voting for
them. Demos did not know how to make laws, would never know how
to make laws, and should not be permitted to try.[2]

Nevertheless, Demos could not be ignored. If order, efficiency, and
progress were imperatives of government, stability and equality were
also imperatives; and these the people were to have and keep:

> If government is to be effective it must be popular with the governed
> and generally acceptable. It must have Vogue. The vogue may be un-
> intelligent and ignorantly idolotrous; but it must exist and be worked
> up by agitation.
>
> I do not mean that Mr and Mrs Everybody should be allowed to
> elect Mr and Mrs Anybody as rulers, though our democratic politi-
> cians still seem to think so. Since women were enfranchised we have
> tried this plan and found that it produces not only stagnant Conser-
> vatism but retrogression checked only by the common sense of the
> Plutocrats it idolizes. Yet Parliament must survive as a congress of
> plaintive and plangent Anybodies with unlimited license, to com-
> plain, to criticize, to denounce, to demand, to suggest, to supply and
> discuss firsthand information, to move resolutions and take a vote on

[1] See the Preface to *The Apple Cart*, p. 171.
[2] Ibid. p. 176.

them: in short, to keep the Government abreast of public sentiment.
. . . for if grievances and desires are not made known fairly
vociferously ('ventitilated'), the Government cannot be expected to
remedy and consider them. . . .

Without such contact the ruling sages may get dangerously out of
touch with the spirit of the age.

But these assemblies of agitators and petitioners must not be
legislators. . . . Legislation must be by 'the quality', not by the
mob.[1]

So much for Demos and, incidentally, Parliament and the Party
System as we know them.

The questions of who constitutes 'the quality', how this is to be
chosen, and how it is going to rule need not keep us long. The quality
is the 5 per cent of the population who, whether their parents are
dustmen or dukes, are the natural bosses; from these the 'ruling sages'
of the foregoing quotation will be chosen, generally by means of
anthropometric tests, and will rule the country from a super-Whitehall
disestablishment. Will rule the country, but will never take over the
country, for frequent elections and the overriding privileges of the
mob will hold the sages in check.

*   *   *

Shaw might well have spared himself for all effect his proposals have
so far had on British or other governments. But so might Plato.
British or other governments do not readily take to political idealism,
unless – to echo Shaw – they have vogue. Unlike Machiavelli's,
Shaw's ideas do not have vogue and whether they ever will is for
clairvoyants, not us, to consider. More pertinent is an aspect of Shaw's
sensibility which his political thinking brings well to the fore – his
sense of history.

This is precisely what Chesterton does not see in Shaw – a sense of
the past; and a great deal of critical opinion, usually less wise than
Chesterton's, has adopted the same attitude ever since *George Bernard*

[1] *Everybody's Political What's What?*, pp. 29–30.

Shaw appeared. It is the 'great defect of that fine intelligence', Chester-ton says, '. . . a failure to grasp and enjoy the things commonly called convention and tradition'.[1] And twenty-five years later he adds: '. . . Shaw has never had Piety. . . . The cult of the land, the cult of the dead, the cult of that most living memory by which the dead are alive, the permanence of all that has made us.'[2] He is partly right. Shaw never made a cult of the past; he preferred revering the possibilities of the present:

> If you cannot believe in the greatness of your own age and time and inheritance (he wrote to Ellen Terry), you will fall into the most horrible confusion of mind and contrariety of spirit. . . .[3]

But Chesterton is also partly wrong, as these lines indicate. The past is the inheritance of the present, an inheritance not to be hallowed or deferred to by any special devotion, but always to be known and critically interpreted, always to be applied in meeting the challenge of the present and used in building a future. This was the way Shaw's Caesar looked at history and the way Shaw's constant allusions to both the secular and the spiritual past should be read; for he made it clear that he was an exception to the rule that we learn nothing from history. He was, as Barzun rightly insists, in the highest degree aware of history.[4] It is difficult to see how a serious evolutionist could have been anything else.

Shaw's proposals for political reform are based quite simply on the lessons that history has taught him:

> We clamor for a despotic discipline out of the miseries of our anarchy, and, when we get it, clamor out of the severe regulations of our law and order for what we call liberty. At each blind rush from one extreme to the other we empty the baby out with the bath,

[1] Chesterton, *George Bernard Shaw*, p. 79.
[2] Ibid. p. 116. (The chapter 'The Later Phases' written in 1935.)
[3] *Ellen Terry and Bernard Shaw: A Correspondence*, ed. by Christopher St. John, London, Reinhardt and Evans, 1949, p. 58.
[4] Jacques Barzun, 'Bernard Shaw in Twilight', *George Bernard Shaw: A Critical Survey*, ed. by Louis Kronenberger, Cleveland and New York, The World Publishing Co., 1953, p. 171.

learning nothing from our experience, and furnishing examples of the abuses of power and the horrors of liberty without ascertaining the limits of either.[1]

He speaks in terms of the present but it is a present fully conscious of both recent and distant past. And his solution, which we have seen is to take one part despotic discipline and one part popular liberty, to mix these in the bath, and to put the retrieved baby back, will, he has no doubt, ensure a vigorous stripling for the future.

But 'the horrors of liberty'? The phrase may challenge the presuppositions of a permissive decade; and now that the foundations of Shaw's Socialism have been laid, we may take the discussion a stage further and see how far he admitted individualism in his collectivist society.

2

To begin at a comparatively mundane level: Shaw made it perfectly clear that Social Democracy as preached by the Fabians did not envisage the abolition of all private property. What would become collectively owned were 'the means of production, distribution, and exchange', which could not sensibly be extended to include a person's bicycle or his typewriter.[2] He would retain the right to call his bicycle and typewriter his own, and, one presumes, call a man a thief who abstracted either article on a collectivist assumption.

The rights of private ownership were comparatively easy to decide. A more complex and delicate problem faced the Fabians: the rights of individual liberty. They tackled these boldly, and a youthfully hopeful Shaw told his audiences:

Establish a form of Socialism which shall deprive the people of their sense of personal liberty; and, though it double their rations and halve their working hours, they will begin to conspire against it before it is a year old.[3]

We should bear these words in mind.

[1] *The Intelligent Woman's Guide*, p. 318.
[2] *The Illusions of Socialism*, p. 19.
[3] 'The Impossibilities of Anarchism', *Essays in Fabian Socialism*, p. 85.

In addition, Social Democrats did not forget to affirm that in matters of Socialist reform 'character is the condition of conditions' and, as the Fabian, Sidney Ball, went on to say:

Its (Socialism's) animating idea is neither pity nor benevolence – at least, not as usually understood – but the freest and fullest development of human quality and power. It is characteristic of modern Socialism or Collectivism that its typical representatives are men who have been profoundly influenced by the positive and scientific conception of social life; while its popular propagandists have derived their inspiration from Ruskin, who is, in economics at least, a profound humanist. What is common to the indictment of modern Industrialism, set out in 'good round terms' by Ruskin, Morris, Wagner (not to mention others), on the one hand, and *Merrie England* on the other, is their sense of the frightful and quite incalculable waste and loss of quality (in producers and product) that it seems to involve. Whether this finding is just or not, Socialism is a principle which stands or falls by a qualitative conception of progress. It is bound up with ideas of qualitative selection and competition, and with the endeavour to raise in the scale the whole machinery, the whole conception and purpose, of industrial activity, so as to give the fullest scope to the needs and means of human development.[1]

Perhaps the most interesting thought to arise from this passage is the tacit acceptance of an ideal which has animated the minds of men since, if not before, the Renaissance: the humanistic ideal of full self-determination. Shaw never revoked the ideal. It is necessary to state this at once because his writings seem to assert the opposite at times. He does not indeed subscribe to John Stuart Mill's proposition that the individual's own good, either physical or moral, is not sufficient warrant for State interference; he categorically affirms a contrary:

[1] Sidney Ball, 'The Moral Aspect of Socialism', *Socialism and Individualism*, Fabian Socialist Series No. 3. London, Fifield, 1909, p. 74. This passage is not unique. Sidney Webb's essay, 'The Difficulties of Individualism' (in the same collection), speaks of the proven invalidity of the belief that 'the best possible social state will result from each individual pursuing his own interests in the way he thinks best.' See p. 8.

Never give the people anything they want: give them something they ought to want and dont.[1]

Which raises the questions: who can be so sure of himself that he knows what the people ought to want? The answer, in Shaw's opinion, is Shaw. What the people ought to want is a decent livelihood, a decent society, a decent nation. Therefore the inescapable condition of a man's liberty is his giving to society that which he owes to society – a decent sense of social responsibility.

It will be observed that this condition whittles away somewhat on the concept of a 'sense of personal liberty' but it does not exclude it. The sense of personal liberty may be allowed only within the context of social demands. The whole comes before the parts. And the whole emphatically prescribes the right of the state to interfere in the affairs of one person, either for his physical or moral improvement or for the improvement of society as a whole.

Thus Shaw's firm answer to Weary Willie, whose fate as a less than reliable member of society has already been touched on. Weary Willie (and his rich relation) have no right to a disproportionate share of liberty. They are not gentlemen (in the Shavian sense) and they have to face the consequences of their idleness: compulsory work; and if they prove incorrigible, the extreme penalty of painless extermination.[2] The sacred injunction of equality says in effect: 'We will not tolerate you as you are. Toe the line as a responsible member of society, or else. . . !'

The sacred injunction of equality must sound disturbingly like tyranny to hapless Willie. Even to responsible members of society it must sound forbiddingly authoritarian.

It should be obvious by now that Shaw is authoritarian in his social and political thinking; and yet, as I say, he never revoked the ideal of full self-determination. He made this conditional on the demands of Nature and of Society (saying in passing that Rousseau had been quite mistaken to imagine that man was ever born free) but he acknowledged that all people desired freedom, or liberty. This, he said, could have only one interpretation:

[1] 'Socialism for Millionaires', *Essays in Fabian Socialism*, p. 119.
[2] See the Preface to *On the Rocks*, in many ways Shaw's most paradoxical (if not positively contradictory) essay.

. . . freedom from any obligation to do anything except just what we like, without a thought of tomorrow's dinner or any other of the necessities that make slaves of us.[1]

And one of the benefits of Socialism would be that more people would have more time of their own than ever before.

But it is customary to believe that controlled liberty, which is what Shaw's concept amounts to, is not liberty, precisely because it interferes with one's sense of personal liberty – with that sense which, Shaw had seen, would drive people to conspiracy and revolt if it were denied them.[2] Shaw answers that controlled liberty is the only permissible liberty: forgo controls as the nineteenth century had done and the commodity in question will sooner or later fall almost entirely into the hands of the unscrupulous few. The commodity in question would be quite lost for most in the anarchy of a *laissez-faire* free for all. Liberty is like money and must be distributed in the same way. That is, equally.

The ideal picture of Shaw's Socialist State, then, is something along these lines: a compulsory working week for all, which leaves an unprecedented amount of time for painting pictures, writing plays, or indulging in any hobby the person likes. A pleasing picture, a wholesome one, and rationally founded. But is it true – true to the irrational desires of man?

Shaw seems to think that it will be true, and his reflections on the matter make us more and more aware of the unvarying yet highly diversified groundbass of his themes. Efficiency, stability, justice, right – truth itself – these are the necessary subjects of his discourse. They are his Platonic Forms but they are not the particular. The particular is human nature, that inconstant denominator man; and consequently, man's inviolable right at all times to be himself – a responsible, creative, decent self – but still himself, bound by the most sacred ties to the Shavian Jesus and the cry for Tolerance:

---

[1] *The Intelligent Woman's Guide*, p. 77.

[2] The Isle of Cats deputation in *On the Rocks* illustrates the irony of the situation. Members of this deputation react sharply against proposed measures of reform (measures that will benefit them and their class first) because they sense in them an infringement of personal liberty.

JESUS: I do not ask you to set me free; nor would I accept my life at the price of Barabbas's death even if I believed that you could countermand the ordeal to which I am predestined. Yet for the satisfaction of your longing for the truth I will tell you that the answer to your demand is your own argument that neither you nor the prisoner whom you judge can prove that he is in the right; therefore you must not judge me lest you be yourself judged. Without sedition and blasphemy the world would stand still and the Kingdom of God never be a stage nearer. The Roman Empire began with a wolf suckling two human infants. If these infants had not been wiser than their fostermother your empire would be a pack of wolves. It is by children who are wiser than their fathers, subjects who are wiser than their emperors, beggars and vagrants who are wiser than their priests, that men rise from being beasts of prey to believing in me and being saved.

PILATE: What do you mean by believing in you?

JESUS: Seeing the world as I do. What else could it mean?

PILATE: And you are the Christ, the Messiah, eh?

JESUS: Were I Satan, my argument would still hold.

PILATE: And I am to spare and encourage every heretic, every rebel, every lawbreaker, every rapscallion lest he should turn out to be wiser than all the generations who made the Roman law and built up the Roman Empire on it?

JESUS: By their fruits ye shall know them. Beware how you kill a thought that is new to you. For that thought may be the foundation of the kingdom of God on earth.[1]

One wonders how Frank Harris could ever have thought Shaw a terrorist at heart.[2] The truth is that Shaw here gives Jesus words which place him, Shaw, more firmly in the liberal tradition of ideas than Western Liberal Democracy has ever been. Individualism could have no more sincere plea.

The problem remains: it is that very creature for whom Shaw has envisaged a Socialist Utopia and for whose sake he has allowed the

---

[1] Preface to *On the Rocks*, pp. 182–3.
[2] Harris, *Frank Harris on Bernard Shaw*, p. 146.

weapon which can destroy the Utopia within a week. What if Man still decides to conspire against the State? What if he actively dislikes what he ought to like? What, in a word, if he behaves exactly as he has behaved since the beginning of history?

One must go on hoping. 'We must believe in the will to good',[1] Shaw says; for everything depends in the last resort on good conduct. At this point we leave facts and the rational mind, we make the leap of faith. 'Good conduct is a respect which you owe to yourself in some mystical way; and people are manageable in proportion to this self-respect. . . . good conduct is not dictated by reason but by a divine instinct that is beyond reason.'[2]

Good conduct is a matter of religious duty.

[1] 'The Religion of the Future', *The Religious Speeches of Bernard Shaw*, p. 34.
[2] *The Intelligent Woman's Guide*, p. 363.

Chapter Two

THE LIFE FORCE

I 'Political Economy and Social Economy are amusing intellectual games; but Vital Economy is the Philosopher's Stone.'[1]

1

Study Shaw as though he were a rationalist and one studies half the man. Study him as though he were an atheist and one studies nothing of him. Here he patiently repeats his view to one of his most perceptive critics:

> I have tried to teach Mr Chesterton that the will that moves us is dogmatic; that our brain is only the very imperfect instrument by which we devise practical means for fulfilling that will; that logic is our attempt to understand it and to reconcile its apparent contradictions with some intelligible theory of purpose; and that the man who gives to reason and logic the attribute and authority of the will – the Rationalist – is the most hopeless of fools.[2]

And the man who has no religion – he says elsewhere – is a coward and a cad.[3]

But Shaw was and remains an out and out heretic, of course, even when one reads 'soul' for 'will', even when one remembers his famous creed: 'I am a resolute Protestant; I believe in the Holy Catholic Church; in the Holy Trinity of Father, Son (or Mother, Daughter) and Spirit; in the Communion of Saints, the Life to Come, the Immaculate Conception, and the everyday reality of Godhead and the Kingdom of Heaven. Also, I believe that salvation depends on redemption from belief in miracles; and I regard St. Athanasius as an irreligious fool –

---

[1] 'Maxims for Revolutionists', *Man and Superman*, p. 225.
[2] 'Chesterton on Shaw', *Pen Portraits and Reviews*, p. 88.
[3] 'Modern Religion I', *The Religious Speeches of Bernard Shaw*, p. 38.

that is, in the only serious sense of the word, a damned fool.'[1] Sheer apostasy, mere irreverence, or profoundly felt paradox? The answer is in the mass of writings Shaw left on the subject.

He was always prepared to render unto science that which belonged to science and conceded that our metaphysical and legendary beliefs remain in constant retreat before the irrefutable categories of scientific knowledge. Within the domain of the knowable pure thought was (as he said) his passion. Beyond the knowable pure thought remained his passion, undergoing a kind of osmosis by which it became something kin to the godhead – kin, however, in pure hypothesis; because the religious philosophy adumbrated in *Man and Superman* and expounded some twenty years later in *Back to Methuselah* (not to mention several comparatively small plays and a number of public addresses) is not a rigid dogma but a provisional creed, a frame of reference within which one could reason. It is a religion for the twentieth century.

Now this was something which the so-called Christian church was not – a modern church propounding a modern lesson. Except when an incisive thinker like Dean Inge of St. Paul's spoke, the contradictions of the Thirty-Nine Articles and the accretions from the past of tribal fetish and superstition made belief a matter of hocus-pocus and terror-inspiring mystery: they put the church back in the jungle. For what, Shaw asked in effect, are the props of the established churches? An elderly gentleman with a white beard and an allegedly swift and awful way of dealing with anyone rash enough to question his omnipotence; a translation of Hebraic prophecies, laws, and histories which were read as though God himself was revealed in them when all that actually could be seen as revealed was the English language at its magnificent best; a belief in the morally reprehensible doctrine of atonement; a host of other puerilities. Such props were hardly intelligent; naturally they were not at all intelligible. Intelligible a religion had to be. 'It is no use falling back on the old evasion and saying that God is beyond our comprehension,'[2] Shaw remarked. We may wonder if he is right: mystery,

---

[1] *On Going to Church*. Reprinted by the Shaw Society, London, as Shavian Tract No. 5, December 1957, p. 11.
[2] 'The Religion of the Future', *The Religious Speeches of Bernard Shaw*, p. 30.

even magic, often seem necessary for religious belief, not only among men and women whose God has given them less brain than Shaw had. Yet right or wrong in this particular instance, his general observation on the Christian church cannot easily be gainsaid. There was a great deal in it which rebuked twentieth-century man – which rebuked nineteenth-century man, as Butler had shown – and many practices and articles of faith travestied the spirit of genuine religion.

As a matter of Shavian 'fact', ever since the Crucifixion, which had practically abolished Christianity, genuine religion had led a fugitive existence, and ever since the nativity of Commercialism it had quite vanished. Commercialism (and here we see Shaw lowering the elevation of his guns from the empty heavens and bombarding the infidel plain) – commercialism was a vicious substitute. Its honour was dishonour and its law anarchy. Its justification was that theory which had 'banished mind from the universe',[1] its canon was 'the survival of the fittest', its rationale was 'chance'.[2]

Lamarck's hypothesis, Butler's rebellion against Darwinism and development of Lamarckism, and Shaw's adoption of Butler's theories do not need to be repeated here. It is enough for our purpose to know that what Butler did against Darwinism Shaw went on doing against neo-Darwinism. This was to attack it for most of his life:

> Most of the natural selection men of the nineteenth century were very brilliant, but they were cowards. . . .

And to uphold his contra-view with great fervour, for Shaw believed above everything else that a universal design, an evolutionary purpose, was the final hope against confusion, alarm, and chaos:

> We want to get back to men with some belief in the purpose of the universe, with determination to identify themselves with it and with the courage that comes from that. . . .

And finally, logically, to align himself beyond dispute:

[1] Butler's phrase, which Shaw often used.
[2] Socialism also saw some justification for itself in the theory of natural selection, but Capitalism could see itself wholly endorsed there. See the Preface to *Back to Methuselah*.

As for my own position, I am, and always have been, a mystic.[1]

A mystic, yes; who saw no remedy in economic Socialism or anything else unless we developed our spiritual life, but a mystic as unlike a Yeats, for example, as *John Bull's Other Island* is unlike *Purgatory*. Shaw was a 'practical mystic'. A religion had to be realized, not for a vague hour or so every Sunday, but vitally every day, every hour of the week: to divorce it from the everyday world was to make it a sort of 'dope', harmful to both the addict and society.

This brings us to Shaw's Jesus, since it is by his retranslation of the Messiah of the western world that he presents and justifies his religion as a force in social institutions. He translated Jesus more than once, with somewhat differing interpretations each time. He once said that Christ was one of the attempts, one of the failures of the Life Force,[2] and his black girl sums him up as 'a lovable man' who means well.[3] But he most generally maintained that not Christ's message so much as the world's anti-Christian interpretation of the message was at fault. The world had all but forgotten what Jesus said in its attachment to an allegedly parthogenetic birth (which was nonsense), to a miracle-worker (who was hardly unique in his gifts), to a man who deluded himself that he was the Messiah (which was pitiful) and to a Pauline transmogrification of the gospel sayings. All this was not the essential Jesus. What was essential could easily be gathered from the gospels – and not altogether surprisingly this gathering showed Jesus to be remarkably Shavian in his outlook.[4]

Once the teaching had been adjusted to the modern world one found that Jesus had taught equality of distribution. That family ties should not hinder one from doing God's work. That the penal code should be based on the instruction 'Judge not that ye be not judged'. Following

---

[1] 'The Religion of the Future', *The Religious Speeches of Bernard Shaw*, p. 33. (There is possibly no more revealing record of Shaw's deep-felt, if thoroughly unorthodox, religious mysticism than his correspondence with Dame Laurentia McLachlan. See 'The Nun and the Dramatist', by a Nun of Stanbrook, London, *Cornhill Magazine*, Summer 1956.)

[2] Ibid. p. 36.

[3] *The Black Girl in Search of God*, p. 44.

[4] To be fair: Shaw called himself a Christian by these terms.

from this, that people should sin no more and *not* that they could comfort themselves in the belief that Jesus had come as an infallible patent medicine for bad consciences.[1] Finally, that the Kingdom of God is within one – that God is immanent. This, according to Shaw, was the revolutionary doctrine for which Jesus was crucified. It was the heart of his message. It was the heart of Shaw's message as well.

2

The egregious Don Juan makes his lonely way to heaven, the Devil and the Statue take the trap to hell, and Ana is alone. 'I believe in the Life to Come', she says devoutly, and then crying to the universe: 'A father! A father to the Superman!'[2]

This thrilling climax to the Hell scene combines biology with mystical yearnings and trembles on the threshold of Shaw's religious philosophy of Creative Evolution. That 'Life to Come', the Shavian Superman, is descended from Nietzsche's *Übermensch*, 'the just man made perfect', and is implicit in Creative Evolution.[3] But in the context of *Man and Superman* – from Preface to 'Maxims for Revolutionists' – it is plain that Ana calls for the fulfilment of a comparatively limited need. As Bentley has said: 'It is out of a deep sense of contemporary political failure that the philosophy of heroism arose in Carlyle, Wagner, Nietzsche and Bernard Shaw';[4] and Shaw's Superman is a political creature in the first, imperative instance.[5] 'King Demos', says Shaw, 'must be bred like all other Kings; and with Must there is no arguing.'[6]

He will be bred, as we have noted, by allowing Nature its lead. Neither money nor – we may now add – marriage should stand in the way. Poor specimens will breed themselves into extinction, good

[1] See the Preface to *Androcles and the Lion*, p. 79. This paragraph is derived from the same preface. Shaw says much the same in his address, 'Christianity and Equality', *The Religious Speeches of Bernard Shaw*.

[2] *Man and Superman*, Act III, p. 131.

[3] See H. C. Duffin, *Creative Evolution*. Printed as Tract No. 1, The Shaw Society, London, 1950, p. 3.

[4] *The Cult of Superman*. Quoted by Roppen, *Evolution and Poetic Beliefs*, p. 356.

[5] See 'The Revolutionist's Handbook', *Man and Superman*, p. 184.

[6] Ibid. p. 207.

specimens will breed the political Superman. This, at any rate, is Tanner's argument; beyond throwing out a few hints in his Handbook that 'What is really important in Man is the part of him that we do not yet understand'[1] and that 'where there is a will there is a way',[2] he seems content to go no further than biology. His illustrious ancestor, Don Juan, has more to say, however, considerably more, on another tack:

> But there is the work of helping Life in its struggle upward. Think of how it wastes and scatters itself, how it raises up obstacles to itself and destroys itself in its ignorance and blindness. It needs a brain, this irresistible force, lest in its ignorance it should resist itself. . . .[3]

Later:

> I tell you that as long as I can conceive something better than myself I cannot be easy unless I am striving to bring it into existence or clearing the way for it. That is the law of my life. That is the working within me of Life's incessant aspiration to higher organization, wider, deeper, intenser self-consciousness, and clearer self-understanding. It was the supremacy of this purpose that reduced love for me to the mere pleasure of a moment, art for me to the mere schooling of my faculties, religion for me to a mere excuse for laziness, since it had set up a God who looked at the world and saw that it was good, against the instinct in me that looked through my eyes at the world and saw that it could be improved.[4]

And again:

> Were I not possessed with a purpose beyond my own I had better be a ploughman than a philosopher; for the ploughman lives as long as the philosopher, eats more, sleeps better, and rejoices in the wife of his bosom with less misgiving. This is because the philosopher is in the grip of the Life Force. This Life Force says to him 'I have done a thousand wonderful things unconsciously by merely willing to live

[1] Ibid. p. 174.
[2] Ibid. p. 204.
[3] *Man and Superman*, Act III, p. 101.
[4] Ibid. p. 123.

and following the line of least resistance: now I want to know myself
and my destination, and choose my path; so I have made a special
brain – a philosopher's brain – to grasp this knowledge for me as the
husbandman's hand grasps the plough for me. And this' says the
Life Force to the philosopher 'must thou strive to do for me until
thou diest, when I will make another brain and another philosopher
to carry on the work.'[1]

Don Juan's loquacity makes further comment unnecessary. But before
going on from where he leaves off, we should glance at the roles played
by the two sexes in the manifestation of the Life Force.

I mean, of course, man and woman, not male and female – terms that
cast too wide a net for Shaw. We have no warrant for doubting his
sympathy for – indeed his feeling of kinship with – the animal kingdom.[2] His much advertised hatred of vivisection and his vegetarianism
probably arise from this attitude; also, his acknowledgement of all life
stems from a refinement of sensibility – an idiosyncratically inclined
aestheticism or fastidiousness perhaps – which has to be respected. In
one sense Shaw does see animate life as a unity, but in another he sees
human beings as having superseded everything else. He is almost
ostentatiously anthropocentric in his view, not for sentimental or
superstitious or egoistical reasons, but for metabiological ones – for the
cause of the Life Force. The animal world has been passed by this
Force: 'brainless magnificence of body has already been tried,'[3] Don
Juan says; it remains, this brainless magnificence, of the tiger for
example, or the brainless insignificance of the amoeba; but discredited,
discarded, reminders of failures of the Life Force, emblems of evil,
anachronisms in an evolving world. Will man also be discarded? If he
goes on as he is, yes, Shaw says; if man and woman desire betterment,
perhaps not.

Given then a physically and mentally superior couple who like a
Tanner and an Ann desire betterment, the Life Force may well be

[1] *Man and Superman*, p. 127.
[2] See the preface entitled, *Killing for Sport*, *The Complete Prefaces of Bernard
Shaw*, London, Hamlyn, 1965, p. 140.
[3] *Man and Superman*, Act III, p. 101.

imagined to be destined for fuller realization. But the problem is not so easily solved. Desire is the important word and the man and the woman each desires a different thing. 'I sing . . . the philosophic man',[1] Don Juan says. He might better have sung the artist–philosophic man but he makes his point: he sings that rare man, the creative genius, whose mission it is to elude the toils of love and to realize the Life Force in him unencumbered (possibly destroyed) by that female spider, the wife of his bosom. 'A father! A father for the Superman!' Ana cries – and immediately the conflict is apparent. For hers is the call of the Life to Come, of motherhood, of the Ann Whitefields who respond to an urge as tremendous as that driving the male genius. Two purposes of the Life Force meet head on; the clash, Shaw says, is sometimes tragic.[2] Whether the plays show him to be right is something to consider later; certainly the duel, if not necessarily the war, of the sexes highlight most of them and in many may be seen as the *raison d'être*.

The abstract of the clash is between the future and the present. Ann overcomes Tanner, the continuance of the race is assured, the longer purpose is served. The Superman may be on his way. But by surrendering himself, by discovering that there may be such a thing as a father's heart, after all, Tanner surrenders something of his individual genius and denies the shorter purpose of the Life Force. As things are, the conflict between the male and female principles is irreconcilable. The abolition of marriage could make things better; the abolition of sex in propagation would certainly make things better; the reconciliation of the now with perpetuity would be ideal. And in that curious excursion into practical struldbruggery, *Back to Methuselah*, Shaw fulfils these conditions.

But twenty years have passed and by this time biology has become metabiology, eugenics has become Creative Evolution; the breeding of political Superman has given way to the willing of a more fully realized God. The Life Force, alias God,[3] is within us. It is imperfect. It is striving for perfection. Man supplies its 'hands' and must work for this

---

[1] Ibid. p. 110.
[2] See 'Epistle Dedicatory': the Preface to *Man and Superman*, p. xx.
[3] Or divine providence, *élan vital*, and Nature. Shaw used these terms synonymously.

perfection, must desire this perfection, and although unconscious of the force working in him, he must will himself to a greater awareness of God's purposes, growing all the while to a greater control over the circumstances of his life; must will himself with all the powers of his accumulating knowledge to take the leap upward from one evolutionary stage to the next; must create a new being, who in turn and by the same processes of desire, imagination, and will, shall create yet another being, so that in time not our time the world – which we know and value as children value their toys – shall be left behind, and matter shall be transcended and a 'whirlpool of pure intelligence'[1] shall be all Life.

Until? There is no 'until': 'It is enough that there is a beyond,'[2] says Lilith. It is, in more academic terms, no teleological system that Shaw postulates. Creative Evolution does not concern itself with the end or the beginning, understandably, since Shaw is either unable or does not wish to conceive of a transcendental as well as an immanent God. The distinction is ultimately unimportant, as are questions concerning first causes, inherent necessity, self-sufficiency, and the nature and occupation of the finally realized God. The philosopher Joad has gone into these matters with a thoroughness that does not need to be reflected here and fails in any case to realize Shaw's purpose. This was not to present a system but to assert a faith – that man could be reborn to the tremendous possibilities of Life, that this Life comprehends a just social and political structure, more than this, that it implies a personal mode of salvation – not for the sake of personal immortality, which was a repugnant idea to Shaw, but for all mankind to inherit the kingdom of God on earth.

This was the necessary, hence the right way. Necessity – the Must of Shaw's argument – informs his message. It is for man's sake that this should be so. Yet – and here again we discover the fused paradox of Shaw's thinking – free will could not be rejected. Only by exercising freedom of choice could man grow to fulfil Life's purposes. This is the essence of Jesus's words to Pilate[3] and the essence of creative genius; this is the beginning of growth towards the infinite. 'Of Life only there

---

[1] 'As Far As Thought Can Reach', *Back to Methuselah*, p. 254.
[2] Ibid.
[3] In the Preface to *On the Rocks*.

is no end,'[1] Lilith says; one may add: 'In Life only is there hope, faith, courage, and the kinship of men.' Shaw thought so:

> ... we may hope if only we give everybody the best possible chance in life, this evolution of life may go on, and after some time, if we begin to worship life, if instead of merely worshipping mammon, in the old scriptural phrase, and wanting to make money, if we begin to try to get a community in which life is given every possible chance, and in which the development of life is everybody's religion, that life is the thing, then cooperation with this power becomes your religion, you begin to feel your hands are hands of God, as it were, that he has no other hands to work with, your mind is the mind of God, that he made your mind in order to work with. Then you not only get an enormous addition in courage, self-respect, dignity, and purpose, get turned aside from all sorts of vile and base things, but you get a religion which may be accepted practically by almost all the churches, as they purge themselves more or less of their super-stitions. ... if I come across religious people, Indian, or Irish, or Mahometan, or anybody else, we can meet on this common ground. You find that this thing is in everybody, the hope of this thing. The moment you clear up people's minds and make them conscious of this, that moment you discover that the roots of this religion are in every person. ...[2]

'Our age needed a new Aquinas', Sir Ifor Evans remarks, 'and we were given G. B. Shaw.'[3] We may legitimately wonder if he knew his man in such passages as this.

[1] 'As Far As Thought Can Reach', *Back to Methuselah*, p. 254.
[2] 'Christianity and Equality', *The Religious Speeches of Bernard Shaw*, p. 78.
[3] B. I. Evans, *A Short History of English Literature*, Harmondsworth, Penguin, 1961, p. 126.

*II 'I am a moral revolutionary, interested, not in the
class war, but in the struggle between human vitality
and the artificial system of morality . . . .'*[1]

Our context is Shaw's religion, our cue a phrase in the passage quoted
from 'Christianity and Equality': 'The moment you clear up people's
minds. . . .' The moment, that is, you get people to question their
morality; the moment they revise their manners, for manners are moral
standards made visible. The moment they purge themselves of decep-
tions and delusions, then all things will be added to them.

Shaw's standpoint is as clear as many paragraphs of crystalline argument can make it: morality is not morality unless it is commensurate
with the facts of social and personal life; further, morality is moral only
if these facts sustain it. This is an axiom and the burden of Shaw's entire
revolutionist creed, implicit in his realization that a change to Socialism
would involve a moral *volte face*,[2] discernible in practically everything
he wrote.

To Shaw, nineteenth-century morality failed on both counts: it was
not commensurate with the facts, it could not possibly find itself sustained by the facts. How, then, did it sustain itself? The answer is: by
humbug, by a fervent belief in words.

Consider, Shaw says in effect, the unholy idols of the 'Infidel Half
Century': Capitalism, Liberal Democracy, Darwinism. What words
were intoned in their temple? – Free Enterprise, Political Emancipation, Survival of the Fittest. What facts were visible in the world at
large? – degrading personal poverty, industrial serfdom, the oblitera-
tion of human hopes. A grinding, shameful, immoral scene – and its
name was Moral.

Adjacent to Capitalism was the pillar of the Church, a massive pillar

[1] In a letter to H. H. Hyndman. Quoted by Henderson, *Bernard Shaw: Playboy
and Prophet*, New York, Appleton and Co., 1932, p. 189.
[2] See *Socialism: Principles and Outlook*, Encyclopaedia Britannica, 1929. Reprinted by the Shaw Society, London, as Shavian Tract No. 4, November 1956,
p. 24.

but crumbling at its base: its word, God. And round and about, a crowd of acolytes: Honour, Duty, Justice – the first three of Don Juan-Shaw's 'seven deadly virtues';[1] the remaining four to be chosen as one wishes from Respectability, Heroism, Patriotism, Romantic Love, traditional Gentlemanliness and Womanliness, conventional Virtue, Private Patronage, Coded Conduct[2] – and probably many more if one cared to sift Shaw's writings for them. These are the words. They may be taken up by one word: Idealism.

Morality informed by Idealism sounds very good: Shaw never gainsaid this; but Idealism which denied the facts was very bad – an admission of a dulled conscience, of supine acquiescence, of a diseased sensibility that fed on and fed in reciprocal perpetuation the unwholesome gods of the age. Idealism represented a disgraceful social and personal morality and (to Shaw) it obviously needed revision.

A semantic card-shuffler of the greatest dexterity (although he cheated a little at times), Shaw entered into the Morality word-game with zest. He surveyed religious practice and declared himself an atheist; he considered the popular myth of Romantic Love and swore by anti-Romanticism; he studied the angels and sided with the devil; for three years he regularly endured moral and orthodox plays and retaliated by writing immoral and heretical ones. In short, he looked upon Idealism and preached the gospel of anti-idealism.

For good measure he created the legend of G.B.S. This legend does not concern us, but because Shaw caused it to become inextricably mixed in the popular mind with his 'immoral' message we may consider it in a brief paragraph. 'The Fool in Christ'[3] Bentley has expressively dubbed the 'mountebank' aspect of Shaw, the 'trumpet and cartwheel' declaimer, the jester who stood on his head and summoned the world to follow his arresting example – for that way lay the deep damnation of Shavian salvation. The jokes were excellent, so instead of crucifying him the world smiled fairly indulgently and on the whole declined to be saved. Perhaps the jokes were too good, for the real joke,

---

[1] See *Man and Superman*, Act III, p. 87.

[2] See Henderson's list, p. 744.

[3] A chapter title in his book, *Bernard Shaw*, New York, New Directions, 1947.

that Shaw was in earnest,[1] did not seem to be generally discerned. Perhaps the real joke was discerned and it seemed easier to pass it off as a joke. At all events, Shaw was not taken seriously except by a few.

Whether since the first incredulous reaction he has come to be taken seriously is a matter to be raised in the final chapter; we should now find out how well Shaw's anti-idealism stood up to the inevitable idealistic reaction – how well it will stand up to similar reactions today.

Because I do not wish to encroach on the subject matter of the plays, I cite only two typical examples, the first a grossly self-flattering one on the subject of Women penned by a man who should have known better – Frank Harris.

> Everybody has noticed this vital defect in Shaw's women, their lack of mystery, grace, divinity, allure, and charm.[2]

By this we are invited to believe that Harris's moral code included an Ideal of Woman which Shaw had desecrated in a characteristically boorish way. Shaw's reply puts his position clearly:

> ... the sort of woman he (Harris) idealized never completely existed except in his imagination. . . .[3]

And by this we may understand that no idealization will do unless it is founded in 'natural history'. Such images of feminity as Harris (and his numerous male counterparts) live by – images redolent of the Age of Chivalry and 'Idylls of the King' – are as much like the real woman as a shrine is like Monday's wash. The analogy is deliberate. 'Home is the girl's prison and the woman's workhouse,' Shaw once wrote;[4] Victorian masculinity had put the girl and the woman where they were and absolved itself by worshipping womanly mystery, grace, divinity, and the rest, in an Arcadian temple as far from home as possible. Shaw came to the rescue of womankind by showing that both the ideal and the fact were unendurable – the first a fatuous impossibility, the second a

---

[1] Clarence Rook, 'George Bernard Shaw', *The Candid Friend*, 1 November 1896. Quoted by Bentley, *Bernard Shaw*, p. 187.
[2] Harris, *Frank Harris on Bernard Shaw*, p. 191.
[3] Ibid. p. 392. (In Shaw's Postscript.)
[4] 'Maxims for Revolutionists', *Man and Superman*, p. 222.

condition of drudgery, both a servitude which no intelligent woman should allow to have inflicted on her. His anti-ideal may finally lack grace, allure, and charm (although this is not likely); it certainly does not lack divinity – the divinity of more fully realized humanity.

Chesterton's feelings about Women were probably not so perfervid as Harris's; all the same, his feeling about other ideals and the morality they inform is intense. Here he criticizes Shaw for his alleged attitude to love and war:

> . . . people who have really scraped the gilt off gingerbread generally waste the rest of their lives in attempting to scrape gilt off gigantic lumps of gold. Such has too often been the case of Shaw. He can, if he likes, scrape the romance off the armaments of Europe or the party system of Great Britain. But he cannot scrape the romance off love or military valour, because it is all romance and three thousand miles thick. . . .[1]

> It may be doubted perhaps whether this realism in love and war is quite so sensible as it looks. . . . The world is wiser than the moderns. The world has kept sentimentalities simply because they are the most practical things in the world. They alone make men do things.[2]

Shaw's opinion of *George Bernard Shaw* was that as an account of his doctrine it was 'either frankly deficient and uproariously careless or else . . . madly wrong';[3] notwithstanding this viewpoint of a man who had every reason to know most about the subject,[4] the book, one of the first on Shaw, is still one of the wisest. But *does* Shaw attempt to scrape the gilt off gigantic lumps of gold? We might refer to *The Illusions of Socialism* and agree that he does not; we may care to suggest that Chesterton should have read this essay before committing himself. It isn't necessary though, because he endorses Shaw in the passages above while in the very process of confuting him. Sentimentalities – illusions – ideals – the words are interchangeable here: they alone make men do

[1] Chesterton, *George Bernard Shaw*, p. 32.
[2] Ibid. p. 53.
[3] 'Chesterton on Shaw', *Pen Portraits and Reviews*, pp. 84–5.
[4] '. . . the best authority on Shaw is Shaw.' In a letter to Henderson, p. xviii.

things, and Shaw would have agreed. Love, for instance, is an undeniable force; it is the irresistible whisper of Life itself – if properly conceived. And military valour is no less necessary on occasion – if properly employed. Yet let love and valour and other 'sentimentalities' not get things done, or get the wrong things done, let love impose an insufferable burden on a person's natural vitality, let valour serve a patriotism that causes wars and is essentially treachery – then a Shaw, and a Chesterton too, assuredly, will protest. Chesterton is wrong about Shaw and Shaw is wrong about Chesterton, but they are both right about ideals. Scrape the gilt off the gingerbread ones, leave the golden ones alone – after making sure they are golden.

Which implies that the arch anti-idealist has ideals. Of course he has. He makes an ideal of the anti-ideal. His golden rule is that there are no golden rules. He denies the incantation 'Whatever is, is right' and cries 'Whatever is can certainly be improved upon'. He stitches another crude name on to his banner – Meliorism – and searches the earth for the Platonic Good, believing as he does so that it is no absolute he seeks. It cannot be an absolute: Creative Evolution cannot accept this, Life cannot accept it. Of Life only, we may remember, there is no end. To know this is to know the golden non-rule; is to know that life and one's living of it is challenging, difficult, varied – and magnificently worthwhile. To know this is to know good conduct as an indestructible ideal.

Chapter Three

AESTHETICS AND ETHICS

I '*The drama's laws the drama's patrons give.*'[1]

l

Sheridan's ebullient entrepreneur, Mr Puff, rang down the curtain on the eighteenth-century stage and rang it up on the nineteenth-century stage with one and the same unabashed flourish. His magnum opus, *The Spanish Armada*, comprehended all the asininity of its contemporaries and anticipated all the puerility of its followers. Although almost clamorously the model of what drama should not be, it stood for nearly a hundred years as the model of what drama should be.

The history of nineteenth-century drama begins with Dr Johnson's maxim. In the early eighteen hundreds the drama's patrons became the mob. It chased polite society from the theatre, bawled elegant sentimentality from the stage, shouted for gobbets of such fare as *The Castle of Otranto* and *The Mysteries of Udolpho* had provided in the Gothic novel, and imposed the tyranny of its rude taste on playwrights of the day. These men – Jerrold, Bulwer-Lytton, Boucicault, Taylor,[2] and others – conceding in an age of extending franchise the democratic (and commercial) principle that the pit and the gallery had a voice to be heeded, gave them what they wanted.

The pit and the gallery wanted spectacle and sensation first and the emergent modern stage was well equipped to provide spectacle and sensation with lavish generosity: glittering ballrooms and murky smugglers' dens, towering forests and lofty hills, castles, lakes, waterfalls, snowscapes, seascapes, landscapes – illusions of illusions, all resplendently grand, gorged the most gluttonous eye. Accompanying

---

[1] Samuel Johnson, *Prologue to the Opening of the Theatre at Drury Lane*, l.53.
[2] These playwrights represent the years 1820–1850, during which period the Gothic play was supplanted by less haunting but no less spectacular theatrical fare.

E

all this was the 'well-made play', that is to say, anecdotage, which contrived situations of baffling complexity, events of frank implausibility, and resolutions of bewildering incredibility. And in intensification of the moment sublime, off-stage music.

If it was an era in which the stage and the actor-manager had their apogee, it was also an era in which drama barely existed. The playwrights were skilled men of the theatre but they were deficient in one vital quality: words failed them. The diction, floundering midway between the highfalutin' and realism, generally reduced character to pasteboard and situation to banality – made lugubrious comedy where passion was meant to soar:

> CLARA: But I too have pride of my own – I too can smile at the pointless insolence.
> EVELYN: Smile – and he took your hand! Oh, Clara, you know not the tortures that I suffer hourly! When others approach you, young – fair – rich – the sleek darlings of the world – I accuse you of your very beauty – I wither beneath every smile that you bestow. . . . No – speak not! – my heart has broken its silence, and you shall hear the rest. For you I have endured the weary bondage of this house – the fool's gibe – the hireling's sneer – the bread, purchased by toil that should have led to loftier ends; yes, to see you – hear you; for this – for this I have lingered, suffered, and forborne. Oh, Clara! we are orphans both – friendless both; you are all the world to me; . . . turn not away! My very soul speaks in these words – I LOVE YOU!
> CLARA: No – Evelyn – Alfred – No! Say it not – think it not! It were madness![1]

Macready is reputed to have had an acting style which made fustian like this quite exciting. One may be permitted to wonder.

And yet nineteenth-century melodrama was not entirely bad. Aesthetically and intellectually inchoate, a play like Jerrold's *Black-Ey'd Susan* has a vigour which eighteenth-century sentimentality lacked; and other plays, such as Bulwer-Lytton's *Money* or Taylor's *Ticket-of-Leave Man*, nibble on issues which were to become staple dramatic diet a few generations later. The playwrights of the day were highly

[1] From Edward Bulwer-Lytton's *Money*.

accomplished men of the theatre, serving it is true a not very exalted Muse but serving her with panache, shaping a dramatic convention in which Shaw was to discover much of his inspiration, and supporting a style of acting – the rhetorical and hyperbolical – which his drama frequently demands.[1] If we tend to regard Shaw as the grand master of the 'new' English drama it should be borne in mind that he was equally – if not more – the grand master of the 'old'.

In fact, the 'new' naturalistic mode which T. W. Robertson inaugurated in the eighteen-sixties may be seen to have had less influence on Shaw than the mode which preceded it. Literary bloodhounds go baying after Robertson, scenting in him the one worthwhile quarry of mid-Victorian dramaturgy, and Shaw himself said that the 'Robertsonian movement' caught him as a boy.[2] It seems that the infection did not last very much longer than the measles. For one thing, he discovered Ibsen, for another, Robertson's drama betrayed the very 'life' which it purported to be restoring to the stage by allowing social conventions to shape its themes. Thus in *Caste*, Robertson's most notable play, the absurd edifice of social privilege is given an interrogative tap and concluded to be 'all right'. Technically an innovator but spiritually complacent, Robertson saw 'real life . . . real relations . . . real mothers'[3] only on their surface and has little to do with Shaw. He is the originator of an English dramatic tradition which came to its first significant fruition in the plays of A. W. Pinero – at a time, as Pinero's luck would have it, when Shaw was drama critic of *The Sunday Review*.

This was in the eighteen-nineties, a decade which brought the century to its close on a high note of dissent. It was a most exciting period; the century went out not with a whimper but a bang. Nietzsche's aphorism that a dancing star was born only from chaos within was manifest, as Holbrook Jackson says, in 'a widespread concern for the correct – that is, the most effective, the most powerful, the most righteous –

[1] Shaw frequently spoke of his indebtedness to the old stock companies. See, for example, his Preface to *Ellen Terry and Bernard Shaw: A Correspondence*, ed. by Christopher St. John, p. xvii.
[2] *Our Theatres in the Nineties*, Vol. III, p. 165.
[3] T. W. Robertson, *Caste*, Act I: in a passage which clearly indicates Robertson's desire to relate his drama to 'real life'.

mode of living'.[1] This is what the adjunctive dramatic revival sought to express; and although Henry Irving continued to produce mutilated Shakespeare, to persist in Scribe and Sardou – all on a grand and sumptuous scale; and although Henry James was jeered from the stage whilst Conan Doyle's *A Story of Waterloo* enjoyed the popularity which the utterly fatuous always seems able to arouse; although, in short, nineteenth-century dramatic practice was still the general habit, it seemed to most critics that in Pinero the English stage was rediscovering its force. But it seemed quite otherwise to the lynx-eyed critic for *The Saturday Review*.

To him Pinero was merely perpetuating the myth of society's omnipotence. There was *The Second Mrs Tanqueray*, which indicted society for not giving a woman with a 'past' a clean slate for the future, but then happily reprieved the accused by having the woman do the 'right' thing in killing herself. Pinero undoubtedly thought that Paula Tanqueray's suicide was the only right thing and by thinking this betrayed his inability to escape from the conventional, to see things, as Shaw put it, from any point of view other than his own.[2] The criticism stands. In all his plays Pinero has heavily diluted the 'new spirit': he would not or could not take any critical thesis through to an honest conclusion, or toughen his drama with anything more daring than a lady's garter. He would not or could not put aside Robertson's world view in favour of the uncompromising terror that smote London in Ibsen's *Ghosts*.

H. A. Jones, the other notable dramatist of the period,[3] was much inferior to Pinero as a man of the theatre but intellectually more honest. The seeds of dissent were more firmly planted in his mind and if these invariably sprouted tendentious plays about adultery they yet succeeded in restoring the odour of challenge to the theatre. He also developed as a dramatist. In 1894 he gave the stage what is now the excruciatingly banal *The Masqueraders* but a year later the genuinely ambitious *Michael and His Lost Angel*. The 'theme of almost heroic

---

[1] Holbrook Jackson, *The Eighteen Nineties*, Harmondsworth, Penguin, 1939, p. 12.
[2] *Our Theatres in the Nineties*, Vol. I, pp. 46–7.
[3] There was the blazing comet called Oscar Wilde, of course; but it flared too briefly to have any immediate impact.

passion is one that made a peculiar appeal to Jones', Allardyce Nicoll comments,[1] perhaps too indulgently, for with Jones heroic passion was enfeebled by that prime falsehood of Victorian morality, an emasculated Tristan. All the same, the critic, Joseph Knight was not far wrong to write in 1896 (Shaw's plays then being virtually unknown) that *Michael and His Lost Angel* was 'one of the most successful dramas of the age'.[2] About a high-minded cleric who imposes on himself the public confession of sexual 'uncleanness' he has imposed on one of his parishioners, it fails as a tragedy but succeeds as an exposure of social prejudice. It is perhaps the most Ibsen-like English play of the period.

All roads led from Ibsen. Jones as well as Pinero, and in due course their lesser contemporaries, could not ignore him. His advent in London was long overdue and when it occurred the response from the general public, consequently from theatre managers also, was such that any desire of English dramatists to follow the Norwegian's forbidding trail must have been tempered by the knowledge that West End audiences would not pay for the journey. Yet to the credit of both Jones and Pinero they infused their drama with a moral purposiveness which the old theatre had lacked. Their work, not Shaw's, began the English revival. Shaw was to emerge as a dramatist only some ten years later. In the meantime it was the weekly *feuilleton* under the initials G.B.S.: it was, characteristically, the theorist who first came into his own.

*II 'The drama's laws the drama's patrons
do not give, nor ever can give: that is the
prerogative of the dramatist, and of the
dramatist alone.'*[3]

Anyone going through Shaw's writings in the expectation of finding a revolutionary and systematic theory of poetics is bound to be disappointed. In the first place, Shaw's theory of drama is less complete than

[1] Allardyce Nicoll, *British Drama*, London, Harrap, 1949, p. 366.
[2] Preface to H. A. Jones, *Michael and His Lost Angel*, London, MacMillan, 1896, p. xiv.
[3] *Our Theatres in the Nineties*, Vol. I, p. 228.

his theory of the Life Force, which is to say that it is far from complete and not remotely a system. He gives the appearance of saying a great deal on what the artist should do and what the drama should be and does indeed devote many thousands of words to the subject in *The Quintessence of Ibsenism*, 'The Sanity of Art', his drama reviews, and several prefaces, but an abstract of all this amounts to what to a devotee might well seem disappointingly little and disconnected. In the second place, he is not at all revolutionary but as old as these remarks, culled from his work, show him to be: 'The claim of art to our respect must stand or fall with the validity of its pretension to cultivate and refine our senses and faculties until seeing, hearing, feeling, smelling and tasting become highly conscious and critical acts with us. . .';[1] '. . . the great dramatist . . . has to interpret life';[2] '. . . the art of the dramatic poet . . . recognizes no obligation but truth to natural history';[3] '. . . art is the expression of feeling'.[4] These pious phrases of literary criticism (as Shaw calls one of them) are enough to show that in broad outline at least his theory of art enters into the 'great inheritance' of poetics, beginning with the Athenians. Since he claimed precisely this inheritance for his plays, it is hardly surprising that his theories should be similarly hallowed.

The belief – by no means a limited one – that he was a revolutionist in the English dramatic tradition arises from the fact that as a critic of and writer for the theatre he took his stand in all-embracing dissent from what passed for dramatic art in the eighteen-nineties. He was the complete dissenter, anti-art for art's sake, anti-'cup and saucer' drama, anti-well-made play, anti-Irving, anti-Shakespeare, anti, in short, the theatrical Establishment. But dissent does not mean revolution, least of all when it is implacably from the stale, the pretentious, and the trashy. It means re-enlightenment.

This seems hardly the word to apply to a person whose most celebrated critical remark was:

---

[1] 'The Sanity of Art', *Major Critical Essays*, p. 315.
[2] Preface to *Three Plays by Brieux*, *The Complete Prefaces of Bernard Shaw*, p. 204.
[3] Preface to *Heartbreak House*, p. 40.
[4] 'Tolstoy on Art', *Pen Portraits and Reviews*, p. 258.

With the single exception of Homer, there is no eminent writer, not even Sir Walter Scott, whom I can despise so entirely as I despise Shakespear when I measure my mind against his. The intensity of my impatience with him occasionally reaches such a pitch, that it would positively be a relief to me to dig him up and throw stones at him, knowing as I do how incapable he and his worshippers are of understanding any less obvious form of indignity. To read Cymbeline and to think of Goethe, of Wagner, of Ibsen, is, for me, to imperil the habit of studied moderation of statement which years of public responsibility as a journalist have made almost second nature in me.[1]

The trouble with this sort of comment is not that it is arrogant so much as too clever by half. Bardolators (that is, most of the English-speaking race) failed to see that it is a piece of studied immoderation; and when a few years later Shaw wrote 'Better than Shakespear?'[2] the sense of outrage occasioned by the earlier comment quite erased the question mark. Thus was begun the myth of Shaw's self-avowed superiority to Shakespeare. Actually he knew Shakespeare's plays very well – some to the extent of having the entire texts by heart – so his judgement has a surer foundation than that of many who would disagree with him; also, although always blatantly non-academic, he was perfectly capable of arguing with academics about textual emendations, printer's errors in the first folio, and so on.[3] More important, he could and did appreciate many of Shakespeare's finer qualities. In 1931 he apologized (to the extent that Shaw *could* apologize) for the excesses of his onslaughts on Shakespeare. 'So forgive', he begged: 'but make the necessary allowances.'[4] But what allowances are strictly necessary when praise of the following order comes directly after the belittlement of the paragraph quoted above? –

[1] *Our Theatres in the Nineties*, Vol. II, p. 195.
[2] A sub-heading in the Preface to *Three Plays for Puritans*.
[3] See 'Shakespear: A Standard Text', *Shaw on Theatre*, ed. E. J. West, U.S.A., MacGibbon and Kee, 1958.
[4] Postscript (1931) to 'The Author's Apology', *Our Theatres in the Nineties*, p. viii.

But I am bound to add that I pity the man who cannot enjoy Shake-spear. He has outlasted thousands of abler thinkers, and will outlast a thousand more. His gift of telling a story (provided some one else told it to him first); his enormous power over language, as conspicuous in his senseless and silly abuse of it as in his miracles of expression; his humor; his sense of idiosyncratic character; and his prodigious fund of that vital energy which is, it seems, the true differentiating property behind the faculties, good, bad, or indifferent, of the man of genius, enable him to entertain us so effectively that the imaginary scenes and people he has created become more real to us than our actual life – at least, until our knowledge and grip of actual life begins to deepen and glow beyond the common.[1]

In the light of such appreciation, at least one critic's assertion, that Shaw's misconception of the function of dramatic poetry was total, is manifestly wrong.[2] On the contrary, his conception of the revelatory power of great poetry is as full as could be desired. Yet in one important respect he does fail as a Shakespearian critic, as a critic of literature generally if not as a dramatist. He failed to recognize the essential unity of form and content: he invariably separated the two, thus creating the ambivalent attitude shown above and perpetrating the fallacy that 'word music' and a 'huge command of rhetoric and stage pathos'[3] existed apart from the ideas which formed them. However: 'make the necessary allowances', especially as Shaw was of his age in practising the separation, and we see that it was the Shakespearian world-picture which he rejected:

It is the philosophy, the outlook on life, that changes, not the craft of the playwright. A generation that is thoroughly moralized and patriotized, that conceives virtuous indignation as spiritually nutritious, that murders the murderer and robs the thief, that grovels before all sorts of ideals, social, military, ecclesiastical, royal and divine, may be, from my point of view, steeped in error; but it need not want for as good plays as the hand of man can produce. Only, those

[1] *Our Theatres in the Nineties*, Vol. II, p. 196.
[2] 'Life and Letters', *The Times Literary Supplement*, 16 June 1966.
[3] Two characteristic phrases. See the Preface to *Three Plays for Puritans*, p. xviii.

plays will be neither written nor relished by men in whose philosophy guilt and innocence, and consequently revenge and idolatry, have no meaning. Such men must re-write all the old plays in terms of their own philosophy; and that is why ... there can be no new drama without a new philosophy.... the humblest author, and much more a rather arrogant one like myself, may profess to have something to say by this time that neither Homer nor Shakespear said.[1]

Shaw is wrong of course to associate even a moderately good play with moral error, but he is also right in a sense: a reasonably well-read fifteen-year-old may profess to 'know' more than Shakespeare and Homer did. Knowing more is the prize of history; and Shaw knew Wagner and Marx and Ibsen, Lamarck and Darwin and Butler, Capitalism and Socialism: he knew a modern world with its brand-new problems.

If he could fault Shakespeare for not being able to 'interpret' the eighteen-nineties, it can be imagined how much more scathingly (but always courteously and wittily) he fell on his contemporaries for barely being able to 'interpret' the seventeen-nineties. There is a notable passage in 'The Sanity of Art' in which he turns his back on 'the platitudes which are "not for an age but all time"' and aligns his work with what he calls 'journalism', that is, a commentary on and an interpretation of people and issues of the present. Journalism, he says, can claim to be the highest form of literature, 'for all the highest literature is journalism'. And being Shaw, therefore one of the assured great men of literature, he concludes that journalism is for him.[2] But not, he declared, for the votaries of 'Art'; or for the 'skilled liars and pandars' in commercial theatres, who were grubbing around in the backwaters of 'Sardoodledum' and the 'cup and saucer' play whilst the mighty life-giving flood of journalism–literature rolled unheeded by.

Life was the business of art, and life to 'pure' art stood as oxygen does to ether. Similarly, Sardou's 'well-made play' – of which Pineroesque 'cup and saucer drama' was a muted, fluting derivative – was capable of as much growth as artificial flowers and clockwork mice are capable

[1] Ibid. pp. xxxi–xxxiii.
[2] *Major Critical Essays*, p. 283.

of growth.[1] The well-made play was like a sandwich, with an all-too-predictable 'situation' as filling and an exposition and unravelling as all-too-stale bread. To Shaw a 'slice of life' was infinitely preferable: this was something with body and energy; it grew in itself out of itself, neither along certain stereotyped lines nor haphazardly, but according to the ineluctable facts of the given situation.

Aristotle's canon about the primacy of plot is never admitted in so many words; as an academic point, it is something Shaw probably never felt called on to discuss. Quite clearly, though, the anathema he pronounced against the 'well-made' plot and his frequent insistence on the organic growth of the play indicate some affinity to classical form. Indeed, as we shall see, he was being far from airy when he announced somewhat late in his career that he wrote in the classical manner.[2] Generally speaking, Shaw accepted the traditional standbys of criticism, citing comedy as drama that chastens morals by ridicule and Aristotle's theory of *catharsis* in tragedy as still the best we have to work with.[3] But pure tragedy was defunct as an effective genre: it had never developed and in any event it had a weakness he could not condone, the element of 'accident'. The new and higher form of dramatic art was tragi-comedy, 'a much deeper and grimmer entertainment than tragedy', with heroes of comedy 'dying without hope or honour ... miserable and not hopeless; for they are mostly criticisms of false intellectual positions which, being intellectual, are remediable by better thinking.'[4]

Better thinking: the phrase brings us back to the axis of the Shavian world; and better thinking was something that simply did not exist in the theatrical world. What did exist was a 'fool's paradise of romance', 'heart-wearying conventionality', 'romantic logic', 'sensuous ecstacy', 'voluptuous reverie' (Shaw had a wide range of telling phrases).[5] He was a professional drama critic for three years; he saw prejudice

---

[1] See 'How William Archer Impressed Bernard Shaw', *Pen Portraits and Reviews*, p. 7.
[2] Preface to *Saint Joan*, p. 54.
[3] 'Tolstoy: Tragedian or Comedian ?', *Pen Portraits and Reviews*, pp. 260–1.
[4] Ibid. p. 263.
[5] See the Preface to *Three Plays for Puritans*.

flattered, illusions pampered, conceit tickled; he saw cant, hypocrisy and humbug, the topsy-turvy morality of a Capitalist society glorified in the topsy-turvy morality of the commercial stage. And as he tells us, having always been a Puritan in his attitude towards art, his moral sense revolted.[1]

*   *   *

When already an established dramatist Shaw affirmed:

I am not an ordinary playwright in general practice. I am a specialist in immoral and heretical plays. My reputation has been gained by my persistent struggle to force the public to reconsider its morals. In particular, I regard such current morality as to economic and sexual relations as disastrously wrong; and I regard certain doctrines of the Christian religion as understood in England today with abhorrence. I write plays with the deliberate object of converting the nation to my opinions in these matters.[2]

Here is the fundamental tenet of Shaw's theory of drama, a personal one in this instance, but given general application by his claim in the Preface to *Pygmalion* that great art can never be anything else but didactic.[3] Unambiguously phrased as both declarations are it might be supposed that nothing more need be said about the matter. But the uncompromising moral crusade here set forth is really compromised time and again, as the pious phrases of criticism, quoted earlier on, will suggest. A literary crusader has a clearly defined 'programme': Shaw's programme was aimed at converting the nation to his opinions— to those opinions outlined in the previous chapters. This being so, it would be legitimate to expect everything else in the play to be subordinated to this aim. Plot would be the merest fabrication, conflict a bore, development mechanical, and the final answer pat. Yet we have already noted what Shaw thought about plot; he stressed the imperative need

[1] Ibid. p. xx.
[2] From 'The Rejected Statement', Part I, the Preface to *The Shewing-Up of Blanco Posnet*, p. 374.
[3] Preface to *Pygmalion*, p. 198.

of vital conflict;[1] he cited Nietzsche in insisting that one should have no convictions[2] and more than once he referred to the Ibsenist answer as the only possibility: this answer was that there was no answer.[3] Quite obviously other criteria than those heretical and immoral ones came into consideration; quite obviously he meant 'didactic' in a special, Shavian sense.

Art had to be true, of course. Artistic truth to Shaw did not mean 'ismatic' truths, in his case Socialism and Creative Evolution, although we may be sure that these informed his versions of the greater truth. Artistic truth was something which comprehended all 'isms' in transcending them. It began in what he called natural history, by which we may understand he implied plain fact. Beginning here, artistic truth was something more: it was the interpretation of the fact, and more than this, it was prophecy based on interpretation of the fact. It was the business of the artist, he said,

> to pick out the significant incidents from the chaos of daily happenings, and arrange them so that their relation to one another becomes significant, thus changing us from bewildered spectators of a monstrous confusion to men intelligently conscious of the world and its destinies.[4]

Although these remarks are misguidedly applied to Brieux, they clearly show the trend of Shaw's thought. It is as far as art can reach. As far as Ibsen had gone; Ibsen, who 'has proved the right of the drama to take scriptural rank, and his own right to canonical rank as one of the major prophets of the modern Bible'.[5] As far as any great artist had gone, for they all, whether in words or on canvas or in the voice of music, revealed something more than themselves in their work, revealed the oneness of art and religious prophecy:

Discernible at first only by the eyes of the man of genius, it (the

---

[1] See Preface to *Plays Pleasant and Unpleasant*, II, p. vi.
[2] *Our Theatres in the Nineties*, Vol. II, p. 93.
[3] Or 'the moral is that there is no moral'. Ibid. Vol. I, p. 191.
[4] Preface to *Three Plays by Brieux*, *The Complete Prefaces of Bernard Shaw*, p. 205.
[5] 'The Quintessence of Ibsenism', *Major Critical Essays*, p. 148.

distant light of the new age) must be focussed by him on the speculum of a work of art, and flashed back from that into the eyes of the common man. Nay, the artist himself has no other way of making himself conscious of the ray: it is by a blind instinct that he keeps on building up his masterpieces until their pinnacles catch the glint of the unrisen sun.

... He cannot explain it: he can only show it to you as a vision in the magic glass of his artwork; so that you may catch his presentiment and make what you can of it.[1]

It may be said, and has been said, that this sort of writing is the merest mush, words piled on words saying nothing at all. If this is so, then not only Shaw but others like Arnold and Wordsworth have said nothing at all when brought to the final excogitation of the nature of art. For art is ultimately a revelation of what we cannot say precisely and never will be able to say precisely; and because we cannot say, the mystery of a divine presence is readily postulated. In this way does the artist become a seer, a visionary, a prophet opening up, perhaps only momentarily, the dazzling vision of heaven on earth or elsewhere and giving us intimations of the glory that is ours to strive for. In this way Beethoven, or Mozart, or Shakespeare are 'didactic'; and this, according to Shaw was the greatness of art, of all art.

But (as his comments on Shakespeare will already have indicated) he distinguished very clearly between 'elemental' art and 'ethical' art, between *A Midsummer Night's Dream* and *A Doll's House* (to take his two examples). The first would still be as fresh as paint when *A Doll's House* was as dull as ditchwater[2] because its themes were those which played round the more stable elements of human nature and so retained their relevance. Not that even the 'elemental' play could be said to be based on immutabilities. In an interesting passage in a theatrical review he attempts the tabulation of ascending values in art, and of the corollary, the survival potential. The first things to date are manners and fashions; then after a time the ethical conceptions no longer apply; all that is then left are the instincts and passions but even

---

[1] Preface to *Plays Pleasant and Unpleasant*, II, p. vii.
[2] See 'The Problem Play – A Symposium', *Shaw on Theatre*, ed. E. J. West.

such 'timeless' qualities, he is prepared to think, may well obsolesce – when humanity has grown into something finer than it has been since the dawn of history.[1] If, however, *A Doll's House*, by being a play which dealt primarily with ethical values should be forgotten relatively soon, it was not less 'great' than *A Midsummer Night's Dream*. It would have done some work in the world and that, Shaw says, is enough for the highest genius.[2]

Enough for the high genius of Ibsen, enough for the high genius of Shaw: art was truth, the truth of ethics, of ethics founded in natural history; and this truth made him not merely an artist, not only a philosopher, but that superior being, the artist–philosopher. So we come to his famous designation and I must say that he perplexes rather than clarifies by using it.

His lengthy attempt in the Preface to *Man and Superman* to say what an artist–philosopher is perplexes even more. Shakespeare and Dickens are not artist–philosophers. Their world is that of diversity, whilst it was the world of a man such as Bunyan that Shaw professed to admire more. Bunyan leads the procession: Blake, Goethe, Shelley, Wagner, Ibsen, Tolstoy, and a few painters and philosophers follow him. They have all a peculiar sense of the world, which Shaw recognizes to be more or less akin to his own. This peculiar sense is manifest in their consistently attacking morality and respectability.

We can agree that Shaw is talking himself into a fine confusion and spinning out distinctions which cannot be pursued. Granted that there is a difference between Bunyan and Dickens – and there is of course an enormous one – it is not in Bunyan's having and Dickens's not having an ethical frame of reference. Unity of conception is implicit in that diversity which Shaw perceived in Dickens; anyway, it was not to be regarded as constituting no attack on morality and respectability that Pecksniff, Pumblechook, and Chadband insinuated themselves into their several novels. And if again we grant a difference between Shakespeare and Tolstoy it is not one that a comparison between, for example, *Measure for Measure* and *The Kreutzer Sonata* will greatly

[1] *Our Theatres in the Nineties*, Vol. II, p. 167.
[2] 'The Problem Play', *Shaw on Theatre*. See Chapter Six for a discussion of these points in relation to Shaw's own drama.

illuminate. But there is something inherently absurd in such couplings. Shaw could well have paused to see what he was in effect doing. The 'apostolic succession' of his frequent iteration included all great artists, and in his less polemical moments he came full circle, so to speak, and admitted this.[1]

If it be recollected that he wrote at generations brought to near stupefaction by such plays as *Lady Audley's Secret, Two Roses*, and *The Bells*, all great successes in their time, all alike in being specially brainless and unedifying, then it can be appreciated how briskly he had to shake playgoers up in order to make them aware of dramatic values. His invariable method was that of the polemicist, who stated the extreme and hoped for the mean. If this is borne in mind we come closest to the essence of Shaw's theory. His shake-up was often excessive, as when he insists that one is not 'entertained' at a theatre but 'educated',[2] or when he condemns all drama except drama of ideas to virtual perdition[3] but (as we shall see) his own plays give the lie to these declarations. 'Ideas' are present in them; so are 'doctrine', 'propaganda', 'edification'. But 'ideas' that, if they affirm his 'isms' and the precedence of intellect over passion, never attempt either to subjugate or pretend unawareness of the emotions. The cerebral ping-pong implicit in his theory of discussion drama is never allowed to subordinate that intensely irrational, unpredictable Will. And his 'educational' purpose is never allowed to subordinate that intensely irrational, unpredictable Wit.

His general philosophy ends in the Life Force, in the affirmation of that divine instinct which drives the earnest seeker ever higher; his theory of drama ascends to the recognition of the same thing. Shaw's 'doctrine' is the doctrine of Life, his 'propaganda' is aimed at promoting this, his 'edification' is of the possibilities in life. Life, the best life, life with a blessing, is the goal. And the play that shows this can be called didactic.

But the play that shows this is never the end in itself, for art, mimesis, is the magic mirror which we make to reflect invisible

---

[1] See Chapter Seven for further remarks on this subject.
[2] *Our Theatres in the Nineties*, Vol. II, p. 72.
[3] Preface to *Mrs Warren's Profession*, p. 161.

dreams in visible pictures, and in the creative evolution of life it will be put aside in time for 'a direct sense of life', for the proposition that one can create nothing but oneself.[1] These are the opinions of the He- and She-Ancients of *Back to Methuselah*, and in citing them we complete our review of Shaw's dramatic theory, finding ourselves where 'two or three are gathered together';[2] in the theatre–church, a place which should be: '. . . a factory of thought, a prompter of conscience, an elucidator of social conduct, an armory against despair and dullness, and a temple of the Ascent of Man.'[3]

[1] See 'As Far as Thought can Reach', *Back to Methuselah*, p. 242.
[2] See the Preface to *Major Barbara*, p. 218.
[3] 'The Author's Apology', the Introduction to *Our Theatres in the Nineties*, p. vii.

PART II: DRAMATIST

Chapter Four

1892-1901: BLUE BOOKS, 'NEW WOMEN', AND DICTATORS

*'I had no taste for what is called popular
art, no respect for popular morality, no belief
in popular religion, no admiration for popular
heroics.'*[1]

1

It is Shaw himself who reminds us of what Karl Marx once said of John Stuart Mill – that Mill owed his eminence to the flatness round about him. The same can be said of Shaw's 'Unpleasant Plays'. They are emphatically not mediocre, neither are they without effective irony and bursts of wit; in fact, for the work of a tyro who began writing plays almost by accident, *Widowers' Houses* and *Mrs Warren's Profession* – but not *The Philanderer*, which I think very poor – can be compared quite favourably with Shakespeare's first plays. But they are 'didactic realistic'[2] plays, their colour is grey, and whatever the *genre* of Shaw's subsequent works it was not didactic realism, whatever the colour it was not grey.

Perhaps one should say that they are blue plays, except that the word has irrelevant connotations. Shaw himself speaks of their blue-bookishness as though they were dramatized versions of Royal Commission reports on housing and prostitution; and (to discuss the first play first) *Widowers' Houses* does even have a blue book turn up in the third act. Here, in sardonic emulation of its counterpart in the conventional romance, it 'reveals all' to the 'heroine', Blanche Sartorius, and gives the audience ground for hoping that if municipal jobbery and shady deals are accorded the priority they call for, love's young dream will

---

[1] Preface to 'Plays Pleasant and Unpleasant', I, p.v.
[2] The phrase by which Shaw designated *Widowers' Houses*.

yet be fulfilled. Love's young dream is duly fulfilled, Blanche and her fastidious lover are happily reconciled – reconciled in the knowledge that the two of them and her father and Lickcheese and Lady Roxdale and Sir Harry and every man, woman and child with twopence to invest in property are morally besmirched and befouled. For, as Shaw puts it, they fatten on the poverty of the slum as flies fatten on filth.[1]

The foundation of the play's thesis is patently Fabian economic theory: Sidney Webb, if not Jevons himself, may be imagined sitting in the wings, prompt-copy in hand, nodding agreement to an argument that develops exactly as 'The Economic Basis of Socialism' says it will. At the bottom of the economic ladder are the poor: propertyless, foodless, and homeless as well, unless one called the tenement warrens for which they pay rent 'home'. The rent collector is Lickcheese who twists, squeezes, and bullies rent out of them in ways that are entirely compatible with legality and his understandable desire to keep himself and his family alive. The first landlord is Sartorius, who twists, squeezes and bullies Lickcheese in ways that are entirely compatible with legality and his blameless, middle-class affluence. Then comes Trench, who does no twisting, squeezing, and bullying, but sits back in gentlemanly indolence and well-bred ignorance of the source of his independent income of seven hundred pounds a year. Sartorius tells him that it is he, Sartorius, who has to pay him the money – and with this, the second landlord discovered, Ricardo's theory of rent is neatly rounded off. At the same time, it is most effectively dramatised. The second act, in which Trench discovers that he is as culpable as Sartorius, is grimly logical, discovery following on discovery with the kind of effect only a natural flair for theatre and sense of dramatic timing can produce. This act is certainly the best of the play – much better than the third, which (written hurriedly five or more years after the first and second acts had been completed) seems to look round in an uncertain way for something that will go one better than twice-paid rent, and settles on a piece of skulduggery which, if it generally confirms the infernal nature of moneyed respectability, is too subtle in its details for the theatre.

[1] Preface to 'Plays Pleasant and Unpleasant', I, p. xxii.

But perhaps Shaw did not think that the finer points of the Lick-cheese–Sartorius–Trench pact much mattered. 'Woe unto you, scribes and Pharisees, hypocrites! for ye devour widows' houses, and for a pretence make long prayer: therefore ye shall receive the greater damnation.' This is what matters, the understood epigraph of the play, as the title hints, one that fuses readily with Fabian economics. But if this denunciation is the yardstick it is reasonable to expect some of its passion to have seeped into the play. None has: although several confrontations are vivid and even intense, the work as a whole is remote and unchallenging.

Not that the play is unintelligent. Shaw may often have done foolish things in his career but he could not ever be unintelligent. Perhaps *Widowers' Houses* is too intelligent – with the intelligence of one who has seen that poverty is a remote thing to wealth, that the broken balustrades and rotten stairways of Robbins's Row *and* the outspoken clergyman are foreign to the middle-class prosperity of Surbiton. But Shaw cannot have it both ways: place the victims of Capitalism far away – but for Lickcheese's few words on their behalf practically out of sight, so far away that Trench has not even heard that their famine puts food on his table and their disease gives his body health – place them there and one has no dramatic warrant (although there is the moral warrant) for crying out 'Woe unto you, scribes and Pharisees, hypo-crites'. A comparison between *Widowers' Houses* and Galsworthy's *The Silver Box* shows that as far as intellectual incisiveness is concerned Galsworthy is Cratyllus to Shaw's Socrates: and yet *The Silver Box* is dramatically more telling because its conflicts are more immediate.

The immediacy of vivid characters is not a lack, however. It will be as well to state at the beginning that Shaw's rendering of stage characters is invariably definite, bold, and vivid. I see this as a merit. Those who object to definiteness, boldness, and vividness – especially definiteness – as faults of delineation demand from the theatre what the theatre dare not give. The muted tones, the subtle pastel shades of portraiture open to the novelist are denied the dramatist, who has very few types of character available for his purpose, the comic dramatist fewer. The result is the 'stock' character, which Shaw used copiously, even (as he once found he had to explain) as Shakespeare had used it.

'I play the old game in the old way, on the old chess-board, with the old pieces . . .,'[1] he said.

So – to return to *Widowers' Houses* – Lickcheese, who is the first Shavian portrait in the drama of an inhabitant of underdogdom, whimpers and whines and wheedles his way through the second act in speeches that do credit to his detachable conscience. Then the grub metamorphosed: Lickcheese ascendant, Lickcheese resplendent, sneering and snarling and scheming his way through the third act in lines that do credit to an utterly forsworn conscience. He is derived from Dickens, he is like his companions in the play in being a bit wooden and predictable, but he is consistently and insistently Lickcheese. The same may be said of Sartorius, Trench, and Cokane: they are themselves, even though what this amounts to is not memorable. But what about Blanche Sartorius, who moved Shaw's 'collaborator', William Archer, to such pained and unavailing protest?[2]

Blanche is not memorable either, but she is very interesting, less for what she does than for what it seems Shaw is trying to express in her. In the first act she is as decorously and obediently in love as the most rigorous convention could expect. Then in Act II a new Blanche – a Shavian Blanche – supersedes the old one. Archer, severely put out in the beginning by a collaborator who used up plot material with feckless disregard of the 'well-made' construction, threw up his hands in disgust.[3] And it must be admitted that the new Blanche is hard to accept, no matter how faithful her behaviour (and Shaw insisted that it was utterly faithful) to her particular category in 'natural history'. The female that throttles its maids and stalks its men with every intention of capturing and annihilating them *may* be explained and justified; but Blanche cannot be, not in the context of the play. She does not have artistic credibility. All the same, one senses that in her sudden proud assertion of independence and in the way she stalks Trench in the last act Shaw is groping for something which he himself cannot be certain of, is reaching out for an as yet insufficiently realized image of woman-

[1] 'I am a Classic but am I a Shakespeare Thief?', *Shaw on Theatre*, pp. 132–3.
[2] See William Archer, *The Old Drama and the New*, London, Heinemann, 1923, p. 346.
[3] Ibid. p. 344.

hood. One senses in Blanche the hesitant, barely articulated beginning of that driving force which was to bring so many of Shaw's women to compelling utterance.

Within a year Shaw had created Vivie Warren. Because of her mother's Profession, Vivie was not presented to the general public in England until 1925, by which time her 'newness' might be thought to have become a trifle old-fashioned, but yet a second world war was required to drive home some of the truths she epitomizes – that young women may have brains, that they may quite possibly be efficient and successful outside marriage and motherhood, that marriage and motherhood are not a necessary consummation of a young woman's dreams. All this Vivie has to prove to herself and we are left reasonably certain that she will prove it. What, though, are one's feelings about her when, having firmly and unambiguously pushed her young man and her mother out of her life, she settles down to her chosen career in actuarial mathematics? Shaw tells us that her 'grave expression breaks up into one of joyous content'.[1] Her demeanour is that of an emancipated woman; justifiably so, for Vivie has won through to the sort of personal freedom which very few women of her time dared hope to achieve. She has won a notable and worthwhile victory.

Run of the mill criticism of *Mrs Warren's Profession* seems satisfied to consider Vivie as far as this;[2] to consider her, it seems to me, only half of the way Shaw succeeded in taking her. Obviously no victory can be without cost, and it is by showing the cost of her victory – which can only be expressed in terms of lost humanity and blighted affections – that Shaw has created very much more than a conventional 'new woman': he has created a woman whose emancipation affords room for our pity.

One should not, of course, sentimentalize over a girl whose hard-headedness and brisk decisiveness finally rout all sentimentality and all 'beauty and romance', and encourage her to take on 'life as it is',[3] but it is clear that she bears the curse of God to the first generation. Vivie is cursed by her terrible inheritance.

[1] *Mrs Warren's Profession*, Act IV, p. 247.
[2] See, for example, Henderson, *G.B.S.: Man of the Century*, p. 531.
[3] *Mrs Warren's Profession*, Act IV, p. 234.

It is a social as much as a personal inheritance. Mrs Warren, forced as a young woman to choose between penury and respectability on the one hand and money and vice on the other, chooses money and vice. Orthodoxy would read her in this way, but Shaw's inversion table, working from the premise that penury is a vice and money a virtue, re-words her career of prostitution as sensible and virtuous. Relatively virtuous, that is, for Shaw does not suggest that life as a prostitute would be preferable to life as a waitress if the waitress were paid as well as the prostitute. Prostitution is a filthy and damnable profession, made wholesome and blessed only by the filthy and damnable social system, which drives women like Mrs Warren to sell their lives so that they may gain their lives. 'Oh', Mrs Warren bursts out to Vivie, —

> Oh, the hypocrisy of the world makes me sick! Liz and I had to work and save and calculate just like other people; elseways we should be as poor as any good-for-nothing drunken waster of a woman that thinks her luck will last for ever. . . . I despise such people: theyve no character; and if theres a thing I hate in a woman, it's want of character.[1]

Woman of distinct character that she is, Mrs Warren has every cause to rebuke the world for its hypocrisy – the Duke of Belgravia, the Archbishop of Canterbury, 'all decent society' in fact, for pocketing its 22 per cent on this questionable investment and that dubious undertaking whilst denouncing her profession. But woman of tireless energy that she also is, Mrs Warren cannot give up her work. She does not put the matter in quite these words but 'whore' is stamped on her honest forehead; besides, as she eventually admits to Vivie, she likes making money; she likes her 40 per cent on the 'hotels' she runs on the Continent:[2] she likes being a conventional Capitalist. So Vivie, who had found it in her heart and mind to forgive and love her mother for having become a prostitute, because this had been an act of sheer necessity, must renounce her finally, because social determinism has been superseded by individual freedom of choice, which Mrs Warren

[1] *Mrs Warren's Profession*, Act II, p. 211.
[2] Ibid. Act IV, pp. 244–5.

cheerfully abuses. Vivie has then to live her life deprived of any gifts from the past.

Deprived it is true of a good deal of sham, for the 'beauty and romance' of Brussels and Ostend can be nothing other than sham when Mrs Warren's dark public secret flourishes in these places; deprived, it may be thought, only of sham, if the general nature of the social circle depicted in the play be considered: Praed, the devotee of 'beauty and romance', whose altogether delightful guiding rule is that life should not be looked into too closely; Frank, whose charm and wit do not begin to hide an almost infinite capacity for idleness; Frank's father, the Reverend Samuel Gardner, whose parental incompetence is the symptom of his spiritual vacuity; Sir George Croft, who is quite simply a vicious man. These people are no loss to Vivie, and a partnership with her friend, Honoria Fraser, is preferable to an association with them, but – and this is the point – these people might well have been, not other people, but altogether cleaner people if their complicity in Mrs Warren's profession had not dirtied their souls.

John Tanner was to say a few years later: 'Sentimentality is the error of supposing that quarter can be given or taken in moral conflicts.'[1] Vivie, succumbing once, will commit no such error again. Abolish the past, bring in the future; send Mrs Warren and Frank packing, bring in Honoria Fraser, remorseless hard work – and actuarial mathematics. This is Vivie's victory: but poor, savaged, victorious Vivie:

> I am sure that if I had the courage I should spend the rest of my life in telling everybody – stamping and branding it into them until they all felt their part in its abomination as I feel mine. . . . The two infamous words that describe what my mother is are ringing in my ears and struggling on my tongue; but I cant utter them: the shame of them is too horrible for me.[2]

Whether or not it was in accordance with one of his own adages that Shaw began doing what he could do and not necessarily what he wanted to do by writing plays, both *Mrs Warren's Profession* and

[1] 'Maxims for Revolutionists', *Man and Superman*, p. 225.
[2] *Mrs Warren's Profession*, Act IV, p. 237.

Widowers' Houses show very clearly that he had discovered his genius. If one's appreciation of these plays must be qualified by the perception of certain weaknesses, chiefly of plot structure, which suggests that 'organic growth' is due to forced feeding (perhaps on blue books), the fact remains that an altogether uncommon talent was finding itself ignored by London. *Mrs Warren's Profession* especially cuts unerringly and deeply through social pretence and pretensions, through several layers of cant and humbug and deceit, opening up the festering sore to shocked discovery – discovery of this guilt and that, of this association and that, of this consequence and that, even the appalling but highly probable consequence of incest. More than this, there is the conflict. Not the conflict between absolutes, in which wares Shaw haughtily says he does not deal,[1] but conflict in which everyone may have a strong case for being thought in the right; in which Sir George Croft may faithfully believe in 'good business', Mrs Warren may sincerely justify starting off as a prostitute and carrying on as a brothel keeper, and Vivie may repudiate her origins in the conviction that *she* is morally right to do so. They are all 'right' according to their individual lights and yet in the end their 'rightness' leaves them terribly impoverished, for they all deny, or are forced to deny, the supreme 'right' of full, generous life.

2

Shaw wrote the last of his 'Pleasant' plays in 1897. If at this date he would have seemed to add to his failure as a novelist failure as a dramatist and to justify in every line of his dialogue William Archer's lament over him,[2] we today are able to see that a major dramatist was coming into his own. He had brought his stage-craft to near perfection, a feat achieved with remarkable, possibly unprecedented speed, he had not perhaps discarded his blue books and 'didactic realism', but he had submerged all this; he had found his true idiom. As Bluntschli, fleeing from death, burst into Raina's bedchamber, Shavian comedy burst on the theatrical world:

[1] See the Preface to 'Plays Pleasant and Unpleasant', II, p. vii.
[2] Archer, *The Old Drama and the New*.

THE VOICE: . . . Excuse my disturbing you; but you recognize my uniform? Serb! If I'm caught I shall be killed. (*Menacingly.*) Do you understand that?

RAINA: Yes.

THE MAN: Well, I dont intend to get killed if I can help it. (*Still more formidably.*) Do you understand that? (*He locks the door quickly but quietly.*)

RAINA: (*disdainfully*) I suppose not. (*She draws herself up superbly, and looks him straight in the face, adding, with cutting emphasis.*) Some soldiers, I know, are afraid to die.

THE MAN: (*with grim goodhumor*) All of them, dear lady, all of them, believe me. It is our duty to live as long as we can.[1]

Thus does *Arms and the Man* start bowling over the romantic clichés of war, and a moment later another romantic cliché, of a maiden's preference for death rather than dishonour – dishonour in this instance amounting to Raina's being seen by rampant rude soldiery in her nightdress:

THE MAN: . . . Now, if you raise an alarm —

RAINA: (*cutting him short*) You will shoot me. How do you know that *I* am afraid to die?

THE MAN: (*cunningly*) Ah; but suppose I dont shoot you, what will happen then? A lot of your cavalry will burst into this pretty room of yours and slaughter me here like a pig; for I'll fight like a demon: they shant get me into the street to amuse themselves with: I know what they are. Are you prepared to receive that sort of company in your present undress?[2]

Raina is definitely not prepared, and so she hides Bluntschli, with consequences which are too well known to be repeated here.

The play, riding the high crest of comic extravagance with a zest that Shaw was to exceed only in *You Never Can Tell*, develops scenes and situations which are undoubtedly more obviously amusing than these two passages, but both of them are characteristic of Shaw's

[1] *Arms and the Man*, Act I, p. 8.
[2] Ibid. pp. 8–9.

technique. It is a technique – one might almost say a formula for laughter – which depends, not on inversion, but on bathos. This is invariably emphasized by vocal scoring, as we see in the first exchange: Raina's declamation, produced *à la* the grand manner, is deftly sabotaged by Bluntschli's rejoinder, produced *à la* Shavian 'natural history', or the alleged fact of the matter. It is not all the fact of the matter, of course: some people – some soldiers – will not be afraid to die; but Bluntschli has not finished. He does so with a statement – 'It is our duty to live as long as we can' – which is palpably true. One does not look for either the academic logician or even Chesterton's 'wild logician' in such lines, here is a dialectic beginning with the thesis, 'Most soldiers are not afraid to die' (which is Raina's implication), then moving on to the antithesis, 'All soldiers are afraid to die', and settling on the synthesis, 'It is the soldier's duty to stay alive'. I laboriously trample on two or three swift and nimble lines of dialogue whose first function it is to be swift and nimble, but I do so because the Hegelian manner here evident is so much a part of the Shavian manner. It is not a necessary progression of thought; it is a dance of ideas – a dance which leaps in anticipation of flight into the empyrean and then suddenly hits the hard earth instead.

In an article written in defence of his 'chocolate cream soldier'[1] Shaw argued for the Bluntschlian 'fact' of soldiering with his usual vigour, citing literature of military campaigns in support of his contentions. That the soldier and the war he has to wage are diametrically opposed to Sergius and the war he tries to wage is made clear in the play as a whole; this is one of the chief anti-romantic themes, handled with such dexterity and effect that it is possible to see Bluntschli's graphic '. . . they shant get me into the street to amuse themselves with' as anticipating the grim cliché of this century. Bluntschli's possible fate is beastly. The fate of his friend – who is burnt alive in a woodyard set on fire by exploding shells – is similarly beastly. Be *Arms and the Man* as lighthearted and gay as operetta it yet pauses to tell us that war is beastly.

But war is also paradoxical, if to be most efficiently conducted by professionals, to be won, it well seems, by amateurs. By death or glory

[1] 'A Dramatic Realist to his Critics', *Shaw on Theatre*.

volunteers. By Sergius. It is Sergius whose magnificent cavalry charge routs the Serbians. He was an ass, he was lucky, yet he won an important battle: it seems highly unlikely that Shaw who so clearly perceived this Byronic hero's unmitigated asininity and arrant luck should not also have seen his role in winning the war the wrong way.[1]

So, despite Chesterton's charge against Shaw's anti-romanticism, the 'higher valour' is given some credit. As a general thing it won't do, though; it won't be able to feed horses or transport troops or do any of the things which Bluntschli does with such consummate ease. As for the 'higher valour', so too for the 'higher love'. Shaw's sub-title is 'An Anti-Romantic Comedy', which should not, as his concession to military valour indicates, persuade one to believe that he is totally unamorous. One can as little be totally romantic or totally anti-romantic as one can be totally anything. Commentators on Shaw have often pointed this out, some with unkind remarks about a suppressed romanticism in his make-up, some like Eric Bentley,[2] with their eyes open to the implications of Sergius's cavalry charge and Raina's indignant accusation of Bluntschli: 'You are a romantic idiot'.[3] Of course Bluntschli is a romantic – to a certain extent; enough of a romantic at all events to deserve Raina's hauteur and to solicit her hand, not as the legatee of six hotels, two hundred horses, seventy carriages, and a staggering number of tablecloths, but as her chocolate cream soldier. But here, we should note, romanticism has become one with fact and has nothing to do with the 'higher love'; this lofty concept is simply too much for mere mortals. By trying to live up to it one succeeds merely in looking foolish and becoming excessively fatigued. Luckily both Sergius and Raina are healthy enough to betray it and not suffer unduly from twinges of conscience.

The gaiety and the exaggeration of *Arms and the Man* are taken up in *You Never Can Tell*, taken up and refined into a play that is not merely a comedy but a farce, an extravaganza – and a serious

[1] See *Arms and the Man*, Act II, p. 28.
[2] Bentley's words are: 'Neither Shaw nor the wiser Romanticists before him advocated the domination of reason by emotion. They said that thought and emotion should work together and not in competition.' *Bernard Shaw*, pp. 47–8
[3] *Arms and the Man*, Act III, p. 69.

'discussion' of, among several things, class distinctions, marriage, parenthood, love, and – Shaw may quite conceivably have averred – the economic straits of light-hearted young dentists at English watering places. It is doubtful whether Shaw could have kept serious discussion out of a play even if he had wanted to, and it is here in full measure, but I feel that *You Never Can Tell* has a buoyancy which it would be a kindness not to disturb by an analysis of the themes. There is one aspect – that depicting the relationship between the lovers – which I comment on in a later chapter; for the rest: the zest and speed of the dialogue (which demands a combination of technical skill and spontaneous vitality not often seen on the stage), the high spirits of the juveniles, the character of William, the waiter – above all, this warm and and warming exemplar of benign, tactful, and gracious service – these qualities keep the play as fresh as a sea breeze.

* * *

Inspiration can come from the most unpromising quarter, if indeed its origin can ever be located, but I advance (as no more than a tentative hypothesis) the West End 'problem' play of the eighteen-nineties, especially Henry Arthur Jones's plays, as one of the sources of inspiration for Shaw's *Candida*. Jones's 'problem' was practically always adultery. To him the seventh commandment was the only commandment, the temptation to break it the only worthwhile subject, the actual breaking of it the only cause of tragedy. As one commentator has wearily remarked, to Jones and his like the Decalogue had become a monologue.[1] Now adultery, whether meditated, anticipated, or consummated, is not a theme of *Candida*; it is sent whizzing out of the play in one line: 'I know well that if I have lost her love and you have gained it, no law will bind her.'[2] This is Candida's husband, James Morell, whose reliance on the 'laws' of convention is total but for this second of grace. When a third person threatens to break up a marriage, more, far more, than the banal switching of bed-fellows is involved; far more

[1] Gilbert Norwood. Quoted by John Gassner, *Masters of the Drama*, New York, Dover, 1951, p. 585.
[2] *Candida*, Act III, p. 129.

than conventional deterrents or orthodox ideals muster their forces to decide the issue; far more than Mrs Grundy's belief in salvation by holy wedlock is challenged. Or so Shaw says, and in saying it advances several leagues beyond the point where Rebellious Susan or Paula Tanqueray or other promiscuous heroines of the time had been left to contemplate their sins. If, then, *Candida* can be seen to derive from Jones's formula, it can also be seen to expose the fallacy by which this formula existed.

Candida is, as everyone knows, also derived from Ibsen's *A Doll's House*, but whereas Nora's journey begins with the famous slam of the house door, Candida's journey consists, so to speak, in staying at home. It is the lover who sallies forth, carrying in his heart the 'secret' which is supposed to constitute the 'mystery' of the sub-title and leaving behind him a scene of apparently blissful domesticity on which the final curtain falls: a curtain which, as Shaw has crossly exclaimed, the New York *Hausfrau* thinks a little paradise but is really a 'greasy fool's paradise'.[1] Is the New York *Hausfrau* wrong – or right?

James Morell, a popular, vigorous, 'advanced' Anglican clergyman, has a wife, Candida, whom he loves and who – he is sincerely convinced – loves him. His is a 'delightful' marriage, a truly 'happy' marriage, firm, secure, sacred, a decisive 'No!' to the philosophy that a marriage can never hope to be anything more than 'convenient'. So Morell believes, so in the course of a single day he is brought terribly to doubt. The assault on his felicity comes from Eugene Marchbanks, a young – a very young – poet who has fallen in love with Candida. He, unable any longer to endure Morell's complacent superiority and his inexhaustible flow of platitudes challenges him:

> A woman, with a great soul, craving for reality, truth, freedom; and being fed on metaphors, sermons, stale perorations, mere rhetoric. Do you think a woman's soul can live on your talent for preaching?[2]

For the first time in his brilliant life Morell is obliged to pause, consider himself, and finally admit, not his shortcomings as yet, but Candida's

[1] Quoted by Huneker in 'The Quintessence of Shaw', *George Bernard Shaw: A Critical Survey*, p. 18.
[2] *Candida*, Act I, p. 98.

right to choose Marchbanks if she so wishes. She is 'put up for auction' and Morell bids for her in these words:

> I have nothing to offer you but my strength for your defence, my honesty for your surety, my ability and industry for your livelihood, and my authority and position for your dignity. That is all it becomes a man to offer to a woman.[1]

Against this Marchbanks bids:

> My weakness. My desolation. My heart's need.[2]

And Candida chooses the weaker of the two – Morell. She explains, and as the truth of his marriage dawns on Morell he has the humility and generosity to acknowledge his need of Candida, his indebtedness to her, his complete dependence:

> It's all true, every word. What I am you have made me with the labor of your hands and the love of your heart. You are my wife, my mother, my sister: you are the sum of all loving care to me.[3]

He remains a windbag but the *Hausfrau* may feel more than satisfied: the Morell marriage is saved; what is more, it will never be brought to ruin, for the cornerstone is that most noble of things, a woman's self-sacrifice for the man she loves.

The *Hausfrau* is not completely deluded. Candida *does* love her husband, her continuous self-sacrifice *is* made in a spirit of love. She *is* industrious, frugal, efficient, cheerful, and affectionate. She *does* have a large and generous spirit. On the whole we should not take either Morell's or Marchbanks's evaluation of her as completely reliable but what we ourselves discern in her makes these qualities clear. But – and with this 'But' we leave the smooth path of sentimental comedy, we turn away from the clichés 'Every Woman Knows', and strike out into purely Shavian territory where the clichés are not repudiated but augmented by their contradictions – but Candida is also her father's daughter.

See her as a paragon of all wifely virtues, then we must see her father,

[1] *Candida*, Act III, p. 138.
[2] Ibid.
[3] Ibid. p. 140.

Burgess, as a more or less irrelevant buffoon tossed into the play to say funny things about Marchbanks's 'poetic orrors' – as someone who cannot be explained as her father. But it will not do to see him in this light. He is Candida's father, which is to say his coarseness, his snobbishness, and above all his eyes for a business opportunity are probably going to be repeated in the daughter he has begotten, reared, and married off. They are repeated, though vastly refined if not completely hidden, by a charm of speech and manner for which Candida can possibly thank money, mother, school – and knowing how to set about getting what she wants from life. She has poetry in her: does not her father sentimentally recollect the fairy stories he told her 'when she was only a little kiddy not that igh' ?[1] She also has prose in her, and it is the prose which directs her to stay at home:

> CANDIDA: . . . Oh! I am to choose am I? I suppose it is quite settled that I must belong to one or the other.
> MORELL: (*firmly*) Quite. You must choose definitely.
> MARCHBANKS: (*anxiously*) Morell: you dont understand. She means that she belongs to herself.
> CANDIDA: (*turning on him*) I mean that, and a good deal more, Master Eugene . . . [2]

It *is* a good deal more; on the face of it cause for leaving rather than remaining:

> . . . Now I want you to look at this other boy here: my boy! spoiled from his cradle. We go once a fortnight to see his parents. You should come with us, Eugene, to see the pictures of the hero of that household. James as a baby! the most wonderful of all babies. James holding his first school prize, won at the ripe age of eight! James as the captain of his eleven! James in his first frock coat! James under all sorts of glorious circumstances! You know how strong he is (I hope he didnt hurt you): how clever he is: how happy. (*With deepening gravity.*) Ask James's mother and his three sisters what it cost to save James the trouble of doing anything but be strong and clever

[1] Ibid. Act III, p. 112.
[2] Ibid. Act III, pp. 137–8.

G

and happy. Ask me what it costs to be James's mother and three sisters and wife and mother to his children all in one. Ask Prossy and Maria how troublesome the house is even when we have no visitors to help us to slice the onions. Ask the tradesmen who want to worry James and spoil his beautiful sermons who it is that puts them off. When there is money to give, he gives it: when there is money to refuse, I refuse it. I build a castle of comfort and indulgence and love for him, and stand sentinel always to keep little vulgar cares out. I make him master here, though he does not know it, and could not tell you a moment ago how it came to be so. (*With sweet irony.*) And when he thought I might go away with you, his only anxiety was – what should become of me! And to tempt me to stay he offered me (*leaning forward to stroke his hair caressingly at each phrase*) his strength for my defence! his industry for my livelihood! his dignity for my position! his – (*relenting*) ah, I am mixing up your beautiful cadences and spoiling them, am I not, darling? (*She lays her cheek fondly against his.*)[1]

Is this the voice of wifely abnegation? To a certain extent it is, but to a greater extent it is the voice of connubial complaint; more, it is the complaint of sisters and mothers, of all women who suffer onions, tradesmen, and other drudgeries and trials of domesticity so that their Jameses may be strong and clever and happy. What price now, we may ask, is James Morell's happiness, what order of 'delight' does Candida find in her marriage? And why, the answers being so much to her apparent disadvantage, does she not leave home?

Partly because there are children in the background, although Shaw has tried to minimize the role they would play in her decision. Largely because of the prose in her make-up: Marchbanks would give her the dew-drenched mountains (or something like that) but Morell, she knows, will give her boots for walking down Hackney Road; life with Marchbanks would be hazardous and uncertain, with Morell safe and secure. For these reasons, and for the reason which comprehends everything: power. The power to belong to herself 'and a good deal more'. To be wife and mother and sisters. To be, not the queen of her little

[1] *Candida*, pp. 139–40.

island but that far more secure, more exalted officer, the person who makes and masters the king.

The question is whether we should qualify Candida's exaltedness by seeing it in its domestic context and allow the greater exaltation to Marchbanks. He proudly spurns Candida as 'mother and sisters' to him and goes out into the mystic night shorn of any desire for mere happiness and in the fullness of his destiny as a poet utterly contemptuous of the life Candida has chosen to lead with Morell. This is generally assumed to be the explanation of the 'mystery'; I wonder though whether a more profound and teasing mystery doesn't remain in Candida's heart.

As far as Beatrice Webb was concerned there was no mystery about Candida: she was simply a woman of bad character.[1] Shaw appears to have cherished this opinion, for he passed it on as his own view to James Huneker some years later: 'Don't ask me conundrums about that very immoral female Candida....'[2] Against this is his assertion to Ellen Terry that 'Candida, between you and me, is the Virgin Mother and nobody else'.[3] We may not feel inclined to take this burst of confidence seriously but it can give us a lead into the woman's personality. A 'bad character' and 'immoral' only in the conventional sense, she is a superbly natural creature, doing the 'right' thing for quite the 'wrong' reasons, playing with the two 'boys' of her life with the skill of a courtesan and the charm of a lady, conquering these 'boys' and making them, embracing domesticity and transcending it, transcending happiness itself. Hers is the sagacity of nature confronted by the actuality of life; the prose of domesticity transmuted, whether Shaw liked it or not, into the poetry of marriage.

Chesterton, at his most mellow and mellifluous, speaks of Candida's choice as expressing what he calls the 'fact', the 'commonwealth' of marriage.[4] What, though, are the facts of this marriage? That it is not

---

[1] *Ellen Terry and Bernard Shaw: A Correspondence*, ed. by Christopher St. John, p. 41.
[2] 'The Quintessence of Shaw', *George Bernard Shaw: A Critical Survey*, p. 18.
[3] *Ellen Terry and Bernard Shaw: A Correspondence*, p. 26. (There are obvious hints to this effect in the play as well.)
[4] Chesterton, *George Bernard Shaw*, p. 53.

Candida's 'goodness' and 'purity' but her love which keeps her with Morell; that she loves him, not in spite of but because of her domestic chores; that, in spite of Morell's happy gassing about the subject, this marriage is not 'delightful' but strictly 'convenient'. That – and this is surely the real 'mystery' of *Candida* – love is neither a free gift from the generous cornucopia of life nor yet a reward: it is a condition. This is a truism, no doubt, as mysteries often tend to be, but how many people, Chesterton not excepted, ever pause to consider it? Certainly not Morell or Marchbanks.

Candida's men are much her inferior as dramatic creations. Morell, it is true, is not merely a pastiche of platitudes but at times an acute and sensitive study of the heart that may beat beneath the platitude. He is also that not uncommon Shavian phenomenon, a person who holds many of Shaw's own views and is set at naught for holding them. Shaw had this habit of shying coconuts at himself in his plays, a habit of searching self-criticism. Conversely, he would set up a member of the idle rich class, a Jack Tanner for instance, as an incipient Prometheus, or a convinced and committed Capitalist, such as Undershaft, as a very Dionysus. This, if it did nothing to the good of his political campaigns was certainly to the good of his art; and in Morell's 'advanced' views we have a substantial addition to the irony of *Candida*. But the short-coming of the character remains: Morell is an oversimplified personality.

Much the same may be said of Marchbanks; the same and a little beside. In several respects Marchbanks is Marchbanks, a perfect foil to Morell, a physically craven, morally fearless, intellectually incisive fledgeling, whose verbal poniards stab Morell's self-esteem. At the same time, we should be mistaken to see him as any less arrogant, conceited, and wrongheaded than his victim, or to hear him as the spokesman of the ethically 'true' and to ascribe any special authority to his summating boast that he understands what a woman is. He does not understand what a woman is, he does not understand the nature of love. He does not, it transpires, understand himself. As far as this segment of Shaw's conception of the character goes, Marchbanks is acceptable, but in several other respects he is not. He is not Marchbanks but Shaw's notion of a poet. I shall have something to say in a later chapter about Shaw's interpretation of the 'artist-genius'; here we need only note that the poet in Marchbanks is an agony of embarrassment – and a slanderous reflection on Shelley, whom Shaw greatly admired and on whom he based Marchbanks's character.

We cannot see Marchbanks as a whole unless we put the boy first and read his poetic speech as adolescent effusion. This was not Shaw's intention but it may be allowed to stand, particularly since, the hour of self-awareness come, the boy grows into the man and in the few minutes allowed him before the final curtain falls, he speaks with a directness that seems to indicate the sloughing off of his former idiom. We may hope for this, at any rate.

These reservations and qualifications about Morell and Marchbanks notwithstanding – and perhaps it is to the benefit of the conflict that neither is a complex or an elusive personality – their confrontations make for intense and exciting drama. This is especially true of their battle in Act IV: the flaming sword *versus* sliced onions, a wretched little nervous disease *versus* pigheadness, archangels with purple wings *versus* fiddlesticks; love that would be freely given *versus* love that would be earned. It is all boldly and vigorously handled and is more, far more, than shadowy drama of 'ideas'.

3

The Perfect Wagnerite, The Man of Destiny, and *Caesar and Cleopatra* all point to Shaw's growing interest at the turn of the century in the strong leader. We have already seen how this concept fitted into his socio-political philosophy; now in Napoleon and Caesar we may see how the man fitted into his drama. Shaw's Napoleon is not important. Created in a hurry to fill a theatrical need, he engages our passing attention because he anticipates Caesar in some ways, chiefly in his scrupulous disregard of the public school code. This is his virtue. His vice is to follow his star without a trace of humorous self-perception. He is only mildly original.

Caesar is a true original, a lonely man in a world of conventional behaviour, where empty-headed posturing, cant, and attitudinizing have come to be regarded as the expressions of universal truths. Shaw is the original playwright, a lonely man in the theatre, where the same mindlessness has come to be regarded as the representation of artistic truths. He has simply and effectively dramatized the conflict of ideas between Caesar and his opponents: by putting it into a play that has all the trappings of popular melodrama. And while Caesar is baffling, surprising, and horrifying his world, constantly showing with devastating affability that its values are false, Shaw baffles, surprises, and amuses his his audience, constantly showing with devastating precision that its melodrama is equally false. The two aims are not really to be separated: they meet in Caesar, the anti-heroic, anti-romantic hero, whose words and actions ridicule Victorian morality and the theatre which images it; for Egypt of *circa* 100 B.C. is patently also England of *circa* 1900 A.D.

This is our introduction to Caesar:

THE MAN: Hail, Sphinx: salutation from Julius Caesar! I have wandered in many lands, seeking the lost regions from which my birth into this world exiled me, and the company of creatures such as I myself. I have found flocks and pastures, men and cities, but no other Caesar, no air native to me, no man kindred to me, none who can do my day's deed, and think my night's thought. In the little world yonder, Sphinx, my place is as high as yours in this great desert; only I wander, and you sit still; I conquer, and you endure; I work and wonder, you watch and wait; I look up and am dazzled, look down and am darkened, look round and am puzzled, whilst your eyes never turn from looking out – out of the world – to the lost region – the home from which we have strayed. Sphinx, you and I, strangers to the race of men, are no strangers to one another: have I not been conscious of you and of this place since I was born? Rome is a madman's dream: this is my Reality. These starry lamps of yours I have seen from afar in Gaul, in Britain, in Spain, in Thessaly, signalling great secrets to some eternal sentinel below, whose post I never could find. And here at last is their sentinel – an image of the constant and immortal part of my life, silent, full of thoughts, alone in the silver desert. Sphinx, Sphinx: I have climbed mountains at night to hear in the distance the stealthy footfall of the winds that chase your sands in forbidden play – our invisible children, O Sphinx, laughing in whispers. My way hither was the way of destiny; for I am he of whose genius you are the symbol: part brute, part woman, and part god – nothing of man in me at all. Have I read your riddle, Sphinx?

THE GIRL: (*who has wakened, and peeped cautiously from her nest to see who is speaking*) Old gentleman.

CAESAR: (*starting violently, and clutching his sword*) Immortal gods!

THE GIRL: Old gentleman: dont run away.

CAESAR: (*stupefied*) 'Old gentleman: dont run away'!!! This! to Julius Caesar!

THE GIRL: (*urgently*) Old gentleman.

CAESAR: Sphinx: you presume on your centuries. I am younger than you, though your voice is but a girl's voice as yet.

THE GIRL: Climb up here, quickly; or the Romans will come and eat you.

CAESAR: (*running forward past the Sphinx's shoulder, and seeing her*) A child at its breast! a divine child!

THE GIRL: Come up quickly. You must get up at its side and creep round.

CAESAR: (*amazed*) Who are you?

THE GIRL: Cleopatra, Queen of Egypt.

CAESAR: Queen of the Gypsies, you mean.

CLEOPATRA: You must not be disrespectful to me, or the Sphinx will let the Romans eat you. Come up. It is quite cosy here.

CAESAR: (*to himself*) What a dream! What a magnificent dream! Only let me not wake, and I will conquer ten continents to pay for dreaming it out to the end.

(*He climbs to the Sphinx's flank, and presently reappears to her on the pedestal, stepping round its right shoulder.*)[1]

The setting for this scene, the opening of Act I, is vital to Shaw's purpose: it is constituted of very nearly everything a playwright bent on providing romance and 'sensuous ecstasy' would require. There is darkness, suspense – for a few moments the engendering of tension,

[1] *Caesar and Cleopatra*, Act I, pp. 101–3.

thoroughly artificial tension because it arises out of nothing; then 'the blackness and stillness break softly into silver mist and strange airs', and slowly, solemnly, the scene becomes visible. It would have filled a Boucicault[1] with joy. A rising moon, a vast horizon, the haunting music of the wind; the Sphinx 'looking straight forward and upward in infinite fearless vigil'; between its paws a splash of vivid colour, a heap of red poppies, and in view of the audience, a girl asleep on the flowers. A shaft of moonlight touches her braided, glittering hair, and the picture of stock romance, tritely mysterious, is complete.

Sounds to match the scene float across the desert: a distant 'vaguely fearful sound', silence, then a 'few faint high-ringing trumpet notes'. This is the cue for the heroic entry. Radames might now appear and the night could ring to 'Celeste Aida', Antony might stride on and resonantly challenge the ranged empire to fall. Both heroes, and countless others from the annals of considerably cheaper romance, would fulfil conventional expectations.

Shaw's hero does not. He comes quietly, with 'stealing steps', a man in an infinity of space, never for a moment appearing to measure up to his surroundings. Before a word has been spoken, the belief that the hero can bestride the wide world like a colossus – which with the belief that love is an infallible solvent of all conflict is probably the hopeful major premise of the romantic convention – is subtly derided.

Less subtle and so much more effective on the stage are the hero's first words: 'Hail, Sphinx ... I have wandered in many lands....' No speaker, least of all a 'rather thin and stringy' one, can hope to make this reverberate; in word and phrase the greeting is flat, prosaic. An audience will probably sense the reduction of the heroic mode, the shift to the anti-heroic mode, but, the question is, does Caesar himself sense this? It is indeed a fine speech he makes, fluent, earnest, sober, and confiding. This is his testament of faith, a confession of immortal longings, a repudiation of the Roman 'madman's dream'. But which is the dream, which the reality? As Caesar's words mount to their sonorous climax we may wonder if they have not begun to work a delusion:

[1] Dion Boucicault may be regarded as the paragon of mid-nineteenth-century sensationalism in the theatre.

My way hither was the way of destiny; for I am he of whose genius you are the symbol: part brute, part woman, and part god – nothing of man in me at all. Have I read your riddle, Sphinx?

As if in reply the hidden girl calls out and in one superbly comic phrase we see the man of destiny deflated to size. By the standards of popular romance Cleopatra's timid, high-pitched 'Old gentleman' is anti-climax; by Shavian standards it is comic climax. The goddess of melo-drama is briskly up-ended – and Caesar is found to have a fair amount of man in him after all.

'Immortal gods!' is the first incongruity from this familiar of the Sphinx; and then Cleopatra's plea that an intimate of the gods should not run away and his reaction – a compound of stupefaction and wounded vanity – comments ironically on a person whose reality a mere thirty seconds before was celestial. It would be an exaggeration to say that Caesar is being purged of vainglorious delusions: he has no need of violent medicine; but he is certainly being teased out of a momentary aberration. His reality is yet but a dream, the dream the reality, and from the moment he clambers on to the Sphinx, exclaiming as he does so, 'What a dream! What a magnificent dream!' the ugly, false, inescapable fact is forced on him. First his 'Queen of the Gypsies' expresses her ambitions in a spate of vindictiveness made more horrid by coming from a child:

> . . . and I shall live in the palace at Alexandria when I have killed my brother. . . . When I am old enough I shall do just what I like. I shall be able to poison the slaves and see them wriggle, and pretend to Ftatateeta that she is going to be put into the fiery furnace.[1]

Then she gigglingly confesses her fear of Caesar, an 'old, and rather thin and stringy' man, no rival in romance for 'young men with round strong arms';[2] makes Caesar's opening speech seem a trifle silly by tell-ing him that his 'eternal sentinel' is only 'a dear little kitten of a sphinx';[3] and a few minutes later jabs a pin into his arm to convince him that he is not dreaming.[4]

---

[1] *Caesar and Cleopatra*, p. 103.   [2] Ibid. p. 104.
[3] Ibid.   [4] Ibid.

There are no more moonlight soliloquies for Caesar after this. Ineluctably an elderly gentleman, bald and thin and stringy, awake and not dreaming, he pursues his course as one who fully recognizes the necessities of this world.

Caesarian necessity is not Egyptian or Roman necessity, however. Hence the conflict in the play, and the danger that the battle of ideologies will be deprived of everything but the most specious suspense. This is the danger of all doctrinaire art, of course, but *Caesar and Cleopatra* is authentic drama. Its action is swift and varied, Caesar's opponents, if doomed always to defeat, have a rich and varied propensity for making themselves look ridiculous, and Caesar himself is presented in episodes that lend themselves perfectly to both his propaganda of sanity and the shock of delight this affords:

THEODOTUS: ... Oh, worse than the death of ten thousand men! Loss irreparable to mankind!

RUFIO: What has happened, man?

THEODOTUS: (*rushing down the hall between them*) The fire has spread from your ships. The first of the seven wonders of the world perishes. The library of Alexandria is in flames.

RUFIO: Psha! ...

CAESAR: Is that all?

THEODOTUS: (*unable to believe his senses*) All! Caesar: will you go down to posterity as a barbarous soldier too ignorant to know the value of books?

CAESAR: Theodotus: I am an author myself; and I tell you it is better that the Egyptians should live their lives than dream them away with the help of books.

THEODOTUS: (*kneeling, with genuine literary emotion: the passion of the pedant*) Caesar: once in ten generations of men, the world gains an immortal book.

CAESAR: (*inflexible*) If it did not flatter mankind, the common executioner would burn it.

THEODOTUS: Without history, death will lay you beside your meanest soldier.

CAESAR: Death will do that in any case. I ask no better grave.

THEODOTUS: What is burning there is the memory of mankind.

CAESAR: A shameful memory. Let it burn.

THEODOTUS: (*wildly*) Will you destroy the past?

CAESAR: Ay, and build the future with its ruins. (*Theodotus, in despair, strikes himself on the temples with his fists*) But harken, Theodotus, teacher of kings: you who valued Pompey's head no more than a shepherd values an onion, and who now kneel to me, with tears in your old eyes, to plead for a few sheepskins scrawled with errors. I cannot spare you a man or a bucket of water just now; but you shall pass pass freely out of the palace. Now, away with you to Achillas; and borrow his legions to put out the fire. (*He hurries him to the steps.*)

POTHINUS: (*significantly*) You understand, Theodotus: I remain a prisoner.

THEODOTUS: A prisoner!

CAESAR: Will you stay to talk whilst the memory of mankind is burning?[1]

Theodotus's passion, Caesar's calm reasonableness, each one's apparent sincerity, set more than one's mind working. The conflict is between personalities as well as between attitudes. The pedant's cries come from his heart. However misguided an instrument this may be and however deserving of ridicule from Caesar and common humanity his first claim may be – 'Oh, worse than the death of ten thousand men!' – his appeal comes in moving words: 'Caesar: once in ten generations of men, the world gains an immortal book.' The power of such appeals provides the scene with sufficient tension and allows greater weight to fall on Caesar's inflexible replies. The contrast of tones, aided by the rhythmic descent and pause whenever Caesar speaks, has the effect of a see-saw that leaps with Theodotus and comes down with a bump with Caesar's answers.

Obviously it is the quality of these answers which will determine the dramatic value of the scene. Caesar is right: so is Theodotus; but while Theodotus is platitudinous, Caesar is refreshingly sceptical. His point of view challenges the other's adoration of a moribund past. 'Will you

[1] *Caesar and Cleopatra*, Act III, pp. 131–3.

destroy the past?' Theodotus cries. 'Ay,' Caesar affirms, 'and build the future with its ruins.' Of course, the past cannot be destroyed, a fact both men seem to forget in the extremity of their views. But while Theodotus pleads like a man possessed for the protection of history, Caesar rebuffs him because present humanity is more important. 'I cannot spare you a man or a bucket of water just now,' he says casually, thus admitting the faults of the particulars in his argument but reinforcing the major point. One suspects that he regards this skirmish of words as a small exercise in dialectic. He is not very fair, either in imposing the discussion on the distraught bibliophile or in his observance of the rules of argument. When Theodotus asks, 'Caesar: will you go down to posterity as a barbarous soldier too ignorant to know the value of books?' his reply is cheating, a generalization about Egyptians dreaming away their lives with books, which Theodotus has neither asked for nor deserved. But a good deal of Caesar's charm lies in his excluding such fixed notions as 'fair play' from his code of conduct, and oddly enough, his slight dishonesty makes him seem benevolent and humane, especially since his 'new' ideas healthily devitalize Theodotus's 'old' ones and as he allows his opponent his freedom. The unlucky teacher cannot escape before the ironically amusing little climax. Even he is caught living in the present. Caesar's sarcastic demand: 'Will you stay while the memory of mankind is burning?' catches Theodotus unawares, and as he scurries off to save his precious books our laughter is directed as much at his discomfiture as at our realization that he cherishes a dream that vanishes before the sharp reality of the moment. The entire passage becomes a small dramatic allegory which lightly chastens our unquestioning deference to the past.

Act IV is the dialectical and dramatic climax of the play. It brings to a head the most serious issue which Caesar's invasion of Egypt has aroused; it also offers an outstanding example of Shaw's manipulation of the constituents of melodrama – deceit, vengeance, sensuous thrills, blood and bombast – for his own ironic purposes. Cleopatra, the kitten, has grown up and become the cat. This is an expressive image, implying first (as it does in Act I) that she has all the softness and playfulness of a kitten. She has no effective claws yet but when she promises herself the delight of seeing slaves wriggle in their death agony, we fancy their eventual hardening and sharpening in the soft paws. At the beginning of Act IV it seems that she is learning to curb her monstrous desires and is well on her way in the spiritual pilgrimage many of Shaw's heroines undertake. She remains, as she confesses, 'as cruel at heart as my father'[1] and entertains herself and her ladies by threatening the most diabolical punishment on a musician[2] (although her reasons for doing so, if not the threat itself, have a touch of Caesar). But Caesar has plainly influenced her. The cat may yet lose its claws, we feel, if it has begun to recognize its own ferocity and is ashamed to let its master see its cruelty. Wanting, as Ftatateeta puts it, to be 'what the Romans call a New Woman',[3] thinking that through Caesar she has achieved wisdom, greatness, and the ability to govern her country, and looking on Caesar as a god,[4] she is beginning to achieve victory over her baser passions. She knows Caesar, she proudly tells Pothinus, 'by instinct'.[5]

It is the phrase on which Pothinus pauses. From this point onwards blind passion controls the action. White with fury Ptolemy's minister declares to Ftatateeta that a 'woman with a Roman heart' will never rule while he lives, and as he goes out, snarling 'So guide yourself accordingly',[6] we may recall the braying cry of Act II, 'Egypt for the Egyptians' and all the insensate nationalism it fostered. He betrays Cleopatra to Caesar, not falsely, as Caesar blandly assures her, but in terms which do no justice to her aspirations. The Queen is destroyed. She had been a long way from governing herself and now as she commands Ftatateeta to avenge her she is a blind, instinctive creature, as much unlike a Caesar as it is possible to be:

CLEOPATRA: Listen to me. If he leaves the Palace alive, never see my face again.

FTATATEETA: He? Poth —

CLEOPATRA: (*striking her on the mouth*) Strike his life out as I strike his name from your lips. Dash him down from the wall. Break him on the stones. Kill, kill, kill him.

[1] *Caesar and Cleopatra*, Act IV, p. 161. [2] Ibid. p. 160.
[3] Ibid. p. 162. [4] Ibid. p. 163–4.
[5] Ibid. p. 164. [6] Ibid. p. 166.

FTATATEETA: (*showing all her teeth*) The dog shall perish.
CLEOPATRA: Fail in this, and you go out from before me for ever.[1]

This is Cleopatra the cat, the personification of bristling, feline savagery. Within a second the claws are retracted and she becomes a caressing creature, winding her soft charms round Caesar, and the Act enters its orgiastically melodramatic first climax.

From Cleopatra's eager little cry, 'I have ordered such a dinner for you, Caesar!' to Pothinus's death scream[2] the play is a calculated assault on one's senses, on one's palate, eye, and ear; the Puritan Shaw casts aside his asceticism, even as Caesar wryly does his —

Well, for once I will sacrifice my comfort . . . I no longer believe anything. My brains are asleep —

and wallows in a surfeit of sensuousness. With its peacocks' brains, nightingale tongues, roast boar, English oysters, fieldfares with asparagus, fattened fowls, and variety of Greek wines – each name lingered over and savoured – the dinner conjures up fatness and luxury, extravagance and excess, the exotic and the romantic. One notes that each person selects a dish which is in character: Rufio, the professional soldier, smacks his lips over roast boar, Apollodorus, the aesthete, prefers nightingales' tongues, Cleopatra, with catlike relish, orders fieldfares, and Caesar, with his happy instinct for bathos, orders the 'pearl' of 'that western land of romance', the English oyster. Here Shaw shows that when peddling voluptuous reverie more thoroughly than the most acclaimed theatrical 'liar and pandar' of the nineteenth century, he had a keener eye for character than any of the writers he was imitating and a savage insight into the very stuff he was writing, as events a few minutes later will prove.

But first the blandishment of the banquet scene passes on to a discussion about the source of the Nile. Caesar's vision of 'a new kingdom' with a 'new holy city' is subtly corrupted by the effluence of qualities which 'destroys a nation of men who are not great': Apollodorus would consecrate this city with Lesbian wine, Rufio sees the

---

[1] *Caesar and Cleopatra*, p. 172.
[2] Ibid. pp. 173–6; the ensuing analysis refers to these pages.

exploration as a conquest of arms, Cleopatra would have the city named 'Caesar's Gift to his Beloved' – a name not unlike those given to the nostalgically romantic verses with which Yeats and other March-banks-like poets were popularizing themselves in the eighteen-nineties. This is a short passage, but long enough for Shaw to create a new mood, one of spurious mystery, which ushers in the priest with the incense-smoking tripod and the miniature sphinx. The sky grows magenta-purple. Cleopatra, with gruesome irony, mentions that the invocation of Father Nile should be fortified by a human sacrifice:

CLEOPATRA: ... To do it properly, we should kill something to please him; but perhaps he will answer Caesar without that if we spill some wine to him.

APOLLODORUS: (*turning his head to look up over his shoulder at Ra*) Why not appeal to our hawkheaded friend here?

CLEOPATRA: (*nervously*) Sh! He will hear you and be angry.

RUFIO: (*phlegmatically*) The source of the Nile is out of his district, I expect.

CLEOPATRA: No: I will have my city named by nobody but my dear little sphinx, because it was in its arms that Caesar found me asleep. (*She languishes at Caesar and then turns curtly to the priest.*) Go. I am a priestess, and have power to take your charge from you. (*The priest makes a reverence and goes out.*) Now let us call on the Nile all together. Perhaps he will rap on the table.

CAESAR: What! table rapping! Are such superstitions still believed in this year 707 of the Republic?

CLEOPATRA: It is no superstition: our priests learn lots of things from the tables. Is it not so, Apollodorus?

APOLLODORUS: Yes: I profess myself a converted man. When Cleopatra is priestess, Apollodorus is devotee. Propose the conjuration.

CLEOPATRA: You must say with me 'Send us thy voice, Father Nile'.

ALL FOUR: (*holding their glasses together before the idol*) Send us thy voice, Father Nile.

The death cry of a man in mortal terror and agony answers them.[1]

[1] Ibid. pp. 175–6.

Pothinus's sudden, taunting death cry, the 'answer' to the call on Father Nile, rends the façade. Cleopatra's sumptuous banquet, her incense-heavy rite, the whole gorgeous edifice of melodrama she has so carefully constructed to soothe and flatter the physical appetites and dull the intellect – all this is false. Behind in the dark the fact is established, a man is murdered. Father Nile, the god of life to a nation, does not answer his call: Ra's scream of blood supervenes with perfect timing and the truth. It is a shocking and superbly managed moment.

We see now that the dialogue preceding it is highly ironical. Cleopatra's true god is 'the hawkheaded friend', Ra, whose voracity is at this moment being served. Rufio's remark, 'The source of the Nile is out of his district, I expect', is perfectly true: Ra's district surrounds them. Cleopatra refers back to the first scene, to 'my dear little sphinx, because it was in its arms that Caesar found me asleep'. It was also in its arms that she had anticipated such a deed as Ftatateeta is busy performing for her, and it was in its arms that Caesar had been aroused from the dream into which he is again allowing himself to be lulled. The 'conjuration' of Father Nile is indeed not the superstition Caesar lightly supposes it is: in ten seconds it will produce the most shattering response.

*   *   *

At this point we may leave the action and consider what seems to me to be the most serious question raised by the play. It is in fact the ultimate question of power politics. When may authority pass the death sentence on a human being? The question is present throughout, from Ra's address to the audience in the Prologue to Caesar's exculpation of Rufio in the last act. The play reeks of blood. Besides having on the stage one of the most gory murders we are likely to see outside Grand Guignol, it has another, a highly audible murder, off-stage, an exchange on severed hands and heads, and a liberal scattering of remarks (chiefly but not exclusively by Cleopatra) on poisoned slaves, fiery furnaces, and hungry crocodiles. Life is expendable in the world of Caesar and Cleopatra; nor should we object to this on the grounds that such a disturbing note should not underscore a comedy. It does underscore this comedy, for the excellent reason that artistic integrity could not allow it not to.

Neither can humanity itself allow life not to be expendable. This conclusion arises from the paradox of Caesar's mission. His way is the way of the gods, the way of life; it becomes also the way of the soldier, the way of death.[1] The way of the gods cannot be won by evading death; it can only be won by overcoming death. So Caesar marches in conquest through Egypt (at least, he conquers when reinforcements arrive), one hand gripping the sword, the other raised in benign salute. Caesar kills that he may bring enlightened peace to prevail.[2]

But even when he lays down his arms he may not also lay down this responsibility for death – his responsibility to life. It is his burden as a leader of men. How shall he carry his burden, how decide whether a man shall live or die?

The issues are raised for the first time when Lucius confronts Caesar in Ptolemy's palace:

LUCIUS: ... You have seen severed heads before, Caesar, and severed right hands too, I think; some thousands of them, in Gaul, after you vanquished Vercingetorix. Did you spare him with all your clemency? Was that vengeance?

CAESAR: No, by the gods! would that it had been! Vengeance at least is human. No, I say: those severed right hands and the brave Vercingetorix basely strangled in a vault beneath the Capital, were (*with shuddering satire*) a wise severity, a necessary protection to the commonwealth, a duty of statesmanship – follies and fictions ten times bloodier than honest vengeance! What a fool was I then! To think that men's lives should be at the mercy of such fools! ...[3]

This is clear enough, and Caesar emerges from the exchange with the increased stature an honest confession of fallibility will always impart. Then Pothinus is murdered and the second part of the debate takes place:

---

[1] *Caesar and Cleopatra*, Ra's Prologue, p. 86.
[2] Cf. two of the Undershaft mottoes, *Major Barbara*, Act III, p. 326.
[3] *Caesar and Cleopatra*, Act II, p. 123–4.

CAESAR: (*with quiet bitterness*) And so the verdict is against me, it seems.

CLEOPATRA: (*vehemently*) Listen to me, Caesar. If one man in all Alexandria can be found to say that I did wrong, I swear to have myself crucified on the door of the palace by my own slaves.

CAESAR: If one man in all the world can be found, now or forever, to know that you did wrong, that man will have either to conquer the world as I have, or be crucified by it. (*The uproar in the streets again reaches them.*) Do you hear? These knockers at your gate are also believers in vengeance and in stabbing. You have slain their leader: it is right that they shall slay you. If you doubt it, ask your four counsellors here. And then in the name of that right (*he emphasizes the word with great scorn*) shall I not slay them for murdering their Queen, and be slain in my turn by their countrymen as the invader of their fatherland? Can Rome do less then than slay these slayers, too, to shew the world how Rome avenges her sons and her honor. And so, to the end of history, murder shall breed murder, always in the name of right and honor and peace, until the gods are tired of blood and create a race that can understand. (*Fierce uproar. Cleopatra becomes white with terror.*) Hearken, you who must not be insulted. Go near enough to catch their words: you will find them bitterer than the tongue of Pothinus. (*Loftily, wrapping himself up in an impenetrable dignity.*) Let the Queen of Egypt now give her orders for vengeance, and take her measures for defence; for she has renounced Caesar.[1]

So the murder of Pothinus was wrong, damnably wrong, a crime against the gods, against nature. But are Caesar's views here consistent with what he said to Lucius? We may leave the question to hover while we outline the third and final part of the debate.

By the end of Act IV Caesar is again ascendant. Cleopatra, deserted by her 'four counsellors' but not defeated, threatens Rufio. He grimly acknowledges the threat and slips away. The Roman soldiers greet Caesar in the courtyard below, 'Hail Caesar! Hail! Hail!' at which moment Rufio is slitting Ftatateeta's throat. As the soldiers salute

[1] *Caesar and Cleopatra*, Act IV, p. 180–1.

their all-conquering hero, the apparently converted disciple of Caesar kills the handmaiden of melodrama and leaves her before her god, her blood deluging the altar.[1] And now the question becomes: is the murder of Ftatateeta right or wrong?

RUFIO: .... Now tell me: if you meet a hungry lion ..., you will not punish it for wanting to eat you?

CAESAR: (*wondering what he is driving at*) No.

RUFIO: Nor revenge upon it the blood of those it has already eaten.

CAESAR: No.

RUFIO: Nor judge it for its guiltiness.

CAESAR: No.

RUFIO: What, then, will you do to save your life from it?

CAESAR: (*promptly*) Kill it, man, without malice, just as it would kill me. What does this parable of the lion mean?

RUFIO: Why, Cleopatra had a tigress that killed men at her bidding. I thought she might bid it kill you some day. Well, had I not been Caesar's pupil, what pious things might I not have done to that tigress! I might have punished it. I might have revenged Pothinus on it.

CAESAR: (*interjects*) Pothinus!

RUFIO: (*continuing*) I might have judged it. But I put all these follies behind me; and, without malice, only cut its throat. And that is why Cleopatra comes to you in mourning.

CLEOPATRA: (*vehemently*) He has shed the blood of my servant Ftatateeta. On your head be it as upon his, Caesar, if you hold him free of it.

CAESAR: (*energetically*) On my head be it, then; for it was well done, Rufio: had you set yourself in the seat of the judge, and with hateful ceremonies and appeals to the gods handed that woman over to some hired executioner to be slain before the people in the name of justice, never again would I have touched your hand without a shudder. But this was natural slaying: I feel no horror at it.[2]

[1] Ibid. p. 185.
[2] Ibid. Act V, pp. 191–2.

If we confine ourselves to the killing of Pothinus and Ftatateeta we see that Caesar admitted a distinction. To Rufio the distinction may be (and very likely is) merely a matter of words and form but to Caesar it is considerably more. It decides an entire way of life. Cleopatra's instigation to murder is wrong, because it was not natural in the sense that Rufio's slaying of Ftatateeta is judged by Caesar to be natural, because she drew her motives from an unnatural, from a positively malignant, source – the claptrap of 'honour', 'dignity', 'pride', and 'justice'.

So far admirably sane; but if we recall Caesar's words to Lucius definitions become badly blurred. Liquidation for the sake of political advantage was (so Caesar confessed to Lucius) abhorrent and vengeance at least was 'human'; but (see the second excerpt) vengeance bred further vengeance and (now the third passage) was not 'natural'; 'natural slaying' was permissible because it was committed 'without malice'. . . . What would twelve good men and true make of this hierarchy? What will a ruffianly Rufio make of this distinction between expediency and 'natural slaying'? And an intensely human Cleopatra of this injunction to eschew humanness? The short answer is – a mess.

However, we should be mistaken to think that the master of the uncategorical imperative has allowed his argument to fold into these untenable categories. The leader, in whom by the fact of his position the law is vested, can rule only as he can and must govern in his own way,[1] which means (be the 'rule of law' as devoutly recited as possible) that his power to adjudicate over rights and wrongs, to decide whether a man is fit or unfit to live, is proportional to his – the leader's – personal stature. Caesar's code is a human impossibility: it will be realized only to the extent that we will become Caesars; for to Caesar the code is not a code, nor merely a distant ideal, but a fully realized habit of mind. No punishment, no revenge, no justice: these to Caesar are not categories but the flat denial of them. He – and he alone – has the insight, the conviction, the strength, and the courage to understand this. He – and he alone – may say 'This man is not fit to live' or better and more often 'This man shall live'.

We see again, as we see so often in Shaw, that the argument runs

[1] See *Caesar and Cleopatra*, Act V, p. 191.

itself out in a Hegelian reconciliation to irreconcilables. There is the triumph of the Superman-Caesar, an acclamation which brings the action to an electrifying conclusion: as Caesar embarks for his journey back to Rome, swords flash, their bright points raised to heaven, and the soldiers acclaim their hero: 'Hail Caesar!'[1] But there is also the tragedy of faltering, erring humanity, of certain idealists in Rome, who wait to assassinate Caesar in the cause of words he has shown to inspire sheer foolishness; of Rufio, whose allegiance to Caesar's way of life must ever be qualified by his instinct to draw his sword first and ask questions afterwards; and of Cleopatra, whose unchanged heart yearns for Antony even as she weeps for the god she has denied. There is this tragedy, and the laughter and delight of the play are tempered by such knowledge.

Caesar and Cleopatra is not Shaw's greatest play but it is a great play, mainly because of Caesar. He is a memorable creation, credible for all his unorthodoxies, convincingly human despite his god-like attributes, the embodiment of super-human sanity as well as of ordinary human frailties. Anti-heroic, anti-romantic, he is probably the outstanding hero of English comedy and paradoxically the most noble hero of English drama since his rival, Antony.

To see him in this light means of course to agree with the way of life he follows. As it is expressed in Shaw's note, this way may seem forbiddingly sterile, but Caesar the man gives it very real warmth. His ideas are often not 'noble', are often selfish and calculating, and they come sometimes with scant regard to their cue and the rules of argument. And yet he stands for an attitude to life which is incontestably worthwhile. To shake loose the dead hand of the past, to free the personality of social and political shibboleths, to have the intellect step forth unfettered and free – this is Caesar's message for mankind and his personal achievement.

Another achievement of his should be mentioned – this to do with the form of the play. Things centre on him, and since his progress through the action seems like a convivial and not overtly purposeful stroll, it may be thought that form has given way to carefree improvization. In fact, the play has a contained resonance. It is in the diction, a

[1] Ibid. p. 193.

daring fusion of the colloquial and the archaic, which imparts a fluid sonority to the dialogue, in the immediate objects on which the abstract conflict is grounded – in the Sphinx, in 'our hawkheaded friend', in the shortage of chairs in Ptolemy's council hall, in Pothinus's death, in the allusions back and forward to these concrete things and to the predominant image of Cleopatra the Cat. It is in the changes of mood, in the swings to the four points of the dramatic compass – from comedy to tragedy, melodrama to discussion – swings that point to no improvizatorial carelessness but to a most audacious yet controlled imagination. The resonance of all this implies a pattern, some unifying principle, and Caesar's progress, meandering though this appears, provides it. His benign glance binds the play, and as his feet tread their course from this initial aberration to his triumph we see a constant spiritual ascent from his immediate environment. Shaw was still to formulate the realm of 'pure intelligence', but had Caesar been created twenty years later it is to this realm he would have been going. Fortunately for the play, the brawling, sprawling, sensuous world has taken hold of his ankles even while his thoughts soar to an apex. The pattern (to indulge in essentially unhelpful but tempting pictorial analogy) may be seen as an apt, simple, and noble one, that of a pyramid, the huge monument sunk in the sands of Egypt, its lines converging on a still, infinite point. The base may be too sprawling, too shifting, to support the structure and to give it the definition that the unities of place and time and the music-like rhythms give such a play as *Heartbreak House*, but if the grand design is not wholly successful, there is enough to explain the resonance, contain the kaleidoscope of scenes and the multitude of characters, and to suggest a finer purpose of the artist in Shaw than accusations of structural laxity do.

*   *   *

The Devil's Disciple came just before, *Captain Brassbound's Conversion* just after *Caesar and Cleopatra*. The first is about the irrationality of the Will and is a seriously religious play set in melodramatic and irreligious Puritan New England; the second is about the futility of vengeance and is set in Morocco. The first is notable for its engaging portrait of General Burgoyne; the second for its transmogrification of Shelley's Witch of Atlas in Lady Cicily Waynflete. Both plays are predictably Shavian and more than mere fun, but neither measures up to *Caesar and Cleopatra* nor gives any hint – as this play does – that Shaw was on the threshold of a masterpiece.

Chapter Five

1901-1903: MAN AND SUPERMAN

'Talking!'[1]

ı

The Hell scene of *Man and Superman* provides a good opportunity for introducing, though not concluding, a discussion on that aspect of Shaw's art which should be reckoned as one of its distinguishing features. I mean its affinities to music.

It has been said that Shaw's plays are full of colour.[2] His stages are, but his words are not – not visually colourful. Far from ignorant about painting – many boyhood hours in the Dublin Art Gallery enabled him to become an entirely competent art critic[3] – he yet does not have the gift of literally colourful speech, nor does his imagination move easily among verbal pictures. Analogy, comparison, antithesis, the 'free use of all the rhetorical and lyrical arts of the orator, the preacher, the pleader, and the rhapsodist'[4] – all this is evident, and always vivid with the vividness of the concrete image, because his instinct as an artist was to weld his ideas to things. But the swiftness of his prose and the excitement of his dialogue leave only a blaze of white behind them. His writing is not sensuous in that a kaleidoscope of ideas is not his; it is sensuous, however, in that the music of ideas is his.

A father who 'destroyed ... domestic peace by immoderate indulgence in the trombone',[5] a mother whose ardour for music was well

---

[1] *Man and Superman*, Act IV, p. 166.
[2] See St John Ervine, *Bernard Shaw: His Life, Work and Friends*, London, Constable, 1956, p. 380.
[3] From 1886–1889.
[4] The 'Quintessence of Ibsenism', *Major Critical Essays*, p. 146.
[5] *London Music in 1888–89 as Heard by Corno di Bassetto*, p. 76. This may be a fiction: Shaw senior indulged more in liquor than the trombone.

served by her talent as a singer,[1] a friend of the family, George Vanda-
leur Lee, who introduced a unique method of voice production and
brought an increased ardour for music into the Shaw household, an
atmosphere of opera and oratorio, of Handel, Haydn, Mozart, Beethoven, Rossini, Bellini, Donizetti, and Verdi, which the young Shaw
inhaled as practically the only cultural benefit of his home – a benefit
which his inclinations later helped him to augment by his gaining a
thorough knowledge of instrumental music and of harmony and
counterpoint, until, as he says, he knew more about music than any of
the great composers:[2] the callow Dubliner who went to London in
1876 to try his hand at novel-writing knew comparatively little about
that discipline; he knew, he was saturated in, the pre-Wagner musical
tradition. Music was and remained an indispensable part of his life;[3]
and so, perhaps inevitably, it was as a music critic for *The Star* from
1888–89 that he began to realize himself.

Corno di Bassetto, by which Italianate name Shaw called himself,
began tentatively and even – though this may be hard to believe –
diffidently. Neither tentativeness nor diffidence afflicted him for long,
though; 'the critic who is modest is lost',[4] he declared and he suited his
method to these words, affirming in every weekly *boutade* his intention
to be anything but lost. As a result, Corno di Bassetto was waggish,
irreverent, and highly readable. Highly readable he would always be,
but when G.B.S. took over from di Bassetto in 1890, writing the *feuille-
tons* on music for *The World*, the waggishness was curbed, the irreverence made more serious: the finished critic took over from the
apprentice.

Art is long, life is short, criticism shorter still; and of all fugitive
critiques of this or that work of art none is more fugitive than the music
review. And yet, astonishingly, certain music critics are able to over-
come the oblivion that waits on their every word. Shaw was one such
critic. He is quite clearly as 'great' as Newman and Tovey are 'great'.

---

[1] 'She . . . had a mezzo-soprano voice of remarkable purity of tone.' Preface to
London Music in 188–89 as heard by Corno di Bassetto, p. 9.
[2] Ibid. p. 27.
[3] Ibid. p. 28.
[4] Ibid. p. 257.

The petty details of so and so's recital shrink away; what is left is a sensitivity, a tact, a surety of judgement that stamp him as one of those rarities whose words endure alongside the music they describe. Or, as frequently happened with Shaw, alongside the music they do not describe:

> That light-hearted body the Bach Choir has had what I may be-fittingly call another shy at the Mass in B minor. . . . [The critic] does not on such occasions prime himself with Spitta's biography of Bach, and, opening his mouth and shutting his ears, sit palpitating with reverent interest, culminating in a gasp of contrapuntal enthusiasm at each entry and answer of the fugue subject.
>
> On the contrary, the first thing he does is . . . simply listen to the body of sound that is being produced. And what clothes his judgement in terror is that he does not, like the ordinary man, remain unconscious of every sound except that which he is expecting to hear. He is alive not only to the music of the organ, but to the rattling and crashing caused by the beating of the partial tones and combination tones generated by the sounds actually played from in the score; and he is often led thereby to desire the sudden death of organists who use their stops heedlessly. He hears not only the modicum of vocal tone which the choristers are producing, but also the buzzing and wheezing and puffing and all sorts of uncouth sounds which ladies and gentlemen unknowingly bring forth in the agonies of holding on to a difficult part in a Bach chorus. And his criticism of the choir is primarily determined by the proportion of vocal tone to mere noises. . . .
>
> When the critic has duly estimated the quality of the vocal material, he begins to take Bach into consideration. An untrained singer can no more sing Bach's florid choral parts than an untrained draughtsman can copy a drawing by Albrecht Dürer. The attempts of ordinary amateurs to make their way through a Bach chorus are no more to be taken as Bach's music than a child's attempts to copy one of Dürer's plumed helmets is to be taken as a reproduction of the original. The critic accordingly must proceed to consider whether the ladies and gentlemen before him are tracing the lines of the

great Bach picture with certainty, mastery, and vigilantly sensitive artistic feeling, or whether they are scrawling them in impotent haste under the stick of the conductor.[1]

This was seventy-five years ago. Today the Bach Choir, for that matter any choir, preparing to have a 'shy' at the Mass in B minor or any great work, may still profitably recite these lines as a Prayer Before Performance, and not merely in propitiation of the critics.

Perhaps the most signal triumph of Shaw's music criticism is that it maintains itself without resource to the jargon of musicology. His first editor requested him to avoid 'Bach in B minor'[2] by which he meant the sort of review that eked out a halfpenny of critical appreciation with a pound of 'scientific analysis' – with the sort of comment which Shaw so successfully lampooned in his 'analysis' of Hamlet's soliloquy on suicide:

> Shakespear, dispensing with the customary exordium, announces his subject at once in the infinitive, in which mood it is presently repeated after a short connecting passage in which, brief as it is, we recognize the alternative and negative forms on which so much of the significance of repetition depends. Here we reach a colon; and a pointed pository phrase, in which the accent falls decisively on the relative pronoun, brings us to the first full stop.[3]

But no editor was needed to tell Shaw how not to respond. It was instinct with him to hear music, not as diminished sevenths or augmented sixths, but as 'poetry', as an emotion, a manifestation of 'intelligence' and, ultimately, as a sort of explicitly inexplicit 'philosophy'.

This led him to dogmatize somewhat rashly on absolute and programme music and to offer debatable judgements on the basis of this dogma. Brahms, for example, may well be allowed to be less pettily absolute and more 'profound' than Shaw reckoned him to be; Mozart at his best is not necessarily the manifest superior of Beethoven; Wagner's 'Ring' does not need to be read as a Socialist apocalypse for

---

[1] *Music in London, 1890–94*, Vol. II, pp. 55–7.
[2] Ibid. p. 322.
[3] Ibid. p. 321.

its more perfect understanding. And yet, read him on these masters (Brahms excepted),[1] read him on the lesser masters, Schumann, Mendelssohn, Dvořák, or on the forgotten 'masters' of his day – and his sense of the fitness of things and fine insight into relative qualities, make one realize and almost regret that in gaining a major dramatist the world lost a giant among music critics.

Wagner, as the anti-Christ of musical orthodoxy in England at the time, was naturally the man Shaw championed. He urged him on the opera-going public as forcefully as he came to urge Ibsen on the theatre-going public. He urged Wagner – and he explained him, setting forth a socio-political interpretation of his major works which need not concern us here, though I should remark that it is not as far-fetched as some might think. More pertinent is his understanding of Wagner's aesthetic aims: the fusion of the word and the music in an artistic whole; the creation of 'music drama', not of 'opera'; the insistence that the accompanying sound does not decorate or elaborate but simply *is* the emotion, the sensation, the word in depth. One may discern the connection, although it is not a direct one between Wagner and Shaw, for the entire field of dramatic music informed Shaw's sensibilities: 'musical drama', in very nearly the literal sense of the term, is the Shavian mode.

We have his own assertion to this effect:

> ... nobody can really understand my art without being soaked in symphonies and opera, in Mozart, Verdi and Meyerbeer, to say nothing of Handel, Beethoven and Wagner, far more completely than in the literary drama and its poets and playwrights.[2]

Perhaps more revealing than this, because it shows his frequent practice as a critic, are these remarks:

---

[1] However, in 1935 Shaw confessed that Corno di Bassetto had been unfamiliar with Brahms. See the Preface to *London Music in 1888–89*, p. 31.

[2] In a letter to Norah Ervine, 12th May, 1934. Quoted by Ervine, op. cit., p. 555. In the Preface to *London Music in 1889–90* (p. 28) Shaw relates how 'Harley Granville-Barker was not far out when, at a rehearsal of one of my plays, he cried out "Ladies and gentlemen: will you please remember that this is Italian opera."'

... a musician only has the right to criticize works like Shakespear's early histories and tragedies. The two Richards, King John, and the last act of Romeo and Juliet, depend wholly on the beauty of their music. There is no deep significance, no great subtlety and variety in their numbers; but for splendor of sound, magic of romantic illusion, majesty of emphasis, ardor, elation, reverberation of haunting echoes, and every poetic quality that can waken the heart-stir and the imaginative fire of early manhood, they stand above all recorded music.[1]

There is some confusion here and the literary criticism is jejune, but the cast of Shaw's mind is clearly evident.

It is equally evident in many of his plays; in *Don Juan in Hell* more so than before: indeed, it does not seem possible that this could finally have been successfully executed by other than 'musical' means.

*   *   *

The foursome in the scene – Ana, Don Juan, the Devil, and the Statue – are not dramatic creations in the normally understood sense of the words; they are voices issuing from figures of fantasy, creatures derived from Mozart's *Don Giovanni*, and as little likely to arouse positive human sympathy as talking dolls. Nor are the arguments in this scene likely to engage the usual participation; attention yes, but not participation. Shaw could hardly have expected such a conventional response – he could hardly have desired such a response, his 'characters' and themes being what they are. This scene is not 'drama', then; neither however – to forestall the well-worn verdict[2] – is this, the most 'Platonic' of Shaw's dialogues, at all Platonic. Mild Socrates would never have endured these loquacious and opinionated shades: their method is quite foreign, their manner would be quite repugnant to him. Their method and their manner is, in fact, of the stage for the

[1] *London Music in 1888–89*, p. 82.
[2] It may have been Max Beerbohm who set the fashion. See his *Around Theatres*, London, Rupert Hart-Davis, 1953, p. 268. (One should add that Shaw himself spoke of his Shavio-Socratic method.)

stage. They are, if one likes, puppets, but puppets so fully loaded with Shaw's theatrical genius that their remoteness, their physical inaction, their abstract argument become immediate, active and concrete. How has Shaw done it?

First, by means of conflict. Shavian drama and conflict are virtually synonyms. Accord among his characters is as rare as a slack moment in his plays – that is, extremely rare. His characters are created to disagree; it seems that they are not really happy unless they are banging away at someone whose point of view differs from theirs, the banged one will not be happy unless he gives as good as he receives, and both sides are usually happy to go on until the moral, if not actual physical, death. Here in the Hell scene the banging is quite splendid. Don Juan against Ana, Don Juan against the Statue, Don Juan against the Devil – Don Juan against the world. The tension is unremitting, the pace tremendous. Brief, sharp, witty exchanges bring moments of relief but these increase rather than diminish the intensity of the struggle.

An oddity of this conflict – and it is quite patently a calculated oddity – is that a 'third man' is involved. Consider the scene – the platform before the eternity which faces us all; consider the questions debated – what is the good life, the right life?; consider the issue – Life or Death; and it should be obvious that the opposition between, for example, the Devil and Don Juan is really nominal, that neither seriously expects to bring about a spectacular conversion on the stage, that, anyway, they have probably had this argument before. They are speaking, not to, but through one another and at this 'third man', who quite unmistakably is you or me. Thus involved, thus addressed, harangued, declaimed at, philosophized over, exhorted, cajoled, and insulted, we are hardly likely to remain unaffected. We may not, it is true, willingly suspend our disbelief, but paradoxically we may willingly find ourselves accepting and enjoying our mute role in the debate; and we shall certainly relish these speakers who so brilliantly fling about the ethical imperatives of our existence.

The most vitally interesting subject can be made dull in a hundred different ways. To the credit of Don Juan and the others they do not know of any one of these ways. They have passionate conviction and, more important, the gift of vigorous, vivid words. They are all masters of debate, exemplars of oratory, paragons of rhetoric. They flaunt their argument in the uncompromising face of time and compromise it, they insolently challenge our mental endurance and know that their supremacy of language will make it endure. Their words ebb and flow, rise and fall; altercation heightens dispute, invective balances rhapsody, colloquialisms offset rhetoric; the orator, the pleader, the preacher, and – I should add – the poet have their moments. No, this is not drama; it is something unique and inimitable, having no criterion but itself and gathering as it develops a hard, naked force that drives thought upward and outward on a journey it has rarely ventured to take before.

The Hell scene realizes more nearly than any other work the Shavian ideal of 'intellectual passion'. An anaemic thing, some may say, a masquerade of true passion, but to Shaw it was the only worthwhile passion, a noble exercise, God-given and the most suitable means of approaching the Godhead, of apprehending morality and knowing the truth. Hence 'moral passion', the phrase on which John Tanner rests his revolutionist creed:

> No: the change that came to me was the birth in me of moral passion; and I declare that according to my experience moral passion is the only real passion. . . . If it were not a passion – if it were not the mightiest of the passions, all the other passions would sweep it away like a leaf before a hurricane. It is the birth of that passion that turns a child into a man.[1]

And it is this same passion that gives the Hell scene its special tone: even Don Juan's opponents, especially the Devil, press moral passion into the service of the humbug of Hell.[2]

We may conclude then that moral passion is the summating element of the scene. Now, its manner is musical. Although one recognizes the Mozartian strain[3] (at the beginning of and right through the scene) in the end it is not Mozart, or any other composer, we should look for: these elusive analogies between the spoken word and the sounded note

---

[1] *Man and Superman*, Act I, pp. 34–5.
[2] Ibid. Act III, p. 90.
[3] Ibid. p. 84.

– risky as they are in any event – would become fatuous if carried to extremes. But still, the manner of *Don Juan in Hell* is musical, specifically operatic.

Henderson reports in a footnote on the first production of this piece in 1907: 'The costumes, designed by Charles Ricketts, R.A., were gorgeous: and there was little movement, the characters looking like jewelled figures pinned against a black velvet back drop.'[1] Ricketts himself recounts that Shaw (who was producing) 'rather approved' a suggestion of his – Ricketts' – that 'at a signal given by Mephistopheles, four gilded [*sic.*] thrones should rise from the floor, to the strains of Mozart's minuet in *Don Giovanni*, a lit chandelier descend from the roof, and the black curtains part before an altar bearing flowers and candles surrounding a gilded Venus de Medici.'[2] Nothing came of this because the Vedrenne-Barker management of the Court Theatre could not allow costs much in excess of a shoe-string, but the fact that Shaw approved is significant. He wrote to Ricketts: 'It seems to me that we (I say 'we' much as an organ-blower uses the plural pronoun when speaking of an organist's performance of a Bach fugue) hit on a most valuable and fascinating stage convention. William Morris used always to say that plays should be performed by four people in conventional costumes, the villain in a red cloak, the father in a bob-wig, etc. etc. etc., and I have always loved Harlequin, Columbine, Sganarelle, etc. in eighteenth-century Italian Comedy and French Champetre painting. If only we could get a few plays with invisible backgrounds and lovely costumes like that in a suitable theatre, with fairy lights all round the proscenium, there would be no end to the delight of the thing. . . .'[3]

If these snippets of theatre history reveal anything, it is that *Don Juan in Hell* was visualized as akin to opera. The costumes, the black velvet curtains, the unattained but wished for thrones, chandelier, and statue, the absence of movement – in a word, everything the eye lights on fosters those prime illusions of opera, which even the most footling

[1] Henderson, *G.B.S.: Man of the Century*, p. 580.
[2] In a letter to the actress, Lillah McCarthy, in *Bernard Shaw's Letters to Granville Barker*, ed. C. B. Purdom, London, Phoenix House, 1956, p. 89.
[3] Ibid. p. 90.

libretto and fiddling score may win to their aid: figures larger than life, momentousness of occasion, elevation of sentiment. The style of opera is as far removed from 'real life' as Ruritania is from Covent Garden market, justifiably removed, because its aesthetic value does not and should not depend on the external fidelity with which it represents nature. It depends on hyperbole and turns a petty story about a consumptive courtesan, or a group of conscienceless Bohemians, or a betrayed husband into epic; opera is exactly what Dr Johnson called it, 'an exotick and irrational entertainment'; for all this it can be indestructably exciting and completely artistic. Shaw knew; and so he used the convention as being best suited to reflect the magnitude of what were to him the most genuinely heroic themes the intellect of man could conceive.

From visual effects to its sibling, tonal effects; to our hearing the four speakers as the traditional vocal quartet: Ana is soprano, Don Juan tenor, the Devil bass, and the Statue, his Mozartian role usurped by the Devil, fills in the gap as counter-tenor, or alto. There can be no question that this distribution of 'parts' has behind it several deeply considered purposes. Certain 'Mozartian strains' haunt the air as the scene opens and three Mozartian characters take part in the debate, although lack of practice (and Shavian requirements) has done odd things to two Mozartian voices, and a hundred years or more of history (and Shavian philosophy) have done odder things to Mozartian ethics. But of course *Don Juan in Hell*, whilst straightaway announcing its reliance on the old formal conventions, relies equally on *Don Giovanni* to show how opposed it is in spirit.

Apart from descending from Mozart, Shaw's quartet carries out one or two essential functions in its own right. Together the four singing voices would cover five octaves, the speaking voices, with exclamations, cries, and shrieks, a trifle less, still enough to enrich the debate with distinct shifts and slides of tone. How important this is will be appreciated when we remind ourselves that the scene, if played at the required pace, takes 110 minutes, which is two or three times longer than most people are normally able to pay attention, especially when the pace is as swift, the debate as concentrated as here. Those qualities of the scene already discussed – the conflicts, the humorous

I

interludes, the verbal brilliance – will probably keep theatre-goers from nodding; at the same time, the discipline of using one's ears, the sheer effort of thinking hard for an hour and fifty minutes, obviously needs to be made as easy as possible by all possible means. Therefore these shifts of tone, these contrasts of aural colour, Ana's clear, thrilling soprano with the Devil's seductive depths, Don Juan's firm, determined notes with the Statue's thinner, unconvincing strains.

It should be evident by now that Shaw's quartet accomplishes more than the tender caress of taxed hearing. Like the setting, the individual voices add resonance to the themes. The Devil's bass, so often the tone of romantic blackguardism, accords perfectly with the enticements of his Hell, the Statue's alto (more often the contralto of an over-anxious mama) captures the essence of that perturbed guardian, Roebuck Ramsden, Ana's soprano is the voice of the conventional heroine. And as for Don Juan, no better reflection of his heroic vision can be realized than by the traditionally 'heroic' tones of the tenor. Any number of operas will confirm these observations.

This is my impression of the absolutes of *Don Juan in Hell*, this the 'opera' that does so much to complete this remarkable piece. 'Hell' – Don Juan exclaims at one point – 'Hell is full of musical amateurs: music is the brandy of the damned.'[1] I bow before the rebuke. But after all, Shaw was writing for the damned.

2

To speak of a 'romance' between Ann Whitefield and John Tanner may seem wilfully perverse, especially from Tanner's point of view. Yet how very much is romantic in their association. Theirs is, Shaw disparagingly says, a 'trumpery story of modern London life':[2] but to have the man you love appointed your guardian, to rescue him from bandits in the majestic Sierras, to become his affianced wife in sunny Granada – forget for a moment that Ann has contrived or brought about every one of these and any number of other situations to capture her mate, and what greater cause could the romantically minded have

[1] *Man and Superman*, Act III, p. 95.
[2] 'Epistle Dedicatory': the Preface to *Man and Superman*, p. xv.

for pronouncing the benediction 'and they lived happily ever after'?
And despite Ann's machinations and Tanner's expostulations, happy
they will certainly be. Like Candida and Morell, this is their fate; our
aunt Edna's aunt Edna would in 1905 or thereabouts have been merely
the first of many to leave the theatre happy in the couple's happiness,
though, possibly, bemusedly under the impression that the Superman
is the Woman and somewhat affronted that the wrong sex did the
chasing and that Tanner should protest his unhappiness so resolutely.

In fact – and here is the recurring Shavian idea beneath the romantic
convention – Tanner is right. His capitulation to happiness is his
acceptance of unhappiness. He will be Ann's husband and the father of
her children, he will – if Ann has anything to do with it – enter politics,
he will go on talking, talking, talking. He will live happily ever after
and know himself to be lost and damned.

Hearing such undertones in the comedy of *Man and Superman* may
seem another perversity, like experiencing pity and terror in the face of
laughter. But laughter should – as far as possible – be left to look after
itself; certainly the inverted convention – man the hunter becoming the
hunted – and the first act satire on a 'fate worse than death' (on Tanner's free thinking, as well); the portraits of Straker, the 'new' snob of
Sherbrooke Road Board School, of the American, Malone, who
romantically wants to work to support his wife; the sketches of the
brigands – among these the mild-mannered Anarchist, the three disso-
nant Social Democrats, and the Jew, Mendoza, whose ode to Louisa
achieves a soaring bathos supremely compatible with those who, in
Ruskin's phrase, have 'pleasure in making a melodious noise about it';
the supercharge of wit, shrewd observation, and vitality: all this, the
laughter of the play, piling effect on effect to vertiginous heights, may
safely be left to look after itself. When two spirited and determined
people, a woman and a man, engage in the duel of sex, there may be,
and in this instance there is, cause for amusement, but there may also
be, and in this instance there is, occasion for serious thought – even,
perhaps, tragedy.

A digression on the subject of Shaw and Sex is called for here. To the
shallow and muddy-minded, a self-proclaimed Puritan writing a play –
as a matter of fact, writing many plays – about sex must seem a denial

of very principle, as though John Bunyan were to have gone whoring. Such an attitude may be disposed of at once as prurient. The Puritan Shaw expended a great deal of Puritan energy in wresting sex from precisely this sort of crooked thinking.

His platform and pamphlet campaign for sexual reform need not keep us. It dwelt on such matters as the nature of sexual love, the nature of marriage, the nature of female, as opposed to male, urges, the question of birth, birth-control, children, adultery, promiscuity, divorce, the laws relating to all this – in short, the sociological and psychological aspects of sex. In his day he was in the vanguard of sex, and was as 'advanced' and 'enlightened' – as 'free', if one likes – as D. H. Lawrence though he retained for himself the old taboo on certain verbal forms which fastidiousness rather than prudery declared necessary.

Many of his views on sex were translated into drama. As he said (I quote at greater length than is strictly necessary, but for an obvious reason):

> There are two effects to be considered in any definite measure of sexual reform. There is the psychological effect, and there is the political effect. Now, it is on the psychological side that I wish to speak tonight, because I am speaking as an expert. (*Laughter.*) I do not in the least know why that remark of mine has elicited laughter; but as a matter of fact I am an expert in sex appeal. What I mean is that I am a playwright. I am connected with the theatre. The theatre is continually occupied with sex appeal. It has to deal in sex appeal exactly as a costermonger has to deal in turnips; and a costermonger's opinion on turnips is worth having. He is an expert. In the same way the opinion of playwrights and other theatre people is worth having because they know how the thing is done through having to do it as part of their daily work.
>
> One very important function of the theatre in society is to educate the audience in matters of sex. . . .
>
> And yet when sex appeal has to be discussed scientifically nobody ever calls in a playwright, and he himself does not come forward without an invitation. But the priest always rushes in and demands to be accepted as an authority on sex. . . .

The Pope represents the priest in this matter. The Pope is the Chief Priest of Europe, and he speaks very strongly on the subject of sex appeal. I, of course, should never dream of appealing in that matter to the Chief Priest of Europe, but if there were such a person as the Chief Prostitute of Europe I should call her in immediately. I should say: 'Here, clearly, is a person who deals professionally in sex appeal, and will lose her livelihood if her method is wrong. She can speak to us with authority.'[1]

This is fine and clear but it does not set aside a very frequent charge that Shavian expertness resulted in plays which are almost sexless.[2] There may be some warrant for the charge. By his frequent attacks on 'voluptuousness' and his disdainful refusal to pander to it, Shaw may simply have been defining the scope of his drama, may have been saying in effect: 'The voluptuary, the sensualist, the lecher are incorrigible; they can have no place in a modern, social morality play'; but he may equally have been making a vice of what could be a literary, if not an actual, virtue, and a virtue of what might be seen as a literary short-coming. These are all possibilities; but if we have to agree that Shaw is not remotely a poet of the flesh, we have no right to infer from this that he was sexless. It all depends so much on what, in art as well as in life, we are to understand by the word.

We may briefly consider two of his early plays, first *Mrs Warren's Profession*. Here he, as an apprentice expert on sex, attempts to delineate a good lady who to all intents and purposes qualifies as the Chief Prostitute of Europe – and we find a bleak asceticism supplanting whatever hothouse expectations adolescent fantasy and casual literature of the bordello may have induced in us. Sex, we may think, is not here at all. It is, though, but terribly deformed, withered stumps on a savage plain: here, clearly, is a writer whose intellectual honesty would not concede Mrs Warren one night of voluptuous sin and his audience one second of vicarious licentiousness.

---

[1] 'The Need for Expert Opinion in Sexual Reform', in *Platform and Pulpit*, ed. by Dan H. Laurence, pp. 201–2.
[2] See, for example, G. J. Nathan, 'Mr. Shaw and the Ogre', in *George Bernard Shaw: A Critical Survey*, ed. by L. Kronenberger, p. 117.

Suppose that for this reason we are disappointed in the play. Would our disappointment not then be in inverse proportion to our opinion that sex, whether bought or not, is a voluptuous experience? To a voluptuary it will be this and very little else. But to a moralist? or a theologian? or a sociologist? or a statistician? Quite obviously we understand sex by what we bring to it. Now Shaw brought metaphysics to it; this was, so he said, 'the real thing',[1] the quintessence, the eternal jewel within the gaudy casket. Metaphysics does purport to make this discovery but as there is no saying whether 'the real thing' is true or not, we may legitimately question Shaw's confident claim. Also, however, we should appreciate the fact that he cut away a great tangle of conventional verbiage that passed in literature as talk about sex; verbiage that, when transferred to real life, may for some few couples be 'the real thing' but for most of us turns out as destructively false as it is possible for anything to be.

> You propound a certain social substance, sexual attraction to wit, for dramatic distillation; and I distil it for you. I do not adulterate the product with aphrodisiacs nor dilute it with romance and water.[2]

Of course, this distillation can amount to nothing more than another, a Shavian, convention, and another, a Shavian, idiom.

If this is an important consideration, it is not yet enough to have us concede any artistic validity to Shaw's sexual convention. We may, as I say, understand the subject in the light of personal supposition, but the subject, when communicated through a work of art, must have some general reference. Here is a passage from another early play, *You Never Can Tell*. What is its effect on us?

> VALENTINE: But why did I do it? Because I was being tempted to awaken your heart: to stir the depths in you. Why was I tempted? Because Nature was in deadly earnest with me when I was in jest with her. When the great moment came, who was awakened? who was stirred? in whom did the depths break up? In myself – myself. I was

---

[1] '. . . when the question of passion arises, it is the real thing, not the conventions. . . .' *The New York Times*, Apr. 13, 1924. As quoted by Henderson, *G.B.S.: Man of the Century*, p. 501.

[2] 'Epistle Dedicatory', the Preface to *Man and Superman*, p. xv.

transported: you were only offended – shocked. You are just an ordinary young lady, too ordinary to allow tame lieutenants to go as far as I went. Thats all. I shall not trouble you with conventional apologies. Goodbye. . . . Let us part kindly.

GLORIA: (*enormously relieved, and immediately turning her back on him deliberately*) Goodbye. I trust you will soon recover from the wound.

VALENTINE: (*brightening up as it flashes on him that he is master of the situation after all*) I shall recover: such wounds heal more than they harm. After all, I still have my own Gloria.

GLORIA: (*facing him quickly*) What do you mean?

VALENTINE: The Gloria of my imagination.

GLORIA: (*proudly*) Keep your own Gloria: the Gloria of your imagination. (*Her emotion begins to break through her pride.*) The real Gloria: the Gloria who was shocked, offended, horrified – oh yes, quite truly – who was driven almost mad with shame by the feeling that all her power over herself had broken down at her first real encounter with – with – (*The color rushes over her face again. She covers it with her left hand, and puts her right on his left arm to support herself*).

VALENTINE: Take care. I'm losing my senses again. (*Summoning all her courage, she takes away her hand from her face and puts it on his right shoulder, turning him towards her and looking him straight in the eyes. He begins to protest agitatedly.*) Gloria: be sensible: it's no use: I havent a penny in the world.

GLORIA: Cant you earn one? Other people do.

VALENTINE: (*half delighted, half frightened*) I never could: youd be unhappy. My dearest love: I should be the merest fortune-hunting adventurer if – (*Her grip of his arm tightens; and she kisses him.*) Oh Lord! (*Breathless.*) Oh, I – (*he gasps*) I dont know anything about women: twelve years experience is not enough. (*In a gust of jealousy she throws him away from her; and he reels back into a chair like a leaf before the wind.*)[1]

It must strike us immediately that, apart from the conventional manipulation of anxiety over the outcome, Shaw has virtually nothing else

[1] *Man and Superman*, Act IV, pp. 292–3.

that is conventional. What husband[1] or mother or society will say is beside the question; what maiden modesty or manly gallantry should say is immaterial; what abstruse idealistic considerations, tenuously associated with Love, may be uttered are not uttered. There are simply no aphrodisiacs worth commenting on; there is no romance and water.

Yet the passage is forceful, and the forcefulness is that of sexual attraction. Gloria and Valentine are in love, deeply in love. But it must be understood (and it is felt) that 'in love' means something approaching, not placidity and peace, but emotional tumult and fear, something – an irresistible force which Valentine vaguely calls 'Nature' – that whisks away anger, pride, self-control, reason itself, and presents each to the other in a state of moral nakedness. They are mere children in the grip of an urge – a specifically sexual urge – larger than their claims to individual notice can ever be.

The couple stands on the threshold of an experience which Shaw subsequently tried more than once to put into words. Here A, the male voice of his little play, *Village Wooing*, describes what we may call the Shavian metaphysic of copulation:

> ... You are the dupe of thoughtless words like sensuality, sensuousness, and all the rest of the twaddle of the Materialists. I am not a Materialist: I am a poet; and I know that to be in your arms will not gratify my senses at all. As a matter of mere physical sensation you will find the bodily contacts to which you are looking forward neither convenient nor decorous.... Your secondhand gabble about gratifying my senses is only your virgin innocence. We shall get quite away from the world of sense. We shall light up for one another a lamp in the holy of holies in the temple of life; and the lamp will make its veil transparent. Aimless lumps of stone blundering through space will become stars singing in their spheres. Our dull purposeless village existence will become one irresistible purpose and nothing else. An extraordinary delight and an intense love will seize us. It will last hardly longer than the lightning flash which

---

[1] There is no husband in this case. Had this been a play by Jones there would have been, though.

turns the black night into infinite radiance. It will be dark again before you can clear the light out of your eyes; but you will have seen; and for ever after you will think about what you have seen and not gabble catchwords invented by the wasted virgins that walk in darkness. It is to give ourselves this magic moment that we feel that we must and shall hold one another in our arms; and when the moment comes, the world of the senses will vanish; and for us there will be nothing ridiculous, nothing uncomfortable, nothing unclean, nothing but pure paradise.[1]

One doubts if a hectoring tone and metaphors of lamps in the holy of holies could ever begin to realize anything, let alone stars singing in their spheres: Shaw was sometimes distressingly inept when he attempted 'poetry'; he could also be surprisingly naïve about a 'poet', as witness his distinction here between that person and a materialist. But this is by the way. The point at issue is the matter, not the manner; and the matter is, quite unambiguously, that the sexual climax is a consummation of an 'irresistible purpose' which is not sensory but spiritual, mystical, metaphysical.

With this in mind, we may now turn back to *Man and Superman*. Writing some twenty years later about this play, Shaw half disparagingly and half proudly referred to the enormous length of the entire work and its too lavish and brilliant decorations.[2] Even without the Hell scene, the play is very long by modern standards, for reasons that have everything to do with that inscrutable though evident relationship between magnitude and theme. The play is given very nearly epic proportions because its main conflict is one that Shaw sees in this light. Accordingly, his two main characters must each have the stature for their parts in the epic. This is most important. Tanner is not an ordinary man, Ann is not an ordinary woman. They are wonderfully portrayed as recognizable human beings, but they are palpably more than this. They are the heroes of epic; they are champions, geniuses.

We note Shaw's careful description of his hero and wonder if he did not wish to suggest something even of the god in him: a 'lofty pose

---

[1] *Village Wooing*, Third Conversation, pp. 137–8.
[2] See the Preface to *Back to Methuselah*, p. lxxxiv.

of the head', an 'Olympian majesty', 'an imposing brow', a suggestion of 'Jupiter rather than Apollo';[1] another suggestion, a very strong one, not made here but to be inferred from the attitude of Don Giovanni's singular descendant, is of Prometheus. Prometheus wasted no respect on Zeus; neither does Tanner on the Zeus of his day. Prometheus was the friend of man; so is Tanner. Prometheus was, one might say, the original revolutionist; Tanner is a revolutionist as well. This is Tanner's genius. He has written a book, 'The Revolutionist's Handbook' (which Shaw has obligingly appended to the play), a veritable munitions dump of anti-establishment ideas. Its collection of 'Maxims', a treasure trove for the compiler of a book of quotations, is startling, witty, and wise, much wiser than a casual glance would seem to justify. Its main essay scourges modern society, the modern political animal in particular: it advocates selective breeding, pours scorn on the institution of marriage, calls for the political Superman. It must rank as one of the most scathing attacks on humanity since Swift's day, and it is very, very Shavian.

Tanner the man, 'prodigiously fluent of speech, restless, excitable . . . possibly a little mad',[2] is full to the brim with his moral passion. He is bent on saving the world. In the course of the play he becomes fairly exclusively bent on saving only himself, but we may easily believe in his greater mission. He is a wit and a philosopher, utterly committed and utterly sincere; he has discovered the true joy in life, the being used for a purpose recognized by himself as a mighty one.[3] Also, unluckily for him, he is as blind as a bat about his personal fate.

The opposing genius, Ann, is Candida magnified several times. To the casual world at large she is a model of propriety, apparently delegating all considerations to the imperatives of duty, duty to her deceased father, duty to her guardians, duty to her younger sister; to poor lovelorn Tavy she is the poetic ideal of woman made manifest; to Tanner she is calculating, hypocritical, unscrupulous, selfish, a liar, and a boa-constrictor. Truth has many facets and all this is true of Ann.

---

[1] *Man and Superman*, Act I, p. 9.
[2] Ibid.
[3] See 'Epistle Dedicatory: the Preface to *Man and Superman*, p. xxxi. See also the reference to the relevant passage in Chapter One of this study.

She is utterly proper, utterly the ideal, utterly immoral. Shaw says: '... every woman is not Ann; but Ann is Everywoman'.[1] She is a genius of Life. She too has a mighty purpose, to bring children into the world; she too is committed and sincere, and delegates everything to her ultimate duty. She too is full to the brim with passion – a passion for procreation.[2]

Tanner, that man of scant illusions, can explain other people with ease: he has Ann's deeper motives off pat:

> You think that you are Ann's suitor; that you are the pursuer and she the pursued; that it is your part to woo, to persuade, to prevail, to overcome. Fool: it is you who are the pursued, the marked down quarry, the destined prey. You need not sit looking longingly at the bait through the wires of the trap: the door is open, and will remain so until it shuts behind you for ever. . . . Why, man, what other work has she in life but to get a husband? It is a woman's business to get married as soon as possible, and a man's to keep unmarried as long as he can. You have your poems and your tragedies to work at: Ann has nothing.

And he adds this dire warning to Octavius:

> Marry Ann; and at the end of a week youll find no more inspiration in her than in a plate of muffins,[3]

which is very ironic, awful, and amusing when Tanner learns that he is the destined prey. He flees. Ann pursues and overtakes him. Watching her approach, he knows that he can escape no further. He groans, 'The Life Force! I am lost'[4] and meekly allows himself to be led off to Granada.

But Tanner is no impoverished little dentist submitting to his Gloria with scarcely a backward glance on the days of his felicity. Lost he may be, but he will talk to the last em and fight to the last ditch.

---

[1] 'Epistle Dedicatory': the Preface to *Man and Superman*, p. xxviii.
[2] This is not to be confused with sexuality. See Shaw's description, *Man and Superman*, Act I, p. 16.
[3] Ibid. Act II, pp. 51–2.
[4] Ibid. Act III, p. 133.

Before we look at the final confrontation between Tanner and Ann, we should consider the conventional objections to the terms of the conflict. As a Member of the Idle Rich Class, Tanner can have no anxiety about providing for a wife and family; also, though he is neither the slave of love nor its dupe, he freely admits to being in love with Ann.[1] Why then, should he draw back from marriage? Because, quite simply, marriage will mean the forfeiture of his self-respect. There is no alternative, no possibility of compromise: either freedom out of marriage or slavery in marriage, either the revolutionist's mission or abject husbandhood.

'Either . . . or': one of the finest of the many fine arguments Bentley advances in favour of Shaw is that, contrary to popular supposition, the Shavian thesis is not presented in 'either . . . or' ultimatums. As Bentley says, 'both . . . and', or what I have called the fused paradox or been associating with Hegelian dialectic, is the general manner.[2] However, *Man and Superman* is the exception that proves the rule. The basis of the conflict is absolute irreconcilability of interests; we may not ask for a measure of give and take: we can really not expect it. Each is so completely self-absorbed that neither begins to comprehend, much less allow for, the genius of the other. Thus, whilst Tanner equates Ann's vitality with muffins, she equates his mission with a talent for party politics.

All this being so, we may feel inclined to foresee a dismally failed marriage, in which Tanner submits to the form but not the fact of his union, and follows the long line of artists and philosophers who neglect their wives scandalously for the greater glory of their work. This is a possibility but not a likelihood. As I will shortly attempt to show, Tanner has a 'tragic flaw'. This will lose him his self-respect and save his marriage.

Now the final scene:[3] Tanner brandishing his refusal to marry like a weapon and speaking with an urgency and force that we would be fools to see as only funny; and Ann, now that the moment has come at

---

[1] *Man and Superman*, Act II, p. 52.

[2] See Bentley, *Bernard Shaw*, p. 32 et seq.

[3] *Man and Superman*, Act IV, pp. 160–66. Unless otherwise indicated, all quotations in the remainder of this chapter are from these pages.

last, demurely evasive but as inflexible as iron against the most stren-
uous argument, the most desperate plea, the most candid thrust.
Tanner despairingly cries: 'Oh you are witty: at the supreme moment
the Life Force endows you with every quality.'

Pretence is swiftly set aside. Romance, love, prevarication, the 'other
man', all the clichés of the immemorial situation, are whisked away by
the gusts of the Life Force, this instinct which makes Ann a pawn and
Tanner a victim. Now the scene moves away from argument, persua-
sion, recrimination; it mounts to the final phase, the dialogue concen-
trates, the sentences harden, the conflict comes to a fine, hard point:

> TANNER: I will not marry you. I will not marry you.
> ANN: Oh, you will, you will.
> TANNER: I tell you, no, no, no.
> ANN: I tell you, yes, yes, yes.
> TANNER: No.
> ANN: (*coaxing – imploring – almost exhausted*) Yes. Before it is too
> late for repentance. Yes.
> TANNER: (*struck by the echo from the past*) When did all this happen
> to me before? Are we two dreaming?
> ANN: (*suddenly losing her courage, with an anguish that she does not
> conceal*) No. We are awake; and you have said no: that is all.
> TANNER: (*brutally*) Well?
> ANN: Well, I made a mistake: you do not love me.

Tanner's refusal and Ann's affirmation are like a comic duet, yet
underneath it we sense the straining of will against will, especially
when the rhythm broadens into Ann's exhausted 'Yes. Before it is too
late for repentance. Yes.' The repeated, long-sounding 'yes' seems to
draw on Tanner's obduracy. It is the crucial moment. Tanner is struck
by the echo from the past. When did he hear all this before? –

> THE STATUE: Repent, scoundrel!
> DON GIOVANNI: No, you old fool!
> THE STATUE: Repent, etc.
> DON GIOVANNI: No! etc.
> THE STATUE: Yes!

DON GIOVANNI: No!
THE STATUE: Yes!
DON GIOVANNI: No!
LEPORELLO: Yes!
DON GIOVANNI: No! No!
THE STATUE: Ah, your time is up![1]

And just before this, Da Ponte gives the Statue these words:

Repent! Change your ways,
For this is your last hour![2]

Here is the origin of the echo. (One wishes it were possible somehow to reinforce the thin sounding words with the thunderous and terrifying music of Don Giovanni's damnation.) Mozart's hero is true to himself to the end. For a second it seems that his modern counterpart will stand as firm, will cleave to his heaven as indomitably as Don Giovanni goes to hell. For a second: then, even as Ann wilts under his brutal 'Well?', the great theorist succumbs, seizes her in his arms, and cries: 'It is false: I love you. . . . I have the whole world in my arms when I clasp you.' We may in this moment of his submission recollect the Devil's courteous parting words to Don Juan:

Heaven, as I said before, suits some people. But if you should change your mind, do not forget that the gates are always open here to the repentant prodigal.[3]

The gates are wide open and Tanner stands near. Compromised but not yet committed he must still hold back:

TANNER: . . . I have the whole world in my arms when I clasp you. But I am fighting for my freedom, for my honor, for my self, one and indivisible.
ANN: Your happiness will be worth them all.
TANNER: You would sell freedom and honor and self for happiness?

---

[1] *Don Giovanni*, Act II, Sc. 5. Translation by Capitol Records Inc. (1961). Published by E.M.I. Records Ltd., London; p. 75.
[2] Ibid.
[3] *Man and Superman*, Act III, p. 129.

ANN: It will not be all happiness for me. Perhaps death.

TANNER: (*groaning*) Oh, that clutch holds and hurts. What have you grasped in me? Is there a father's heart as well as a mother's?

He holds back, yes, but his admission of a father's heart, a sentiment which, as Chesterton justly says, makes for a really noble moment,[1] brings him fatally nearer. He cannot go back now and yet he cannot go forward. Annihilation, the only escape from this agony, is all he craves; and Ann, having dared to the limit of her strength and *still* not elicited a proposal of marriage from him, feels the malaise of sheer exhaustion overwhelming her. With a final supreme effort, she rectifies Tanner's oversight: 'I have promised to marry Jack', she says to the people who come in, and quickly faints.

It is finished. The Life Force has whirled the unrepentant prodigal willy nilly through the gates of hell. They close behind him; with the icy stoicism of despair bravely borne he declares to Octavius: 'I never asked her. It is a trap for me.' Octavius is justifiably petrified.

But is Tanner speaking the whole truth? Perhaps not. There had been a second when his victory seemed won, when the echoing chords of *Don Giovanni* commingled with his defiant 'no's' and gave him the strength and resolution to withstand Ann. And yet he had thrown his advantage away. Why? Apparently because, as he exclaims, the Life Force enchants him; but as the Life Force has had three long acts in which to accomplish this and not done so, we may press the point and ask 'Why at this precise moment?' It is again from Don Giovanni that we might be led to an answer:

The poor woman is in love with me, and out of pity I must pretend to love her, for it is my misfortune to have a kind heart.[2]

Give this the necessary Shavian twist, see the betrayed Donna Elvira as Ann in the moment of her anguish, and we have arrived at the cause of Tanner's submission. It is his misfortune, it is his 'tragic flaw', to have a kind heart. The weakness of the father has been visited on this

[1] *George Bernard Shaw*, p. 92.

[2] *Man and Superman*, Act I, Sc. 3, p. 31. And of course in Act I (on p. 37) Tanner speaks feelingly about Ann's 'damnable woman's trick of heaping obligations on a man. . . .'

son of the fourth generation. For all Tanner's aspirations to the philosopher's heaven, it seems certain that his 'hamartia' no less than external events would have brought him finally to hell and the obligations of a loving father and a kindly husband.

The phrase, 'the Life Force', occurs several times in the play, in this final scene with great emphasis. It is perfectly true that intelligibility is a prerequisite of the stage but when Tanner cries out at the very climax 'The Life Force enchants me' we may uneasily wonder if intelligibility is not being driven to over-explicitness. If a dramatist does not trust his play, incongruities may easily develop; and the very real danger in 'The Life Force enchants me' is the same as if a committed stage neurologist in a similar situation were to exclaim (shall we say), 'My ganglions are stimulated'; in other words, terms which to the layman are gibberish, may too easily create bathos. This has not happened in the scene with Tanner and Ann because the play as a whole and this scene in particular give the phrase the necessary significance. It may even be felt by some (and no doubt this was Shaw's intention) that the repetition of the phrase induces an incantatory effect and the suggestion of a transcendental force; but for my part, the incantatory effect to be derived from a 'crude new name' is not worth striving after; not when the dialogue is as powerful and the suggestion of a transcendental force as evident as they are in this scene. Labels are for critics to use but not, I think, for dramatists.

The play ends swiftly, with an ironic finale which brings everyone onto the stage to wish the couple joy. Tanner protests – from within the very gates of hell he protests – and then he is allowed the last 'aria'. As assertive, as fluent, as provocative as ever, he harangues his audience:

> I solemnly say that I am not a happy man. Ann looks happy; but she is only triumphant, successful, victorious. That is not happiness, but the price for which the strong sell their happiness. What we have both done this afternoon is to renounce happiness, renounce freedom, renounce tranquillity, above all, renounce the romantic possibilities of an unknown future, for the cares of a household and a family. . . .

Violet responds in the manner beloved by revolutionaries. 'You are a brute, Jack', she says with intense conviction. This is Tanner's element, the hot water he desires. Then swiftly, cruelly, the final blow falls: 'Never mind her, dear. Go on talking.' Ann, looking at him with fond pride and caressing his arm, fondly dipping him into the cold water of wifely support, fondly assuming the cosy domesticity of 'dear', fondly intimating that 'this is *my* Jack, my amusing, eccentric, lovable Jack.' There is all this, and more. John Tanner, who only a few days before had proudly announced his life's work: 'I shatter creeds and demolish idols',[1] hears himself reduced to the greasy-eyed mediocrity of husbandhood and his stirring vision of a new, wholesome, revitalized world reduced to . . . words. Poor Jack, at last bereft of speech, can do no more than echo his wife-to-be and echo as well the despair of his soul: 'Talking!'

* * *

This is Tanner's 'tragedy' and the poignancy underlying the comedy. We would, I think, be indifferently perceptive if we understood the play as merely a burlesque of the convention with a lavish display of intellectual fireworks as a sideline. Shaw intended, and achieved, very much more than this. Tanner, it is true, is a vastly entertaining person, but the fervency and profound emotion of his loquacity demands that we see him more deeply, ultimately as a latter-day Prometheus felled by the terrible force of Nature and bound again to the rock, the secrets of Life locked once more in his breast.

But it does not follow that either he or Ann, for all their largeness of stature, sustains a general philosophy. To derive a general philosophy from their behaviour would be absurd. The propositions are entirely valid for them: there is a duel of sex, the woman is the hunter, the man the hunted; but the most that can be said after this is that the general rule *may* be true. As far as the play is concerned, the truth or otherwise does not matter. Tanner and Ann are superb as themselves. This is enough. Although Shaw wanted us to do so, we cannot and should not try to establish a universal metaphysic on their 'romance'. *Man and Superman* is an abundant and rewarding 'morality', but not an allegory.

[1] *Man and Superman*, Act I, p. 35.

K

Chapter Six

1904-1912: WOT PRICE SALVATION?

I 'There is no wicked side: life is all one.'[1]

I

In the ten years between *Man and Superman* and the outbreak of the war Shaw was probably more active than he had ever been before and would ever be again. His output was amazing, his energy inexhaustible. For most of this period he relentlessly continued his Fabian activities, writing – so to speak – *The Commonsense of Municipal Trading* one day and quelling H. G. Wells the next. He threw himself into the Court Theatre productions, perhaps finding in these (and in his close association here with Granville-Barker) the most complete satisfaction of his generally satisfying career. He preached and pamphleteered like any Encyclopaedist.[2] And he wrote twelve plays, eight of which may be considered important.

Of these eight plays, very nearly any one could be chosen as representing Shaw, not necessarily at his best, but in his prime. Some of the titles alone speak of eminence: *Major Barbara, The Doctor's Dilemma, Fanny's First Play, Androcles and the Lion, Pygmalion;* some are clearly better than others, *The Doctor's Dilemma* than *Androcles*, for instance; but they are all rewarding plays, intellectually as well as dramatically, and may all be justified to a greater or lesser degree as works of art.[3] However, I am not being entirely arbitrary by selecting *Major Barbara* to discuss at length, while relegating subordinate status to *John Bull's Other Island* and *Pygmalion*, and passing over *Fanny's First Play* in silence.

[1] *Major Barbara*, Act III, p. 338.
[2] See the Preface to *Major Barbara*, p. 221.
[3] The two 'disquisitory plays', *Getting Married* and *Misalliance* are briefly discussed in Chapter Seven. The 'tragedy', *The Doctor's Dilemma*, is also discussed in Chapter Seven.

Major Barbara is one of Shaw's best-known plays. It is in many ways the most vehemently didactic, if not ultimately doctrinaire. It is exceedingly challenging, even today, sixty years after its first performance. To many people it is normally reprehensible. To many others it is baffling. And to yet others, who want to throw the onus of failure on Shaw's shoulders, it is confused. Here Archer speaks for himself, but we may reckon on a fair amount of assent in his audience:

> . . . I confess that the main line of doctrine entirely eludes me. I cannot help thinking that there are two main lines, which eventually cross each other, so that the trains of thought which run on them collide, to their mutual destruction. . . . No one can think or expound his thought more lucidly than Mr Shaw, when he sets himself to do so; but in the rapture of dramatic composition, in the dust and heat of *Donnybrook Fair*, he often, I think, loses the thread of his argument, and lets himself go in orgies of fine confused cerebration.[1]

This is simply not true. If anyone is guilty of 'confused cerebration', it is not Shaw. Quite the opposite. He is honest, straight-thinking; and – as I shall attempt to show – he has written a play which achieves the validity of work rooted in the soil of religious experience. If, as Tolstoy believed, the highest form of art was religious art, then *Major Barbara* may be granted a foremost position in the Shavian canon. Overtly or implicitly religious though nearly all Shaw's plays are, this play succeeds in a way special to itself: it is a religious allegory.

The claim may possibly be substantiated in more ways than one: I propose to substantiate it by going back to what seems the source of inspiration of the play. This – the discovery of 'indebtedness', 'parallels', 'affinities', 'influences', and the rest – may very easily degenerate into that frequent academic exercise, 'Catch the Red Herring'. We caution ourselves by bearing this in mind. But red herrings sometimes turn out to be live, natural-coloured ones, like Fiske's *Bernard Shaw's Debt to William Blake*[2] or Barzun's 'Shaw and Rousseau: No Paradox',[3]

[1] Archer, *The Old Drama and the New*, p. 353 4.

[2] Shavian Tract No. 2, The Shaw Society, London, 1951. Also printed in *G. B. Shaw: A Collection of Critical Essays*, ed. R. G. Kaufmann, Prentice-Hall, Englewood Cliffs, New Jersey, 1962.

[3] *Shaw Bulletin*, New York, I, 8 May 1955.

and of great help in understanding Shaw better, especially since he was as reticent as most artists and more reticent than some on certain elements in his work, for all his voluble helpfulness on others. The most he would normally say about the composition of a play was to the effect 'The Life Force guides me',[1] which is not very helpful, and true only to the extent the Life Force could guide a wide-eyed and wilful companion. As more than one critic has remarked, Shaw was an extraordinarily conscious artist: inspiration for him was the outcome of nearly full self-awareness. So, I proffer 'Shaw and Euripides', more correctly, 'Shaw and the Euripides of Gilbert Murray', persuaded that Shaw was conscious of the affinities, though he preferred to keep silent about them; I am also persuaded that by an examination of Shaw's relationship to Euripides, especially the relationship of *Major Barbara* to *The Bacchae*, we shall greatly increase our understanding and appreciation of *Major Barbara*.

That (in Aristotle's phrase) 'the most tragic of the poets' should have fired a response from someone whose tragic view of things was usually alleviated by exuberance and laughter is not necessarily a contradiction. Farce may conceivably grow out of tragedy, and tragedy out of farce. The drawing-room comedy may drive from the standard commercial model and expand to comprehend the spiritual fate of mankind. It depends on the people in the drawing-room; and three people in Lady Britomart's drawing-room are able to command belief there, in a Salvation Army shelter, at Undershaft's munition works – to command belief, not merely as drawing-room characters but as emblems in a spiritual conflict quite as critical and momentous as that in Greek tragedy.

Shaw knew classical drama well and he followed its form very often, not, of course, because it was classical, but because it served his purpose. He wrote in the short prefatory note to *Getting Married*: 'I find in practice that the Greek form is inevitable when drama reaches a certain point of poetic and intellectual evolution.'[2] Here is he referring only to the Unities, to which he was uncommonly faithful, in several of his orthodox no less than in his disquisitory plays, but there are other

---

[1] See for example the Preface to *Buoyant Billions*, p. 4.
[2] *Getting Married*, p. 180.

characteristics of Greek drama, which we shall refer to *Major Barbara* (since this is the play we are discussing). The *parabasis*, for example, is custom-built for Undershaft as he swings into one of his Shavian speeches on poverty. The chorus is Cusins as he stands between Undershaft and Barbara, commenting on each and interpreting their religious conflict to the audience – a perfectly natural thing for a 'collector of religions' to do. The messenger is Bill Walker: at least, his return to the shelter after his humiliation under the knees of the terrible Todger and his tale of ignominy may be seen as the old practice turned to excellent modern account. Then, there is the Discovery, or revelation of hidden identity, which Shaw employs in Cusins's disclosure of his origins. The disclosure is perhaps of non-identity – an amusing inversion – but whichever way up it is, it provides one of the big surprises in the play. Cusins is indeed something of a compendium of classical devices, for as Murray tells us:

> An element in the Year Ritual in most Greek communities was a mysterious foundling, recognized at the end of the story as a semi-divine being, son of a God and the local princess. At one time (this was) a common theme of tragedy. . . .[1]

Cusins may now be seen as this foundling, whose father becomes the 'God' Undershaft and mother the 'princess' Lady Britomart – much to her annoyance.

In all this and no doubt in further general resemblances we see that Aeschylus, Aristophanes, Sophocles – and also of course the great writers of more modern dramatic literature, all of whom explicitly or implicitly acknowledge certain classical imperatives – were basic knowledge to Shaw, but there are reasons to believe that Euripides was more than this. These reasons begin in theatre history. *Hyppolytus*, *The Trojan Women*, and *Electra*, in translations by Gilbert Murray, were produced at the Court Theatre between 1904 and 1906, and a translation, though not a production, of *The Bacchae* added further lustre to Murray's reputation shortly before Shaw wrote *Major Barbara*. We may believe that these translations, coupled with

[1] Gilbert Murray, *Euripides and his Age*, London, Oxford University Press, 1965, p. 59.

Shaw's friendship with Murray, who may well in these years have been expounding the ideas which formed the nucleus of his classic study, *Euripides and his Age*, in 1918, encouraged Shaw to acknowledge a fundamental spiritual kinship between himself and Euripides.[1]

We have only to dip into Murray's book to see how remarkably alike the two are. Euripides came at a time of social and political reaction: so did Shaw. Euripides was a traditionalist about dramatic form and was opposed to traditional patterns of thought: so was Shaw. He was a patriot who scourged his country for its betrayal of political integrity: Shaw was and did the same. He portrayed among other un-conventionalities the baseness of war, the wrongness of vengeance: so did Shaw. He dissented from the orthodox religious habit to the point of blasphemy: so did Shaw. And he was, as Murray says, 'steadily admired by some few philosophers . . ., he enjoyed immense fame throughout Greece; but the official judges admired him reluctantly and with a grudge.'[2] Very much the same could be said of Shaw in his day.

All this would probably amount to little more than the schoolboy refrain about great minds thinking alike if it were not for a certain fact. The fact is *Major Barbara*. Shaw acknowledges his debt to Murray in a note placed before the preface:

> *N.B.* The Euripidean verses in the second act of Major Barbara are not by me, nor even directly by Euripides. They are by Professor Gilbert Murray, whose English version of The Bacchae came into our dramatic literature with all the impulsive power of an original work shortly before Major Barbara was begun. The play, indeed, stands indebted to him in more ways than one.[3]

The esoteric last sentence is generally supposed to allude to the portrayal of Murray in the character of Cusins, but it seems to me that

---

[1] This is not entirely new. A comparative study of Shaw and Euripides was made as long ago as 1921. See Gilbert Norwood, *Euripides and Shaw, With Other Essays*, London, Methuen, 1921.

[2] Murray, op. cit., p. 2.

[3] *Major Barbara*, p. 202.

Shaw implies considerably more, so much more that we may suggest *The Bacchae* as the direct cause and inspiration of *Major Barbara*.

At this point I am obliged to summarize the plot of *The Bacchae*, even at the risk of spelling out common knowledge.

The god Dionysus, with his Wild Women in fairly remote attendance on him, arrives in his own land, 'changed in shape from God to man'[1] but determined

> ... to show me in men's sight
> Manifest God.[2]

Because they have mocked and scorned him, he has sent a madness on the women of the royal household, and he now proposes to put an end to King Pentheus, who is bent on repudiating him. He allows himself to be captured by Pentheus, to be bound and led into the palace. An earthquake shakes the palace and Dionysus emerges unbound. In a great fury Pentheus rushes after him but he gradually succumbs to the God's will. He agrees to go disguised as a woman to watch the Bacchae (whose rites to Dionysus a messenger brilliantly describes). Pentheus goes, is discovered, and in accordance with the divine prophecy is torn to fragments. His mother, Agave, returns with his head, which in her transport of madness she thinks is that of a lion. The bacchic blindness is slowly lifted and she discovers the truth. Pentheus's body, painstakingly put together, is brought in. Dionysus appears, pronounces his doom on the wretched humans, and ascends in triumph to heaven.

The myth of Dionysus, which, according to Murray, is the source of Greek drama, hence of western drama, and which Euripides repeats in essential structure in *The Bacchae*, was bound up with early pagan religion, the beliefs and rituals surrounding which were an exaltation of a recurring revolution in the natural order of the world. Dionysus was specifically connected with the advent of the new year and the retreat of the old. He is therefore a god of vegetation and new growth (and only incidentally a god of wine and the bibulous orgies attributed

---

[1] Gilbert Murray's translation: *The Bacchae* by Euripides. In *Collected Plays of Euripides*, London, Allen and Unwin, 1954, p. 7.
[2] Ibid. p. 8.

by the Tintorettan school of art); he is a god of both death and life, of both impotence and fertility; a destroyer as well as a creator, a prince of the Underworld come to assert his kingdom in the world of men. We may go further. The Dionysian principle seems a primitive articulation of the polar mysteries, birth and death, which are explicable only in terms of antithesis – the antithesis which that enigmatic philosopher, the 'Dark' Herakleitos, declared in:

> God is day and night, winter and summer, war and peace, surfeit and hunger. . . .[1]

and in:

> Men do not know how what is at variance agrees with itself. It is an attunement of opposite tensions, like that of the bow and the lyre.[2]

We seem to be drifting away from Shaw and *Major Barbara*, and although this is not really so, we may leave Dionysus for the moment and return to Cusins, Undershaft, and Barbara.

Is there a resemblance between the foregoing and Shaw's play? Obviously no absolute resemblance, but there is so insistent an echo of *The Bacchae* that we cannot regard it as accident. Consider Cusins first. This Professor of Greek is practically a spokesmen of Euripides. He cites him readily, 'quotes' some Euripidean stanzas (very poor stanzas), equates the work done by the Salvation Army with the Dionysian ecstasy. He refers to Undershaft as the Prince of Darkness and as Dionysus. He loses himself completely to this modern god and leads the dithyramb with resounding bangs on his bass drum. Then as though Shaw were putting the final archetypal touch to Cusins's 'conversion', he has him spend the evening imbibing the god's Spanish burgundy: Cusins explains: 'I think it was Dionysus who made me drunk. . . . I told you I was possessed.'[3]

Possessed by Undershaft, who whether 'manifest God' or not, has returned to his home and visits the Salvation Army shelter to claim his

---

[1] Fr. 36 (according to Bywater's arrangement). In John Burnet's *Early Greek Philosophy*, London, Black, 1958, p. 136.

[2] Fr. 45, ibid.

[3] *Major Barbara*, Act III, p. 304.

favourite daughter, Barbara, for his own. At the Shelter he brings his 'divine alchemy' to bear on Cusins, on the entire Salvation Army, eventually on Barbara: the 'divine alchemy' of Money. A short while later, at his armaments factory, the second part of his creed is presented: Gunpowder. The destructive power in this, so vividly and 'brutally' indicated in the mutilated dummy soldiers on the stage and Undershaft's 'callous' talk of slaughtered armies, may be related to the dismembering and mutilation of Pentheus in *The Bacchae*; in the old mysteries this represented the death of the old order and the accession of the new. But Pentheus's body, we may remember, was put together again: this signifies that restoration grew out of death. So Money and Gunpowder shall destroy poverty and the ideals that tolerated poverty in order to restore prosperity to the world.

Barbara herself plays no active role in the Dionysian mystery: she is acted upon, and finds herself, as she says, as though in the midst of an earthquake:

I stood on the rock I thought eternal; and without a word of warning it reeled and crumbled under me. I was safe with an infinite wisdom watching me, an army marching to Salvation with me; and in a moment, at a stroke of your pen in a cheque book, I stood alone; and the heavens were empty. That was the first shock of the earthquake: I am waiting for the second.[1]

The second shock comes; then the revelation of what a power for good hers may be if she grasps the power of Money and Gunpowder; then – again in accord with the classical myth – comes the epiphany, which is granted her: this we shall leave until later.

To conclude this review, there is the contrast of sets – the miserable, cold, and dingy Salvation Army shelter and the spacious view of Perivale St Andrew. This points of course to the poverty-money thesis, and accentuates Shaw's belief that salvation of the soul without the prior salvation of the body was hopeless. But we may detect something more than sociological comment here, for Undershaft's city, as Shaw describes it,[2] surely suggests a panorama of the Grecian idyll,

[1] Ibid. p. 328.
[2] Ibid. p. 317.

with tall, slender factory chimneys imaging the pillars of ancient temples, and the eminence from which we gaze down (here, where a huge cannon is mounted and the high explosives are made) suggesting the seat of Zeus himself. Alongside this visual contrast is the allegory of change, the implied opposition between hunger and satisfaction, degradation and uppishness, winter and summer. Undershaft's description of poverty suggests the deathly chill of winter; the noisome breath of the plague:

> Poverty blights whole cities; spreads horrible pestilences; strikes dead the very souls of all who come within sight, sound, or smell of it.[1]

Now it will be agreed that all this amounts to fairly loose imitation, and as such is not worth much more than momentary surprise. We may therefore move to higher abstractions and see if *Major Barbara* gains or loses by this.

The Bacchae reflects two transcending characteristics of the Dionysian cult, the first to do with morality, the second with the emotions. Morality is the wrong word, but no other will do, our range of concepts being as limited as they are; morality really stops short of Dionysus, for this god knows no morality; nor does he know immorality, or, for that matter, amorality and unmorality. He was simply the pagan I AM, being neither pitiless nor pitying, neither merciless nor merciful, neither full of hate nor full of love. He is the deification of the natural cycle and supremely true only to himself. It may be that some of the greatness of Greek drama begins here, in the acknowledgement of a divinity as inevitable as the rising sun, as miraculous as bursting leaves. It seems certain that Shaw was fired by these qualities, and by a third, the sheer determinism of the god's declaration of himself. Here, in what we may regard as the prime ethic of nature, in this MUST and WILL BE of the manifestation, is the key to an understanding of *Major Barbara*.

Undershaft's gospel is patently derived from this ethic. He boldly flaunts his motto, UNASHAMED, in the eyes of horrified conventionality, usurps the plaintive 'oughts' of timid liberalism and reinstates the

[1] *Major Barbara*, p. 329.

full-blooded 'shall' of Dionysus, turns his machine-guns and cannons and aerial torpedoes on mankind to wipe out poverty and slavery, dealing in and thriving on death so that the world might be reborn to full life. He proudly quotes his predecessors, all of whom, not necessarily excluding the one who had no literary skill, give evidence of a decided bent for the paradox of mystical utterance. This is the point: Undershaft is an out-and-out mystic who has the power of life in his hands because he has the power of death. The tension of opposites implicit here is no resolution, and for this reason many people who know the play are disturbed. But resolution is impossible: the lyre is not a lyre if the tension is removed; the harmony of the quivering strings resides precisely in opposite tendencies. The harmony of the spheres, as Pythagoras postulated this, derives from the magical numbers of the taut bow. What is at variance agrees with itself: creation strains against itself: life is all one.

To which one may imagine the response that Shaw is taking the Devil out of Hell and putting him back in Heaven. He is not, of course. To him there is no Devil and hell shall be obliterated when poverty is obliterated. If our further response should be that an abolished Devil displays a hopeful rather than realistic view of evil, Shaw's answer in the play is that hope – the hope expressed by Barbara in the epiphany – when coupled with power can be the only admissible religious reality.

But the quarrel goes on, and the most urgent protest, raised by Barbara's cry 'My God: why hast thou forsaken me?'[1] and teased to anger by the glorification of Money and Gunpowder, is: 'What about Jesus?' Which Jesus? the play asks: the Jesus who on the one hand condones and even makes shift to exalt the hideous face of physical starvation and spiritual degradation and on the other hand condones and even makes shift to accept Bodger's bribe for salvation – the Jesus of doublethink and two faces, of deprivation for the many and privilege for the few: the Jesus of Crosstianity? Or the Jesus who condemns and would make every shift to eradicate the crime of poverty and the crime of parasitic wealth, the humanitarian Jesus, who so loves the world that he would destroy it to make his word manifest: the Jesus of Dionysian Christianity? Shaw repudiates the first Jesus; he makes this

[1] Ibid. Act II, p. 300.

the very price of salvation: he cleaves to the second Jesus, and makes this the prize of salvation.

It is a kind of Augean cleansing of the soul that Barbara endures and Shaw would have the world endure. Crosstianity must be scrapped; a religion that fitted the facts must be introduced. We may, if we wish, call this Christian, or Dionysian, or Christian-Dionysian, or whatever else in whatever combinations that appeal. Religion, as Shaw saw it, as Cusins saw it, as Undershaft saw it, and as Barbara comes to see it, is not true by virtue of the name coupled to it:

> The business of the Salvation Army is to save, not to wrangle about the name of the pathfinder. Dionysus or another: what does it matter?[1]

It does not matter one jot. What does matter is the universal of religion, that which makes Moslem, Buddhist, Christian, and pagan, brothers, uniting them in the family of humanity. That which Shaw has attempted to realise by going back to the source of Western (perhaps also Eastern) religious practice; by drawing an ethical philosophy from it. By trying in Acts II and III, and in my view succeeding thrillingly, to recreate the spirit of eternal religion – the excitement, the ecstasy of surrender to something greater than one's self.

This brings us to the second transcending characteristic of *The Bacchae* – the emotion of religious worship. It must be understood that this emotion has nothing to do with the licentious extravagance we tend to associate with the word 'bacchanal'; it is purely religious; purely devotional, even in its extreme form, when fervour gives way to ecstasy and this gives way to madness. Thus Euripides depicts the Bacchae, whose frenzy is the glorification of their god, no matter how outrageous it may seem to those who have not been affected by his divinity. Human tragedy does follow on the divine rage, desolation and horror fill the souls of those on whom the god's hand falls. But over and against this is the triumph of the god, his will done, and the heavens opening to receive him. How small in the scale of things – how tinpot – is the human tragedy, how overwhelmingly vast is the power and the mystery of the divine will.

[1] *Major Barbara*, p. 286.

The unspoken admission of religious practice is that words alone cannot express such power and mystery, and so ritual and song come spontaneously forth to augment the word. This is the intoxicant of worship, that which can so work on a person's spirit that he will lose himself to the rhythms and notes, lose himself to the cosmic I AM and be transfigured.

Dionysus was worshipped in the dithyramb, a song less of praise than of identification with his being. A choral song, it was initiated by one person (perhaps the one most under the influence of wine), who led others. We transfer the pagan custom to *Major Barbara* and Cusins immediately comes to mind. With his big bass drum he beats thunderous praise of salvation, for to begin with he is not aligned with Dionysus; then abstract salvation becomes concrete as Money and Gunpowder; Bodger's money and Undershaft's money saves the Salvation Army; cymbals clash, cornets peal, the trombone blares, the drum booms; shouts of praise and thanksgiving go upward; the march down Mile End Road begins, and the brassy torrent of sound sweeps to a crescendo, clash, peal, and boom, 'Glory, Halleluja!', 'Money and Gunpowder!', crowd one on the other until the air seems a fierce clamour, and violent upheaval seems to shake the Army shelter. Then stunned silence, and Barbara's cry of desolation piercing the emotions. The dithyramb is over.

Add to this thunderous assault the fine, hard thrust and parry between Undershaft and Cusins and the tragi-comedy of the unregenerate Bill Walker, and we may willingly acknowledge the 'impulsive power of an original work', which (in this, the second act, at least) transforms ancient myth into reverberant modern drama.

I hesitate to say the same of the second part of Act III, although the argument, if too long, has its own excitement. Such a speech as this will show the eloquence Shaw was capable of:

Come, come, my daughter! dont make too much of your little tinpot tragedy. What do we do here when we spend years of work and thought and thousands of pounds of solid cash on a new gun or an aerial battleship that turns out just a hairs-breadth wrong after all? Scrap it. Scrap it without wasting another hour or another pound on it. Well, you have made for yourself something that you call a morality or a religion or what not. It doesnt fit the facts. Well, scrap it. Scrap it and get one that does fit. That is what is wrong with the world at present. It scraps its obsolete steam engines and dynamos; but it wont scrap its old prejudices and its old moralities and its old religions and its old political constitutions. Whats the result? In machinery it does very well; but in morals and religion and politics it is working at a loss that brings it nearer bankruptcy every year. Dont persist in that folly. If your old religion broke down yesterday, get a newer and better one for tomorrow.[1]

This is as blatantly doctrinaire as any party politician's speech, let alone a dramatic character's speech. One tends to wish that it were not so baldly what it is, for example, that 'That is what is wrong with the world at present' had been scoured out of the first draft. But Shaw would have been less Shaw (and Undershaft less Undershaft) if this general diagnosis of the world's ills were to have been diluted with more 'art' and cleaned of its didactic grit, and so we must see what we can make of it as it stands. We detect the ghost of Shaw behind the speech, the ghost of a thousand and more platforms and committee rooms and pamphlets. T.S. Eliot would not have approved[2] and neither would many others who insist on the extinguished personality of the creative artist. We can as little have expected Shaw to extinguish his personality as we can expect Ireland to stop breeding revolutionists; besides, the ineffaceable stamp of art, of painting and music, no less than of literature, is the personality of the artist, or if not the person himself, the person in his time always.

The ghost of Shaw may therefore be left to hover. But perhaps this is not the objection; perhaps it is not the ghost but what the ghost is putting into the speaker's mouth that we object to: with apparent justification, because Undershaft, for all his splendid confidence, cannot be thought to be speaking whole truths. Three-quarter truths at most,

[1] *Major Barbara*, Act III, p. 328.

[2] I am referring, of course, to his celebrated essay 'Tradition and the Individual Talent'. That Eliot subsequently qualified the view expressed here is seemingly n ot well known. See his 'Yeats' in *On Poetry and Poets*. London, Faber, 1957.

which is also to say quarter falsehoods. Is the ghost accordingly to be hailed before a self-elected jury of pundits and given a fair trial before banishment? This is what has happened to Shaw more often than bears recounting, and yet the underlying fallacy burrows away unchecked. This fallacy is that Undershaft's quarter falsehoods are Shaw's whole truths and that whatever anybody else has to say in dispute with Undershaft must be ignored as not having any ghostly authority. Which is palpable nonsense, as a glance at the concluding passages of the play – what, in tracing the Dionysian ritual, I am calling the epiphany – will bear out.

With arguments such as that quoted above Undershaft slowly wins Cusins to his side. What, however, about Barbara? During the general conversation outside the high explosives shed she says very little; by her withdrawal from the group and her silence she indicates a spirit yet undecided, yet uncommitted. Then she and Cusins are left alone and she opens her heart and soul to him.

It would seem that Dionysos–Undershaft has won unconditionally, and yet this is not so. Barbara is not the sort of girl who can be won over unconditionally. As Cusins and Undershaft say of her in Act II:

> CUSINS: ... The power Barbara wields here – the power that wields Barbara herself – is not Calvinism, not Presbyterianism, not Methodism –
>
> UNDERSHAFT: Not Greek Paganism either, eh?
>
> CUSINS: I admit that. Barbara is quite original in her religion.
>
> UNDERSHAFT: (*triumphantly*) Aha! Barbara Undershaft would be. Her inspiration comes from within herself.[1]

There is in this girl a spirit of independence, a fervour – or even a 'madness' – for salvation work, which not all the high explosives in the world and not the most compelling arguments of her father can wholly overthrow. In accepting the power of Money and Gunpowder, she accepts as well the four hundred years old tradition of Capitalism; this will not go unchallenged, we feel, nor will the exhortation to scrap the 'old religion' be carried out fully. Dionysos-Undershaft may not know it, but in claiming this redoubtable daughter for his own he seems to

[1] *Major Barbara*, Act II, p. 286.

me to have introduced a new and not fully expected high explosive into the Salvation works of Perivale St Andrew. New and yet as old as human aspiration, a proud, free, fierce religion of life itself:

> BARBARA: . . . My father shall never throw it in my teeth again that my converts were bribed with bread. (*She is transfigured.*) I have got rid of the bribe of bread. I have got rid of the bribe of heaven. Let God's work be done for its own sake: the work he had to create us to do because it cannot be done except by living men and women. When I die, let him be in my debt, not I in his; and let me forgive him as becomes a woman of my rank.
>
> CUSINS: Then the way of life lies through the factory of death?
>
> BARBARA: Yes, through the raising of hell to heaven and of man to God, through the unveiling of an eternal light in the Valley of the Shadow. (*Seizing him with both hands*) Oh, did you think my courage would never come back? did you believe that I was a deserter? that I, who have stood in the streets, and taken my people to my heart, and talked of the holiest and greatest things with them, could ever turn back and chatter foolishly to fashionable people about nothing in a drawing room? Never, never, never, never: Major Barbara will die with the colors. . . .[1]

II '. . . *every jesti s an earnest in the womb*
of Time.'[2]

Connoisseurs. Irishmen, and politicians profess a liking for *John Bull's Other Island*, but – proof, if that were needed, that neither connoisseurs. nor Irishmen nor politicians have much influence on general taste – the play has not maintained its initial popularity or even been very well known. My own taste in this instance is the popular one. *John Bull's Other Island* seems to me a comparatively major attempt and a minor success. Too long by a good twenty minutes, constructed in such an

---

[1] *Major Barbara*, Act III, p. 339.
[2] *John Bull's Other Island*, Act IV, p. 176.

un-Shavianly loose way that it seems to grow by thematic accretion rather than organic development, and talkative even by the standards of the most talkative dramatist in history, it would, it seems to me, have profited from drastic revision.

These strictures are relative to Shaw's achievement at the time. Suppose Pinero had written such a play, there would have been stupefaction to begin with and then wonderment at the unprecedented vaunting of brain-power; suppose Yeats had written such a play, there would again have been stupefaction and then wonderment at the unprecedented flair for comedy. In other words, the play is distinctly Shavian and, being Shavian, has passages of typical strength. For this reason I select it, not for general evaluation but for the pegs it offers to hang discussions of certain characteristics of Shaw's drama.

The first 'peg' is that of topicality. All Shaw's plays – all plays – are topical, of course, but we must distinguish between human topicality and institutional topicality. All Shaw's plays, it is often said, perhaps most often by Shaw himself, are concerned with institutional topicality, consequently are barely able to survive a change of government, or a change of editor, or a change of public interest. It would be hard to find a more politically, socially, or culturally topical play than *John Bull's Other Island*. It was written by request for an occasion for a cause: Yeats asked for a play for the Abbey Theatre for the cause of Mother Ireland. The fact that Shaw's compliance did not turn the withered crone into a beauteous Kathleen is to the point: Mother Ireland, as Shaw perceived her in 1905, is there in all her tattered socio-economic, political, and cultural garments.

The implications for us today are obvious. Mother Ireland (of 1905) is dead and gone. The question of Free Trade, which could so excite Broadbent; the Liberal Party which made so resolutely stiff a backbone for his political thinking; the issue over Home Rule: these are with O' Leary in his grave. To be accurate, they followed him to the graveyard in a fairly short time. Does it follow that *John Bull's Other Island* has gone the same dusty way?

Not necessarily; for institutional topicality is a very frequent ingredient of comedy. We invoke no airy precept for the assertion of the solid example of Aristophanes, Shakespeare, Molière, who knew

L

that institutional topicality was a regular prerequisite of effective satire: it was a ticket at least into the vestibule of the theatre of living
drama, and no cause at all for non-admission. So *John Bull's Other
Island* may (whatever its shortcomings as a play) be allowed to proceed
thus far.

Now its entrance into the auditorium would depend on whether,
say, Broadbent has or has not been bestowed alongside his dead ideas
in that heterodox cemetery for historical knick-knacks, whether he has
transcended his ideas and maintained compellingly and compulsively
an existence in himself. Odd though it may seem, he has: he remains a
splendid exemplar of human topicality.

This – human topicality – the human comedy – rises above the
institution, even while being inseparable from it. It seems very clear
that Shaw's instinct as a creative artist insinuated this admission into
his seemingly most institutional or topical drama.

Widowers' Houses (for example) is based on a discredited theory of
economic rent, yet it reveals a state of affairs which is as rife today as it
was seventy years ago. Sartorius lived on in Rachman. But if Rachman
and all his tribe of landlords were miraculously banished from the face
of the earth, *Widowers' Houses* need not become defunct, for the essential theme is human lust. Similarly – though in differing quantities –
Mrs Warren's Profession and *The Philanderer*; and if not lust, then
prejudice, misconception, delusion, error. We may pitch out of a Shaw
play every scrap of institutionalism and still discover (in character and
ethical conflict) a valid though not necessarily an abiding comment on
the human drama.

Thus *John Bull's Other Island*, despite its structural weakness, despite
its dead wood of Free Trade, Liberal Party, Home Rule, and so on. It
holds out against oblivion by the strength of its characters. There is the
Englishman, Broadbent, a munificent gift to the stage; there are the
numerous minor characters, not easily recollected individually but
forming a conglomerate which in some subtle way seems to contain
the spirit of a people; then there is the unfrocked priest, Father Keegan.
He is the one I want to discuss.

He is among Shaw's most interesting portraits: interesting for his
role in the play, perhaps more interesting in himself and in his represen-

tative quality, which is how we shall look at him. Keegan is a mystic. He holds intelligent conversation with crickets, he regards all animals as his brothers in the family of living creatures, he regards all men, black, yellow, brown, and white, Hindu, Buddhist, Moslem, and Christian (both Protestant and Catholic) as his brothers in the family of humanity; and so, for his evincing such all-embracing charity, everyone thinks him mad. This is how the madman speaks:

KEEGAN: . . . I heard that a black man was dying, and that the people were afraid to go near him. When I went to the place I found an elderly Hindoo, who told me one of those tales of unmerited misfortune, of cruel ill luck, of relentless persecution by destiny, which sometimes wither the commonplaces of consolation on the lips of a priest. But this man did not complain of his misfortunes. They were brought upon him, he said, by sins committed in a former existence. Then without a word of comfort from me, he died with a clear-eyed resignation that my most earnest exhortations have rarely produced in a Christian, and left me sitting there by his bedside with the mystery of this world suddenly revealed to me.

BROADBENT: That is a remarkable tribute to the liberty of conscience enjoyed by the subjects of our Indian Empire.

LARRY: No doubt; but may we venture to ask what is the mystery of this world?

KEEGAN: This world, sir, is very clearly a place of torment and penance, a place where the fool flourishes and the good and wise are hated and persecuted, a place where men and women torture one another in the name of love; where children are scourged and enslaved in the name of parental duty and education; where the weak in body are poisoned and mutilated in the name of healing, and the weak in character are put to the horrible torture of imprisonment, not for hours but for years, in the name of justice. It is a place where the hardest toil is a welcome refuge from the horror and tedium of pleasure, and where charity and good works are done only for hire to ransom the souls of the spoiler and the sybarite. Now, sir, there is only one place of horror and torment known to my religion; and that place is hell. Therefore it is plain to me that this earth of ours

must be hell, and that we are all here, as the Indian revealed to me –
perhaps he was sent to reveal it to me – to expiate crimes committed
by us in a former existence.[1]

Arland Ussher (an Irishman) says that Keegan is convincing because
his speech rhythms are those of ordinary Irish speech.[2] Perhaps this is,
if not the whole reason, a large portion of the reason. It is generally
true that Shaw's visionaries tend to forgo natural speech rhythms in
favour of what we may unkindly but most accurately call vapid blether-
ing whenever the moment sublime, like an end-of-month account,
falls due. I have already quoted one such passage and may refer to
another, Mrs George's trance in *Getting Married*, both of which suggest
that if Shaw was not actually frightened by situations which seemed to
him to call for visionary poetry he could be embarrassed by them.
So embarrassed as frequently to cover them up with a joke, like Broadbent's inanity about liberty of conscience, as though laughter presented
a positive refuge for him; so embarrassed (possibly by literary deficiency
possibly by temperamental inaptitude) as to be incapable of anything
better than visionary gaucheness.

The quoted passage shows that this was not always so, that Shaw at
his best, as he is with Keegan and Shotover of *Heartbreak House*, could
control his mystics with a sure sense of purpose and effect.

Keegan is in fact not being consciously mystical, and in this, his
unselfconscious apprehension of things, his words have a portentous-
ness and a luminousness which 'He's' harmonious spheres or Mrs
George's 'eternity' or any other spuriously poetic afflatus can never
have. The elderly Hindoo, whose tragedy is so succinctly and gravely
described, has revealed the mystery of the world to Keegan because his
– the Hindoo's – fate is quite simply a commonplace of the world conceived in commonplace images.

A remarkable thing about Keegan's two speeches is that they are
built round a conceit – that hell is here, now, on this earth and not in
some sub-terrestrial hereafter – and yet they do not for a second invite

[1] *John Bull's Other Island*, p. 151.
[2] 'Bernard Shaw: Emperor and Clown', *Three Great Irishmen*, London, Gollancz,
1952, p. 31.

anything other than a serious, even solemn, hearing. As I say, this is largely because Keegan is Keegan, but it is also because Keegan is an Irishman whose rhetoric derives straight from the Augustan age at its most spacious and resonant and solemn. The spirit of an embittered and frustrated Irishman – Jonathan Swift – whose bitterness and frustration could so often be made to seem golden by the majesty of his periods, is not far away, we feel.

*   *   *

It is time to say a little more about Shaw's humour; and it is this curate's egg of a play, *John Bull's Other Island*, which offers the opportunity, containing as it does a scene where several people on the stage laugh themselves to near imbecility at a sequence of events which have been absolutely, dogmatically unfunny.

What happened was that Broadbent, his hopes riding high for election as the Member for Rosscullen, rashly undertook to transport a certain pig from one place to another in his motor car. Here, in Barney Doran's words, is the first side-splitting sequence:

> Dhere was Patsy Farrll in the back sate wi dhe pig between his knees, n me bould English boyoh in front at the machinery, n Larry Doyle in the road startin the injine wid a bed winch. At the first puff of it the pig lep out of its skin and bled Patsy's nose wi dhe ring in its snout. (*Roars of laughter: Keegan glares at them.*) Before Broadbint knew hwere he was, the pig was up his back and over into his lap; and bedad the poor baste did credit to Corny's thrainin of it; for it put in the fourth speed wid its right crubeen as if it was enthered for the Gordn Bennett.[1]

The engine of the car thus spectacularly engaged, things happen swiftly. The car leaps forward, Larry Doyle leaps aside, clearing

> six yards sideways at wan jump if he cleared an inch; and he'd a cleared seven if Doolan's grandmother hadnt cotch him in her apern widhout intindin to.

[1] *John Bull's Other Island*, Act III, p. 143. Further references are to this and ensuing pages.

Immense merriment: paroxysms when the old dame's injury is particularized. The car is now tearing down the main street; the pig, its tail caught under the foot brake, is squealing; Broadbent (behind the steering wheel) is powerless to stop the car because the pig's tail is in the way.

Then the pig leaps out and forward into the road in front of the car —

> Bedad I'm sorry for your poor bruddher, Mister Keegan; but I recommend you to thry him wid a couple o fried eggs for your breakfast tomorrow. It was a case of Excelsior wi dhat ambitious baste. . . .

But the pig out of the way and turned into rashers makes no difference. Broadbent has quite lost control of the car, which continues its mad rush, tears through the market, does resounding battle with a solid wall, and only then comes to a halt. Doran concludes:

> Begob, it just tore the town in two and sent the whole dam market to blazes. . . .
>
> Oh, you never heard such a hullabaloo as there was. There was Molly cryin Me chaney, me beautyful chaney! n oul Matt shoutin Me pig, me pig! n the polus takin the number o the car, n not a man in the town able to speak for laughin.

Every man laughing; and every man on the stage (except Keegan) laughing at the memory of the jolly event. But it had not been funny.

Shaw is at pains to make this point. Besides the facts of the happening, which silently deny the humour of Doran's racy and vivid narrative and turn the raciness and vividness stale and flat, two characters, Nora and Keegan, are quick to speak against the amusement. Nora reacts to the account of grandmother Doolan's mishap with spontaneous words of compassion and Keegan reacts with an outburst of angry disgust:

> There is danger, destruction, torment! What more do we need to make us merry?

This laughter scene may serve us as something of an allegory on the moral responsibility of humour. We may briefly enlarge on Shaw's attitude.

Once asked to define 'humour', he answered, 'Anything that makes you laugh. But the finest sort draws a tear along with the laugh.'[1] The first implication in this is that he was not disposed to go along with the anatomists of laughter and differentiate between 'wit' and 'humour', and was probably less disposed to recognize laughter as being caused by 'satire', or 'lampoon', or 'hyperbole', or whatever. All the organs of the body added up to life and, similarly, all the categories of 'humour' added up to laughter: it may even be inferred that to him categories of humour were semantic fiddle-faddle.

The second part of his definition slightly qualifies the first and implies a scale, the greatest value being granted that humour which 'draws a tear along with the laughter'. An unfortunate phrase perhaps, but the meaning is clearly in line with the 'apostolic succession' of dramatic humorists – Aristophanes, Shakespeare, Molière – whose laughter so frequently has serious undertones, both emotional and didactic, and plays like a shimmer of light over ignorance, delusion, and despair. Molière has with reason been described as the most tragic of the great French writers.[2] The best humour, then – or its concomitant, laughter – may be regarded as being instinct with a high moral sense. The following passage as much as says this by its forceful denunciation of the debased currency of mirth:

> To laugh without sympathy is a ruinous abuse of a noble function; and the degradation of any race may be measured by the degree of their addiction to it. In its subtler forms it is dying very hard: for instance, we find people who would not join in the laughter of a crowd of peasants at the village idiot, or tolerate the public flogging or pillorying of a criminal, booking seats to shout with laughter at a farcical comedy, which is, at bottom, the same thing – namely, the deliberate indulgence of that horrible, derisive joy in humiliation and suffering which is the beastliest element in human nature.[3]

[1] 'Who I am, and what I think', in *Sixteen Self Sketches*, p. 54.
[2] 'Eugène Ionesco on the Theatre': an interview by Carl Wildman, London, *The Listener*, LXXII, 24 December 1964.
[3] *Our Theatres in the Nineties*, Vol. II, p. 118.

We may now skip seven years and pluck from that comparatively slight but incandescent play, *Pygmalion,* the scene which is probably the most explosively amusing in the entire body of Shaw's work: Liza Doolittle's introduction into polite society. We may take the delight of the scene for granted and limit ourselves to considering why we laugh and what Shavian purpose underlies the laughter.

Liza enters Mrs Higgins's drawing-room and everyone, not excepting members of the audience, who have last seen her in her Lissom Grove finery, is stunned. As Shaw says, she creates an impression of remarkable distinction and beauty. She greets everybody in the most perfectly articulated English. She seats herself in a graceful and easy – in a completely lady-like – manner. Then:

> MRS HIGGINS: (*at last, conversationally*) Will it rain, do you think?
> LIZA: The shallow depression in the west of these islands is likely to move slowly in an easterly direction. There are no indications of any great change in the barometrical situation.[1]

And Freddy laughs and we laugh. Why? Freddy because he thinks this an example of the new 'small talk' and the quintessence of drawing room wit, we because Liza's remark is so absurdly inappropriate to the polite conventions of an 'at home'. As we know, this absurdity is very shortly to swell to sheer grotesquerie when Liza embarks on her history:

> LIZA: (*darkly*) My aunt died of influenza: so they said. . . . But its my belief they done the old woman in.
> MRS HIGGINS: (*puzzled*) Done her in?
> LIZA: Y – e – e – e-es, Lord love you! Why should she die of influenza? She come through diphtheria right enough the year before. I saw her with my own eyes. Fairly blue with it, she was. They all thought she was dead; but my father he kept ladling gin down her throat til she came to so sudden that she bit the bowl off the spoon. . . .

By now the marriage between manner and matter is not merely inappropriate: it is a fantastic misalliance. And Freddy laughs and we laugh so uproariously that we may quite possibly not listen to Mrs Eynsford

---

[1] *Pygmalion*, Act III, p. 250. Further references are to this and ensuing pages.

Hill's words. She, plaintively ineffectual lady that she is, mentally, emotionally, and socially equipped to see as far as her own genteel distress but no further, accepts this Miss Doolittle on drawing-room terms – and so, of course, finds herself appalled and bewildered by the matter-of-factness of Lissom Grove.

> MRS EYNSFORD HILL: (*to Eliza, horrified*) You surely dont believe that your aunt was killed?
> LIZA: Do I not! Them she lived with would have killed her for a hat-pin, let alone a hat.
> MRS EYNSFORD HILL: But it cant have been right for your father to pour spirits down her throat like that. It might have killed her.
> LIZA: Not her. Gin was mother's milk to her. . . .

And Liza, growing more and more at ease, launches into an account of the redemptive qualities of liquor in family life. She cannot be allowed to go on for too long, for the sake of both Mrs Higgins's 'at home' and the success of the scene, and so Higgins drops the hint: the experiment is over, Liza must now leave. Gracious 'Goodbyes' to Mrs Higgins and Colonel Pickering, a gracious 'Goodbye, all' to the others, then the too well-known conclusion:

> FREDDY: (*opening the door for her*) Are you walking across the Park, Miss Doolittle? If so —
> LIZA: (*with perfectly elegant diction*) Walk! Not bloody likely. (*Sensation*) I am going in a taxi.

With which final, shattering expletive Liza sails out. We must admit that modern faecal-minded drama and the familiarity of the scene to us all has reduced the sensational effect considerably; but it is no damp squib. It can never be, considering the purpose it serves over and above its aim to be shock-provoking.

The point at issue is whether to walk or take a taxi. Taxis, we may remember, had implied a good deal in Act I. To Freddy and his family they had meant simple necessities of existence, without which it became impossible to move; to Liza they had represented the height of luxury, mysteriously associated with Royalty and other symbols of the material ultimate. Now we have Freddy asking her to *walk* across the Park: for him it will mean a pleasant change, but for Liza it will somehow mean a return to the weariness and drudgery of her former life. So she rejects the invitation with all the emphasis and vigour her education in the gutters can muster for her. Her exit line is not simply a lurid piece of theatricality. It is an assertion of the awakening Life Force. It is, in the light of her background, inevitable and peculiarly right. By contrast, how pallid and sluttish the expression sounds when silly, superficial Clara uses it a few minutes later.

This, then, is the climax of a scene which since its auspicious opening has brilliantly balanced laughter against great seriousness of purpose. Liza is, of course, nothing more nor less than a doll, a triumph of artifice. She is a princess or a Cinderella doll at the moment of collision with her former existence. Beautifully intoned, phonetically perfect (if idiomatically unsound) words clothe grim suspicion, covetousness, and jealousy; they hang from the gaunt shoulders of ignorance and drunkenness and disease; they are the shimmering drapes round squalor and brutality and the sheer beastliness of poverty. They – these golden sounds of the phonetician's art – are the grotesques and Liza's squalid tale the truth.

The Eynsford Hill children are vastly entertained, and stand exposed. Deceived by appearances, they hear the comedy of the stricken aunt and drunken father as 'small talk', to be gleefully received and emulated. 'And it's so quaint, and gives such a smart emphasis to things that are not in themselves very witty', Clara says later. She could not damn herself more effectively.

But Shaw exposes Liza as well, and we join Freddy in laughing at her. We should not be sentimentally evasive about this: Liza is an unmitigated incongruity in Mrs Higgins's drawing-room. The more she reveals of her incongruity the more we shall laugh at her – if we have a drawing-room point of view, if we have a middle-class point of view; if, like Doran and his cronies, we can stand in the castle of our self-complacency and delight in 'danger, destruction, torment'.

But we should not imagine that this scene indulges us in the sort of humour which in *John Bull's Other Island* Shaw had forthrightly condemned. To have done so would have been a simple matter – and cruel; would have been merely to have Eliza go on uttering inanities

like her weather report, thereby keeping her at a disadvantage throughout. The very opposite happens, the point of view shifts away from
the drawing-room, the ethic turns upside down, and as Liza proceeds,
it is as though the degradation and viciousness of the poor have gained
the ascendancy. Nor – to the likes of the Doolittles of this world – is
there anything funny in this. All is quite simply just so, normal, in-
offensive, 'proper' and 'right'. The properness and rightness of her
disclosures are points of honour with Liza, which she is prepared to
defend in any squabble. And yet, what sordid proprieties, what squalid
rights: what a guttersnipe soul this Cinderella still possesses!

Everyone stands indicted: Mrs Eynsford Hill by her genteel alarm,
Freddy and Clara by their amusement, we – the audience – by our
laughter, Liza by her poverty: indicted before the high tribunal of fact
and its concomitant, that of common humanity, the implicit ethic that
burns within the particulars of Liza's discourse. That stricken aunt,
that drunken father, that hat, that hat-pin – these are all very, very
amusing, yes. But these are images pointing to the chasm between
money and no money; education and ignorance; privilege and deprivation: the bedrock of our laughter, we are brought to realise, is a social
and human tragedy. Shaw's satire lies deep and may indeed be engulfed
by laughter – but when it is perceived it is disconcertingly sharp.
Comedy cannot be more masterfully realised.

*   *   *

'Wot prawce selvytion nah?' Bill Walker asked Barbara: it may seem
that we have forgotten the question in the second part of this chapter.
Not really. The price of salvation is everything, and in the drama, in
the work of art, should be realized by whatever means the author is
able to summon to his aid. The gap between human ability and immortal longings may be bridged only by complete artistry, and Shaw's artistry lacked several important struts and stays. Yet we may see that
those struts and stays which *were* his, above all, his genius for high
comedy, sustained his bridge. Laughter – the fine exalted laughter of
redeemed souls – is the first statute in the Shavian paradise.

Chapter Seven

1913-1923: THE GREAT PLAYS

I 'Then suddenly Nature takes her revenge.'[1]

2

Speak of the technical aspects of Shaw's plays and we speak of little that is new. As the continuing popularity of even his slightest work suggests, his craft is the craft of the masters of theatre. In fact, as Meisel's book shows, his craft often came from a less exalted (but remarkably efficient) workshop, the joinery of nineteenth-century dramatic practice.[2] He was an original dramatist, yes; but technically he was a traditionalist who, rather than beginning a new style, consummated the old, and out-made the well-made play, out-did the stage characters, and out-wrote the writers of his nonage with seemingly careless ease.

Yet having said this, I invite qualifications. Shaw did of course adapt stage conventions, primarily by subordinating 'story' to what is sometimes unkindly referred to as 'talk, talk, talk': a more tolerant designation is 'discussion'. This is the explicit dogma of his dramatic method, a dogma which, when he carried it too far, imposed great strain on his construction. Talk, talk, talk is sometimes indulged in as though the last word, if there can ever be the last word on anything, transcends form; and yet more talk, issuing from strangers to the action – such as Mrs George of *Getting Married* – add a load of opinion that inflicts near fracture on the structure. The objection, it will be seen, is based on aesthetics and despite Shaw's opinion on aesthetics, the objection must stand.

But of course, the artist in Shaw, which is to say that part of his creative personality that acknowledged 'beauty' as a necessary constituent of drama, usually prevented discussion from going too far and

---

[1] Preface to *Heartbreak House*, p. 7.
[2] M. Meisel, *Shaw and the Nineteenth Century Theater*, London, Oxford University Press, 1963.

instead melted talk into plot, and plot into talk, so that on the whole his plays realise a highly effective unity. But by plot one must understand something other than mere anecdotage; one may occasionally, understand a story but more often a simple, one may say an elemental, situation. Situation is the essence of the Shavian plot: it is, perhaps, a throwback to nineteenth-century anecdotage, and as such a piece of theatrical machinery which Shaw would gladly have discarded. That he did not discard it entirely but relied on something which could set his merry-go-round off shows him to have been of his time, though also ahead of his time in feeling towards the no-plot, no-situation play of Beckett and Pinter.

The spearhead of Shaw's exploration into further possibilities of dramatic technique is three plays, *Getting Married*, *Misalliance*, and *Heartbreak House*, all of which are discussion plays with 'strong' situations but no, or very little, conventional plot. In the present examination of Shaw, plays such as *Getting Married* and *Misalliance*, though interesting in themselves, are significant chiefly in that they lead on to *Heartbreak House*. Both are apprentice plays – from a writer at the height of his power; consequently both are brilliant, witty, and thought-provoking. They have a strong touch of fantasy, not to say implausibility, in them. They are loud, high-spirited, and exhausting. Their effect is of a brass band on a swiftly revolving stand vigorously playing Sousa for two hours or more – though, it would be fair to add, *Misalliance* shows Shaw's orchestra to have grown to a few woodwind instruments.

To have grown as well out of the too cramping specificity of *Getting Married*, from the poser Shall we marry, and if so, on what terms? to the far less limiting question on parent–child relationships. Was such a growth the intuitive sloughing off of the constriction of strict realism? We cannot say; it is enough to discern the freer fantasy of *Misalliance* and the greater effectiveness of this play.

But *Misalliance* is a stepping-stone. *Heartbreak House* was completed six years later, in 1916. This play is a triumph for its genre, a great play by any terms, a harmony of infinitely subtle notes, a fantasia. Not so much a fantasia 'in the Russian manner' generally or in the Tchekov manner specifically; a fantasia in the Shavian manner, a basically despairing yet irrepressibly jocular study of social and human disaster. *Getting Married* and *Misalliance* are far behind now, but they had done well in making this work possible.

*   *   *

Heartbreak House is not merely the name of the play which follows this preface. It is cultured, leisured Europe before the war.[1]

The visible symbol of this Europe is Captain Shotover's house, which looks like a ship. In this – the ship of Europe – Ellie Dunn's 'story', her awakening, her problem, and her final decision, becomes the central issue of the play that is Europe.

Ellie, this ingenuous daughter of the ever-hopeful Mazzini, is recognizably of the genus Shaw, one of those heroines who in the course of their plays journey from self-delusion to more truthful perception of themselves and life in general. These heroines – like Raina or Gloria or Liza – begin as more or less conventional young women dipped (each of course in mixtures to suit her particular situation) in a solution of romantic clichés and socially 'proper' attitudes. One might say that Ellie had been left to soak overnight. Accordingly, she venerates her father as the best man she has ever known, not because Mazzini *is* the best man she could ever have known (he isn't), but because he is her father. She feels herself 'bound in honour and gratitude' to marry Mangan because of his 'kindness to dear Father'. And most enviable but also most pitiable, like Desdemona adrift in the twentieth century, she has quite lost her heart to and her head over the preposterously romantic 'Marcus Darnley'. She learns the truth about Marcus in a swift, cruel, yet to us brilliantly managed anti-climax. He is a lie, his tales of fabulous adventure are lies, the life he had created in Ellie's imagination – one 'better than the happiest dream', a 'life transfigured' – is, though not an absolute lie, quite unattainable in the Europe of 1914; and the bereft girl, a stranger in this noisy, pitching ship, must begin to find a new spiritual home, a new 'reality' for herself.

But everything proves false. Deprived of romance, Ellie is gradually

[1] Preface to the play, p. 3.

deprived of all faith in humanity and of all personal hope. One by one her companions reveal their moral nullity behind their various poses, one by one each is stripped of his 'culture' and shown to be – what? The Capitalist, Mangan, towards whom she seems to turn in violent reaction against her romantic illusions, shows himself to be a cheat, an adventurer, a gambler with other men's money – to be that not uncommon curiosity a virtually penniless millionaire. Lady Utterword, beautiful, patrician, the feminine gender of 'Empire', shows herself to be as utterly heartless as only the proud can be. Her follower, Randall, trailing behind her in the puerile dejection of unconsummated adultery, is in all respects an unconsummated man. Hesione has nothing true about her, except her beautiful black hair, her devastating beauty. And Captain Shotover, this fine and fearsome advocate of the 'seventh degree of concentration', tears aside the curtain of his being – and shows Ellie the horror of an old man drinking.

There is then no hope for Ellie – and so she gains salvation. Driven to become 'one of those who are so sufficient to themselves that they are only happy when they are stripped of everything, even of hope', she gains, as Shotover says, 'the only real strength', the strength to resist and do. 'At your age,' he fiercely tells her, 'I looked for hardship, danger, horror, and death, that I might feel the life in me more intensely. I did not let the fear of death govern my life; and my reward was, I had my life.'[1] Ellie accepts the metaphor, disowns her 'real father', claims the unconscionable Billy Dunn as her new father – the father of her newly discovered, independent spirit – and in the last act of the play commits herself to Shotover-Shaw's Vitalism by 'marrying' Shotover.

Her action is the complete repudiation of 'cultured, leisured Europe', the rejection of personal relations in the careering ship. It means no hope for posterity: in her end is no beginning for the future. For Ellie is the potential future of cultured, leisured Europe. She represents all young women of her class instinctively searching for a worthy father to their children; and the possible fathers in Heartbreak House are glaringly unworthy. The alternative is sterility – an alternative that says as unambiguously as the final disaster: Heartbreak House is doomed.

[1] See *Heartbreak House*, Act II, pp. 113–15.

Ellie's elected bridegroom celebrates his nuptials under the threatening heavens by remaining fast asleep, as unmoved by Ellie's announcement of her marriage (if he hears her at all) as he is by most of the shocks and surprises of the play. Shotover is an enigmatic, an extraordinary, an immense figure. He cannot be defined but he is magnificently definite. Humanity is his despair and rum is his solace; the invention of death-dealing weapons is his hobby, the 'seventh degree of concentration' his desire. He combines the terrible mortality of old age with the unquenchable spirit of an Old Testament visionary. He is a prophet of damnation and an oracle of redemption, the devil's disciple and the elected of God. He is Shaw and Ibsen and Lear and Nature. And Life, realised in all its restless, questing energy, forced to the brink of extinction by the hellish forces of discouragement.

Discouragement – that pander of death. We may look more closely at some of its exemplars. Mangan and Hector Hushabye, the capitalist and the warrior, the villain and the hero of romance – these cannot be the fathers of the future, Mangan for reasons that shriek the man's ignominy, Hector for subtler ones. Hector is a liar, which is not at all a fact to condemn him by, because the lies spring from genuine but thwarted bravery. It might then seem that we may interpret him as the authentic hero of romance, as someone like his illustrious Trojan namesake or Othello ('only, of course, white and very handsome') whose dreams of high daring and glory, like their feminine counterpart in Ellie's dreams, can come to nothing in a world directed by Mangan and Hastings. As the dialogue frequently suggests, he seems genuine enough, so why is he fundamentally unworthy? The answer is not only that he is already married, for marriage in the abstract presents merely an obstacle of convention. It is that he is married to that vampire woman, that demon woman – Hesione; and she has used him up and left him nothing but his dreams. He has become a lapdog, a pampered creature who can 'prove' himself by deeds of physical daring and collect a drawerful of Albert Medals, and who yet lacks the moral courage to escape the bewitchment of his wife. He has exhausted his essential manhood and vitiated his self-respect by languishing in the toils of 'beautiful black hair'.

But – to move to the outer circle of the play – if Mangan is an outcast, even in Heartbreak House, Hector is not. He is very comfortably surrounded by his kind. Everyone, Shotover and Ellie excepted, has exhausted his or her essential manhood or womanhood, everyone has forsaken the creed 'resist and do' and drifts wittily, self-satisfiedly, unthinkingly through life. Lady Utterword and Randall have only to open their mouths and they endorse this judgement, but what about Mazzini – gentle Mazzini, kindly Mazzini? Does he deserve this indictment? He does. He is the sentimental lie of liberalism, the canting rhapsodist of the land that never was England. He is tolerated and even made to feel welcome in Heartbreak House, but he does not really belong there, no matter how amiably at his ease he sits and chats in his pyjamas. He belongs in a place where misty idealism can perform some practical function and where deceit and corruption, self-seeking and greed, ruthlessness and theft are as unknown as they are everyday facts of our public and private worlds. A born 'soldier of freedom', Mazzini Dunn fails his namesake signally and lamentably: he has no sword in his hand; and freedom, or peace, or anything morally valuable, can only prevail if that weapon is wielded in its cause. Or, to use another analogy, derived not from *Major Barbara* but the New Testament: if Mazzini exemplifies the meekness, mercifulness, and righteousness of the Sermon on the Mount, he yet does not temper this with the strength to 'resist and do'; he does not have the moral passion of the Man who could both deliver the Sermon and knout the money lenders from the temple.

*   *   *

Heartbreak House prophesies the destruction of Capitalism and the wholesale correction of the established church at one end of its scale and at the other end delivers a brisk little lesson on infant care. In between these extremes is a rich and varied collection of ideas and comments, most of them so closely interwoven that I hesitate to pull more threads than I have already done, for fear of destroying the dynamic pattern of the whole. But there is one major blemish, the burglar, and before we go on to consider the culminating ideology of the play, we may briefly inspect this scion of the 'drinking Dunns'.

He breaks into the action with startling effect, and making captive his

M

captors, provides a few minutes of undoubted entertainment. He is most amusingly an 'inopportunely contrite sinner', but he is also a thorough scoundrel, who has heard the skeletons rattling in the cupboards of Heartbreak House and realised that no resident would want them yanked out and made to caper in the public gaze. In a word, he is a blackmailer, an uncommonly wily blackmailer, it must be admitted, who plays the morality game with such finesse that he casts a haze of perplexity over the whole question of indictment, guilt, and judgement. But his vocation is not to be endured and he indicts himself sufficiently to deserve his messy end: a bomb on Billy Dunn is unquestionably just retribution – not, however, that during his brief moment in the limelight he had failed to indict the members of Heartbreak House nearly as sufficiently. But once these and one or two associated ideas have been admitted we might wonder if they serve any strictly necessary purpose. It does not seem so; it really seems that, in spite of his contribution to the 'discussions', Billy Dunn has been put into the wrong play, has made a long work longer, and strained our credulity by turning out to be the rascal who had once robbed Captain Shotover. When we have finished laughing at him, we should, I think regretfully ascribe him to that tendency of Shaw already referred to, the tendency to heave 'talk, talk, talk' (the more amusing the better) into his plays, no matter what the cost to dramatic coherence.

*   *   *

The year is 1914. Cultured, leisured Europe sails the high seas to destruction. Never, one is inclined to imagine, was so inexpert a crew of navigators, such moral drunkenness, such delusion about palpable fact. Rarely could so varied a collection of offences against God's laws have been gathered together. Shotover, the ignored Captain on the bridge, gives the savage warning:

> . . . Nothing happens, except something not worth mentioning. . . . Nothing but the smash of the drunken skipper's ship on the rocks, the splintering of her rotten timbers, the tearing of her rusty plates, the drowning of the crew like rats in a trap.[1]

[1] *Heartbreak House*, Act III, p. 138.

Then the central message of the play, delivered with a force that makes the best efforts of most writers of 'pure' drama seem anaemic:

> HECTOR: And this ship that we are all in? This soul's prison we call England?
>
> CAPTAIN SHOTOVER: The captain is in his bunk, drinking bottled ditch-water; and the crew is gambling in the forecastle. She will strike and sink and split. Do you think the laws of God will be suspended in favor of England because you were born in it?
>
> HECTOR: Well, I dont mean to be drowned like a rat in a trap. I still have the will to live. What am I to do?
>
> CAPTAIN SHOTOVER: Do? Nothing simpler. Learn your business as an Englishman.
>
> HECTOR: And what may my business as an Englishman be, pray?
>
> CAPTAIN SHOTOVER: Navigation. Learn it and live; or leave it and be damned.[1]

This is the business of the Englishman, and by legitimate inference, the business of every white, yellow, red, and black man and woman on this earth. There is nothing new in the idea, but the Shavian twist has already been provided:

> Let a man drink ten barrels of rum a day, he is not a drunken skipper until he is a drifting skipper. Whilst he can lay his course and stand on his bridge and steer it, he is no drunkard. It is the man who lies drinking in his bunk and trusts to Providence that I call the drunken skipper, though he drank nothing but the waters of the River Jordan.[2]

'Providence' echoes Mazzini's words and denotes 'the Old Man in the sky' of popular superstition. We know what Shaw thought of this belief, and here he clearly wishes to show that no such 'God' is ever at hand to be conciliated by pious-sounding platitudes, or bottles of holy water, or Mazzini's hopeful mysticism. Shaw's God will hold no basin at ceremonial hand-washings; He abides by his law, which is

[1] Ibid. pp. 138–9.
[2] Ibid. p. 138.

that the hands are cleanest which work for redemption. If we do not help ourselves, if we do not use our hands and hearts and brains to expel the false, the decadent, the corrupt from our lives, to resist the poisonous blandishment of moral sloth and to fight for a pure code of social and personal conduct, then God will assuredly leave us to 'strike and sink and split'.

And this happens to Heartbreak House not many seconds after Captain Shotover's warning. Suddenly – or perhaps not very suddenly – Nature takes her revenge. She balances the long overdue account. Against the follies of the world she enters the *catharsis* of war. When it is over it is seen that the inmates of Heartbreak House have not been much affected, though the burglar and the capitalist are destroyed whilst 'the poor clergyman will have to get a new house'. The war – this war – is over, but it will not necessarily be the war to end wars. Hector, in a moment of godlike comprehension, cries out against Mazzini's pity for Mangan: 'Are you immortal that you need pity him? Our turn next'; and Ellie, 'radiant at the prospect', echoes Mrs Hushabye's exultation, though not, perhaps, the reason for the exultation, in hoping that the bombers will return.[1] The play ends on a grimly ominous note. Nature, like Captain Shotover, may have gone to sleep again, prepared to allow the human race another long term of credit, but we are left uneasily wondering whether the survivors will honour the account. Will they learn navigation or continue to drift? The 1939–45 war has the answer, one which Shaw may well have sensed would come.

I should cite Desmond MacCarthy's criticism of *Heartbreak House* at this point. He says: '*Heartbreak House*, in spite of its rare merits, . . . is zig-zagged by a flaw from top to bottom. . . . As a picture of behaviour and talk in an English country house during the summer of nineteen-fifteen or sixteen or seventeen, or whenever the action is supposed to take place, the play has no relation to reality.'[2]

This comment invites two queries. The first is about MacCarthy's implications in the phrase 'relation to reality', the second is about his doubt when the action takes place. *Heartbreak House* stands in relation

[1] These quotations in *Heartbreak House*, Act III, p. 142.
[2] Desmond MacCarthy, *Shaw*, p. 153.

to reality as fantasy does to realism. The sub-title suggests, the characters advertise, the action proves this. Fantasy is Shaw's medium here. But MacCarthy's objection is based entirely on the demands of realism, that is, on the sort of verisimilitude given by discoverable fact, in this instance historical fact. There is an air raid. Therefore the action takes place during the war. And as the facts of the war prove, the people represented by Hector and Mrs Hushabye, Lady Utterword and Randall, Mazzini and Ellie, were not turning a certain country house of old England into a veritable merry-go-round of talk but were busy helping the war effort (as MacCarthy goes on to argue) – all except the Mazzinis of the country, who were addressing pacifist meetings wherever they could get a hearing! Therefore the play is badly flawed. By the demands of realism it probably is, but by the nature of its medium of fantasy no such criticism as MacCarthy puts forward need be accepted. Fantasy may be related to reality through the symbol, a device which can define eternity, let alone four years, in a single image, if the writer is able and wishes it. It seems beyond question that the air raid in *Heartbreak House* is Shaw's symbol of the whole war, and not, as MacCarthy supposes, an unexpected announcement of the middle of the war. The action before the air raid is what Shaw in his preface has said it is, 'cultured, leisured, Europe before the war', and Mrs Hushabye's 'I hope theyll come again tomorrow night' after the raid refers simply, terrifyingly to the possibilities of the next war.

The end of the play is apocalyptic then. As a revelation of what had happened from 1914–18 to the Capitalist and his poor relation, the burglar, it is hopeful rather than true, but as the final stroke on a picture of a frivolous society going to destruction it has a blinding veracity. After 1914, someone has said, Shaw ceased laughing. This is not so, but here, as the inmates of Heartbreak House collect their scattered wits and look about them, despair breaks through for the first time.

*   *   *

So much, then, for the moral machines and their ideas. But has Shaw reconciled the general to the particular; are his representative figures also human beings, complex, wilful, irrational, emotional? Are they, in short, also moral animals?

It is a deferred question and finally to raise it here, in the context of the play of ideas *par excellence* when a more 'human' drama like *Candida* or *Pygmalion* is to hand, may seem an aberration, as though, to state the obverse, Shaw himself were to proclaim the subtle ratiocinations of Othello. But apart from the fact that the question must be asked and answered sooner or later and that *Heartbreak House* by being an extreme example of one form of drama begs one to inquire how well it maintains itself at the other extreme – apart from these facts, Shaw seems to be inviting – no, coercing – the question here by the operative word of his title: Heartbreak. Moral machines do not suffer heartbreak; moral animals may.

We may begin an answer by taking up the discussion on Shaw's characterization, which was left in abeyance in Chapter IV. The people of *Heartbreak House*, realized in delicately varying speech rhythms which point to their author's superlatively fine ear, are unquestionably tangible. I cite Lady Utterword as an 'average' portrait. Here that paragon of Empire betrays both Empire and Lady Utterword in every sculpted phrase:

> Go anywhere in England where there are natural, wholesome, contented, and really nice English people; and what do you always find? That the stables are the real centre of the household; and that if any visitor wants to play the piano the whole room has to be upset before it can be opened, there are so many things piled on it. I never lived until I learnt to ride; and I shall never ride very well because I didnt begin as a child. There are only two classes in good society in England: the equestrian classes and the neurotic classes. It isnt mere convention: everybody can see that the people who hunt are the right people and the people who dont are the wrong ones.[1]

We know the subject is the political Englishman's home, Horseback Hall, a distant though important mansion in Shaw's analysis of Heartbreak House. So Lady Utterword speaks as the representative of the

[1] *Heartbreak House*, Act III, p. 125.

Hall. At the same time she speaks as herself. There is the 'I', which imparts a faint touch of individuality to the speech, but besides this we find sentences that in their architectural balance, their symmetry, their coldly formal counterpoise, denote both the type and the person, the ambassadress of Horseback statecraft and the woman whose splendid good form is the epitome of Pride and as cold as any stone.

This creature is moved to something approaching anguish in a short scene initiated by Ellie's musings on the numbness of heartbreak and brought to a cold flare by Lady Utterword herself, who takes umbrage at Ellie's remarks. It is over almost before one is aware the exchange has begun, as though Shaw desired no more than a single vivid brush stroke to set M'Ladyship off:

LADY UTTERWORD: I know very well what you meant. The impudence!

ELLIE: What on earth do you mean?

CAPTAIN SHOTOVER: . . . She means that her heart will not break. She has been longing all her life for someone to break it. At last she has become afraid she has none to break.

LADY UTTERWORD: (*flinging herself on her knees and throwing her arms around him*) Papa: dont say you think Ive no heart.

CAPTAIN SHOTOVER: (*raising her with grim tenderness*) If you had no heart how could you want to have it broken, child?[1]

The moment passes and is soon lost in the swirl of discussion, but lifted from the stock shop of melodrama and yet so cunningly touched with new meaning, it lodges in one's memory. This heartless creature has a heart after all, but where perhaps only a father, disappointed, bitter, and unloving, can say. Certainly the daughter cannot – and is afraid to say: she flees from the situation into darkness, madly pursuing Hector and leaving behind her an impression of something pitiful, tortured, and ghastly.

Shotover is the colossus of the play – Triton among the minnows, tormented to near madness by the sanity of his vision, driven to near despair by the fact of a collapsing world. His speech is hard, angry, fierce, as though – even in moments of quiet meditation – the

[1] Ibid., Act II, pp. 108–9.

frustration of his soul pressed and pressed for outlet. In the following passage the strain and tension of his periods is brought to apparent rest, but only apparent: underneath the tranquillity and the seemingly casual colloquialisms is a wedge of iron:

> At sea nothing happens to the sea. Nothing happens to the sky. The sun comes up from the east and goes down to the west. The moon grows from a sickle to an arc lamp, and comes later and later until she is lost in the light as other things are lost in the darkness. After the typhoon, the flying-fish glitter in the sunshine like birds. It's amazing how they get along, all things considered. Nothing happens, except something not worth mentioning. . . .[1]

There is poetry in this singular old man; also an exultant memory of death challenged for the sake of life:

> . . . I see my daughters and their men living foolish lives of romance and sentiment and snobbery. I see you, the younger generation, turning from their romance and sentiment and snobbery to money and comfort and hard common sense. I was ten times happier on the bridge in the typhoon, or frozen into Arctic ice for months in darkness, than you or they have ever been. You are looking for a rich husband. At your age I looked for hardship, danger, horror, and death, that I might feel the life in me more intensely.[2]

And also, in contrast, this terrifying sketch of mortal decay:

> . . . But when you are old: very very old, like me, the dreams come by themselves. You dont know how terrible that is: you are young: you sleep at night only, and sleep soundly. But later on you will sleep in the afternoon. Later still you will sleep even in the morning; and you will wake tired, tired of life. You will never be free of dozing and dreams: the dreams will steal upon your work every ten minutes unless you can awaken yourself with rum. I drink now to keep sober; but the dreams are conquering: rum is not what it was: I have had ten glasses since you came; and it might be so much water.

[1] *Heartbreak House*, Act III, p. 138.
[2] Ibid., Act II, p. 113.

Go get me another: Guinness knows where it is. You had better see for yourself the horror of an old man drinking.[1]

Shotover exemplifies the range and depth of themes Shaw handles in the play. To quote him at length is to give some idea of the variety and richness of *Heartbreak House*, and also, is to quote a fierce indomitable who will die before his heart breaks.

Ellie is the relative failure of the play: Shaw loads too much on her slender shoulders. A starry-eyed romantic, then abruptly someone whose materialism would make her the envy of most gold-diggers, then, just as abruptly, a woman of remarkable serenity and profundity: this presents a changing moral climate as the prison houses of successive generations disintegrate – the final one of materialism crumbling before the advent of Vitalism. This is also supposed to happen to one *ingenué* in the space of a few hours. Ellie's reactions may be psychologically valid, the period of devotion to Mangan may have been more apparent than real – as she says, a trial of her strength – and the atmosphere of fantasy may allow the suddenness of the changes. But there is some incoherency, as though Shaw's 'double time' had split apart at the join, and we are left wondering whether the ruthless predator of Act II can ever really find salvation, and whether the artless young thing of Act I could really be able to learn what heartbreak is.

Heartbreak: we return to it every time; for 'this silly house, this strangely happy house, this agonizing house, this house without foundations'[2] is Heartbreak; is the house built with romance and sentiment and snobbery, with vanity and conceit and illusions; the place where Ellie's heart *does* break and Lady Utterword's cannot break and Captain Shotover's will not break and Mangan's is alleged to break. A house, Hector says, inhabited by heartbroken imbeciles. What, to Shaw, is heartbreak? It may be Mangan howling or Ellie going numb; it is shock and profound personal loneliness, mental turmoil and spiritual deprivation; it is the tragedy of vain hopes, shattered illusions, and self-revelation. All this – and one may still ask for the physical

[1] Ibid., p. 114.
[2] Ibid., Act III, p. 134.

pang, the sickness of the heart, but there is not much of that in this house. There is not much of that in any of the houses Shaw built.

At this point it is necessary to take up yet another issue, this one first raised in Chapter III, where Shaw's distinction between an artist like himself or Ibsen and an artist like Dickens or Shakespeare was discussed. The matter is relevant here because a writer's attitude to humanity will affect his attitude to his characters.

As I indicated, Shaw's distinction was more confusing than revealing and ultimately seemed to be no distinction at all, since great artists were practically at one in the end by their affirming universal human values. But – it is time to concede – these values may be affirmed in differing, possibly even divergent, terms; their very colouring may be altered by altering emphasis: it is here that Shaw's distinction may be seen to have point.

For the sake of clarity, let me state this distinction as Shaw might have, that is in impossible and no doubt provoking extremes. There are as far as matters here two types of man. One is Socratic man, the other – I use the label purely to denote a special sensibility – is Christian man. These two men are alike in many respects, are concerned about good and evil, about life, about human beings. But the sources of their concern are utterly unlike. Socratic man lives in his head; he thinks and therefore is. Christian man lives in his heart; he feels and therefore is. One may hazard a brief history of each. Socratic man was born in pre-Hellenic Greece and resuscitated during the eighteenth-century Enlightenment: he is classical. Christian man was born in biblical Judah and resuscitated during the Renaissance: he is romantic. Socratic man is a philosopher, he tends to think in abstractions, regards man as a species but can and does see him as an individual. Christian man experiences things in concrete images, regards man as so many individuals but can and does see him as a species. Socratic man apprehends life ratiocinatively, Christian man apprehends it intuitively.

Translate these two concepts into literary art and we may see how Shaw's characters differ from Shakespeare's. They are extraordinarily alike in many respects, being (as Shaw says) the same chessmen on the same board, but each artist realizes his characters by emphasizing different aspects. Shaw's characters are full of intellectual curiosity,

Shakespeare's full of emotional curiosity. The Shavian archetype is Undershaft, the Shakespearian Othello. Both of them 'live' in the printed word, but their 'life' is sustained by totally dissimilar forces.

One should not insist, because Shaw's dialogue is such palpable proof, but one does insist, because this proof is so often missed: the question with its implied criticism is asked: 'Where is the vitality, the passion of the characters?' Shaw's Socratic characters do have their 'life'. It is played in the treble clef of thought, with only a touch now and then in the ground bass of the emotions; played brilliantly, compulsively, boldly, with an urgency and energy that affirm the vitality of the characters beyond any doubt, affirm their artistic truth, and Shaw's right as a dramatist to look in his head and sing.

A drawback of this emphasis on the intellectual 'life' is that the characters are not likely to be as memorable as those emerging from the well-springs of the emotions. Shaw's characters are highly individualized and vivid, but they lack immediacy; they do not have that quality which gives them an existence independent of their plays and allows us to experience them direct, as we experience so many of Shakespeare's or Dickens's characters. Furthermore, the 'life' of a character sustained by the intellect is apt to be precarious: his thinking dare not fail him, else he will collapse into mummery. A few of Shaw's characters do fail in this way. Thirdly, as the drama exists almost solely on emotional situations, the Socratic character may frequently find himself in an alien element and, like a stranded fish, expire in futile gasps. That Shaw's characters do not generally expire, that on the contrary they may live with redoubled energy, is indication enough that any Socratic–Christian categories are a mere convenience and not remotely mutually exclusive. We have only to recollect such scenes as those between Mrs Warren and Vivie to see how effectively Shaw could manage the nakedly emotional situation. At the same time, we have only to recollect Dubedat's death in *The Doctor's Dilemma* or Joan's final pleas before her accusers to sense that alien element.

Socratic man is most emphatically not devoid of passion. It is indeed not Othello-like passion that he possesses, but Shavian. Intellectual passion – moral passion – in such scenes as those between Marchbanks and Morell, it shines like a white light, a blaze of energy. Or in such works (to return to the play of the moment) as *Heartbreak House* it sustains the action at an extraordinary pitch of intensity.

We ask, then, for heartpang and find very little; we are, it seems to me, asking that Mozart should be Beethoven. So much is already in *Heartbreak House* it would be captious to ask for more. The words dazzle, shock, delight; the characters have such a protean capacity for self-deceit, each debates, argues, quarrels, with such disregard of humbug (his or her own excepted), that one's response to them is as immediate and full as the Muse of Comedy could desire.

It is Thalia one invokes, not Melpomene, for the despair of the play manifests itself in laughter, frenzied laughter occasionally, and having little of the joy of traditional comedy, but still laughter with no black hatred in it. And no anger either. 'From my mother' – Shaw reminisces – 'I had learned that the wrath on which the sun goes down is negligible compared to the clear vision and criticism that is neither created by anger nor ended with it'[1] – the truth of which *Heartbreak House* endorses. Whatever the delusions, the futility, or the ignominy of the characters, however impoverished their souls, they are people we cannot begin to hate and can barely be angry with. They are charming people. Mazzini, who is in many ways the most charming of all, says as much:

> You are . . . most advanced, unprejudiced, frank, humane, unconventional democratic, free-thinking, and everything that is delightful to thoughtful people,[2]

which is true, and being true, ironic, for Mazzini's testimonial highlights the poise, the flair, the *savoir faire* with which these men and women play at life. Moreover, no one except Mangan is completely unregenerate; some have, as Ellie says, particular 'blessings', something somewhere which the world cannot afford to lose; and all, Mangan not excepted, have the 'blessing' bestowed by Shaw's unquenchable sense of comedy. In the absence of hatred and anger, and in the face of this charm, these 'blessings', the laughter, the tragedy of it all shines forth so much more vividly.

[1] 'My Mother and her Relatives', *Sixteen Self Sketches*, p. 13.
[2] *Heartbreak House*, Act III, p. 135.

Shaw has 'never orchestrated dialogue better', MacCarthy remarks,[1] and the sub-title alone, 'A fantasia in the Russian manner', shows that MacCarthy's metaphor is not a casual one. *Heartbreak House* is a symphonic fantasia in three movements, the total effect of which may perhaps be most fully appreciated in musical terms. Edmund Wilson's celebrated essay on Shaw[2] includes an analysis in such terms of part of *The Apple Cart* – a somewhat loose analysis with no evident insight into the technical discipline underlying the succession of 'arias', 'ensembles', 'duets', and somewhat misapplied when the example of *Heartbreak House* is available. *Heartbreak House* gives us, in fact, the opportunity for continuing the discussion, begun in Chapter IV, on Shaw's musical technique.

Take the following important passage:

ELLIE: There seems to be nothing real in the world except my father and Shakespear. Marcus's tigers are false; Mr Mangan's millions are false; there is nothing really strong and true about Hesione but her beautiful black hair; and Lady Utterword's is too pretty to be real. The one thing that was left to me was the Captain's seventh degree of concentration; and that turns out to be —

CAPTAIN SHOTOVER: Rum.

LADY UTTERWORD: (*placidly*) A good deal of my hair is quite genuine. The Duchess of Dithering offered me fifty guineas for this (*touching her forehead*) under the impression that it was a transformation; but it is all natural except the color.

MANGAN: (*wildly*) Look here: I'm going to take off all my clothes (*he begins tearing off his coat*).

LADY UTTERWORD:		Mr Mangan!
CAPTAIN SHOTOVER:	(*in consternation*)	Whats that?
HECTOR:		Ha! Ha! Do. Do.
ELLIE:		Please dont.[3]

It is a fine, still, moonless evening. The only light is that given by an electric arc, which captures the characters, we can imagine, in an

---

[1] Desmond MacCarthy, *Shaw*, p. 153.
[2] 'Bernard Shaw at Eighty', *The Triple Thinkers*, London, Lehman, 1952.
[3] *Heartbreak House*, Act III, pp. 129–30.

opalescent cocoon. In their small world they are vividly seen, while round them is the darkness of the universe. Isolated and motionless, the group seems entirely sufficient to itself; sufficient also to the drama which it serves, for everything except the voice and the ideas it expresses has been eschewed.

Ellie opens the quoted passage with words that move slowly, held back as much by the balanced phrasing as by the sadness of the thought; they are round, full, and deep. 'Rum' shatters the flow. The word, like a hoarse bark, jerks the tone brutally down; and then apparently unaffected by the interjection, Lady Utterword takes up the strands of sound again. Her phrasing is like Ellie's, although she has none of the girl's fullness of tone; she is louder, brittle – as in the phrase 'Duchess of Dithering' – though she softens perceptibly for Mangan's words to have a more explosive effect. His declaration, a sequence of hysterical monosyllables, falls into four cramped phrases. There is a momentary pause as he begins to undress, then a jarring chorus of voices brings the section to a halt.

It is obvious that the passage relies largely for its impact on changes of rhythm and tone. There is, as I have indicated, no other abstract like colour or movement of 'story' that it can rely on. But rhythm and tone are in themselves not absolutes. They must cohere in a way that will satisfy the ear by its balance and so fulfil the demand for formal 'necessity'. This passage does both in a remarkable manner. Its structure is like that of a musical 'sentence': two 'phrases' (Ellie's and Lady Utterword's lines) end in, first the half-cadence, 'Rum', and then in a full cadence (Mangan's lines resolving into the chorus).

An example in isolation cannot in this instance be said to state the general rule, and no doubt the neatness with which this passage fits musical punctuation is more the exception than the rule. But it is an exception which, by its very neatness, provides the key. Before this passage and following it is a series of exchanges which flow and twine and mesh, is a movement of themes, an accumulation of impressions, succeeding one another in a way that finds its definition only in psychology and its artistic analogy only in musical form. The whole act is built up in this way, in statement and counter-statement, in crescendos

and diminuendos, in Adagio leading on to Allegro, finally in the culminating 'allegro con furioso', where the spirit of Beethoven himself is
invoked. As in the third act, so in the whole play. The fundamentals
of music are the fundamentals of this verbal fantasia. Musical form is
the cohering agent of the action.

Of course such affinities to music are not and should not be ends in
themselves. They merely reinforce the sense (to illustrate which, however, is to impose statism on a law of flux). In the passage quoted
above, Ellie's words sum up what she has found in Heartbreak House
– that everything which had once seemed fine and true to her is now
false; Captain Shotover's 'Rum' signifies his despair; Lady Utterword's
description of her hair indicates her artificial values; and poor Mangan's
sudden decision to undress himself connotes the moral 'undressing'
that has been going on ever since his arrival. This is not all. Here and
throughout the play, echoes reverberate from a wider context than that
offered by the immediate scene. The anger of the heavens and the sea,
the fierce delight of living, which the bold spirit can discover in the
teeth of the gale, the 'splendid drumming' in the sky, which Mrs
Hushabye compares to the music of Beethoven, the tragedies of Shakespeare, which comprehend the grandeur and terror of human, of
universal, suffering – these have their places in the drama, as though
Shaw would call on all that was sublime to witness this tragi-comedy
of the doomed House. In the passage under discussion the vastest
tragedy of all, *King Lear*, is echoed, as it is repeatedly echoed throughout the play, in the diction and in the relationship between the characters. Mangan may here be seen as the grotesquely stunted image of
Lear. By suddenly beginning to tear off his clothes he all unconsciously
claims kinship with Lear in his noble rage and madness – but the gesture
effects only our pitying contempt, for the contrast is between a dwarf
and a Titan.

Shaw regarded *Heartbreak House* as his best play: perhaps it is. He
was unwilling to explain it to anyone, understandably, because it
achieves the unexplainable authenticity of art, which is 'true' only to
itself. What, though, about the didacticism? It is still there, emerging
from the 'talk, talk, talk' with urgent and passionate voice: it is, quite
simply (though not so simply), a plea for 'life with a blessing'.

II '... *the angels may weep at the murder,
but the gods laugh at the murderers.*'[1]

2

Shaw called *The Doctor's Dilemma* a tragedy, and although one may be permitted to wonder why, it seems apposite to preface the discussion of *Saint Joan* with a few remarks on the earlier play.

The first act of *The Doctor's Dilemma* gives no inkling of tragic possibilities and is by any standard a curiosity; yet a successful curiosity combining realism and fantasy with skill, presenting the very real danger of medical quackery in a zestful fantasy of humours. If in the end the act is a trifle too long and a shade too zestful, it remains a fundamentally pointed and grave indictment of our latter-day exorcists.

The foregoing comment is not a digression. When late in the second act the 'tragic' issue does arise, Shaw's doctors maintain the mood of Act I and pursue their medical obsessions in a way apparently calculated to keep detached amusement running hard at the expense of pity. As for terror, there is none: purgation will have to occur, if it is going to occur at all, through some other emotional medicine.

Aristotle's prescription is not the only one, and when we consider the nature of the doctor's dilemma we realize that Hegel's diagnosis of tragedy has considerably greater relevance. This diagnosis, the familiar either-or of, for example, Antigone's choice, is applicable to Ridgeon, who, in a position to save the life of only one patient, must choose between an honest but mediocre doctor, Blenkinsop, and a dishonest but extremely talented artist, Dubedat. In the event there is never much of a dilemma because Ridgeon is practically heaved into choosing Blenkinsop by his disgust at Dubedat's behaviour and his falling in love with Mrs Dubedat. He consigns Dubedat's fate to one of his colleagues and the expected happens: Ridgeon's vicarious murder

[1] Preface to *Saint Joan*, p. 50.

is committed. Dubedat's phagocytes, duly stimulated, react with violent contrariness and their unlucky possessor dies. However, Ridgeon gains no beautiful widow; she marries again, but someone else. All he gains is the realization: 'I have committed a purely disinterested murder!' – which is a doubtful consolation in the evening of his career.

As this outline shows, Shaw squanders Hegel almost at the moment of investing in him, as though he were required only to give the action momentum. So: Aristotle ignored, Hegel dismissed – where is the tragedy?

It will be readily admitted that someone who hunts tragedy by precept will fail to see the quarry under his nose. Tragedy does not *have* to be Aristotelian or Hegelian; it may be Shavian. At the same time, even if Shavian, it must fulfil certain requirements connoted by the word. Accordingly, we may still ask where the tragedy is in this jocular study of the lunatic centre of medicine and barely less jocular study of an unregenerate genius.

The answer is nowhere, as far as our perfectly legitimate expectations need go. This is not a social or even a professional tragedy: when medical practice is designated by phagocytes, nuciform sacs, and greengages we have salutary fantasy but not tragedy. This is not a personal tragedy either; the gods laugh long and loudly at the murderers but no angels weep for Dubedat. He is not worth a single tear.

Shaw's definition of a genius is:

> . . . a person who, seeing farther and probing deeper than other people, has a different set of ethical valuations from theirs, and has energy enough to give effect to this extra vision and its valuations in whatever manner best suits his or her specific talents.[1]

Such persons crop up frequently in the plays: Marchbanks, Caesar, Tanner, Undershaft, and now Dubedat and (shortly) Joan. Shaw could not very well have done without such inspired proponents of the new, Socio-Shavian ethic. Some of the persons are doers as well as philosophers: some are artists as well as philosophers. Some are Caesars, some are Dubedats. It is Shaw's delineation of the Dubedat cast of genius that we should consider here.

[1] Preface to *Saint Joan*, p. 7.

N

That Shaw, a major artist, should have had such erroneous notions about 'artists' is a mystery which his immediate cultural background – of fragile aesthetes in floppy cravats – may begin to explain, and his idea of the artist-seer may finish explaining. Both Marchbanks and Dubedat are externalized as fragile aesthetes and given the spiritual quality of energetic 'extra vision'. The result is two characters whose only apparent claim to genius is a genius for imposing on our credulity. Marchbanks *may* be allowed his outrageous poses, his unfortunate diction: his *raison d'être* as a poet does not come upon him until the end and when it does, he obeys the summons with words and actions that augur a more direct apprehension of his calling. But where Marchbanks may get away with it, Dubedat cannot – because Shaw's conception of him as an 'artist' (as distinct from a moral iconoclast) is unconvincing.

The technical problem is of course great: how does one portray an artist–genius? By presenting him in front of an easel? Shaw does this and we are obliged to believe nothing more than that Dubedat apparently paints pictures. By having *cognoscenti* enthuse over his work? Shaw does this and we are obliged to believe nothing more than that he is an alleged genius. This is the trouble; the painter Dubedat is not and cannot be more than an allegedly good artist. Shaw is aware of this and so allows the painter to *say* something on his deathbed. But now the trouble is that the painter Dubedat can do no better than take on a pose of fragile aestheticism. This artist is not the man; he cannot possibly be.[1]

If, therefore, there is no necessary connection between the alleged artist Dubedat and the proven morality of the man, it must follow that the 'extra vision' of this suspect genius is without substantial authority. It exists on its own account. Let it also be said at once that even if Dubedat's genius had been confirmed beyond any shadow of doubt, his ethical valuations would have been hard to acknowledge. His

---

[1] Had the artist been the man, we may be reasonably certain that an ultra-conservative person like Ridgeon would have thought Dubedat's paintings quite distasteful: that the artist Dubedat was as much 'advanced' as the ethical Dubedat. Shaw has had to evade this high probability in order to keep the axiological part of the doctor's dilemma in the play.

ethic is, quite simply, based on betrayal of trust. Thoroughly Ridgeon-like though this judgement may seem, it is the only one to pass on a person whose virtue is his charm, whose salvation is his plausible tongue, and whose saving grace is his deceit. If highly conventional morality condemns him, it is condemning a thoroughly retrograde young seer.

So, unsatisfying and unsatisfactory, Dubedat succumbs to his maddened phagocytes without a pang from us. But Shaw called *The Doctor's Dilemma* a tragedy and if he failed to make it one, he yet saw a tragedy somewhere. As the matter has a bearing on *Saint Joan* we may develop it slightly.

The tragic situation (as Shaw saw it) has nothing to do with villains and other props of romance. It had to do with the exceptional man or woman, the genius, in a society composed of average men and women, of normally innocent people who act with good intentions in ridding themselves of the genius. Hence Ridgeon's 'disinterested murder' (although it is disinterested only in retrospect). Ridgeon is a pillar of society; whatever his vision as a medical scientist, his ethos is the good, solid Victorian one, and he murders Dubedat with the safeguarding of this ethos very much in view. As Shaw says:

> The tragedy of such murders is that they are not committed by murderers. They are judicial murders, pious murders; and this contradiction at once brings an element of comedy into the tragedy.[1]

With these thoughts in mind, we may turn from the tragedy that is not to the tragedy that is: to *Saint Joan*.

2

This play may or may not be Shaw's greatest. It is certainly his best known, his most celebrated, his most discussed. *Saint Joan* is history and not history, less than history and more, a reasonably faithful chronicle of Joan's career in time and place, an interpretation of this career as a universal truth for twentieth-century man. The play is, perhaps, the rationalization of the miracle that the romantic imagination and thirty million Frenchmen see as the Blessed Maid. Equally it is an

[1] Preface to *Saint Joan*, p. 50.

imaginative acknowledgement of a miracle that the rational mind cannot see. Shaw's Joan is the Life Force brought to an extraordinary pitch of intelligibility and is yet ultimately intelligible only in itself.

Joan was also (so he insisted) one of the first Protestants at a time 'when the whole world was Catholic and when the Reformation had not yet taken place'. Why Protestant? Because:

> . . . she said that God came first with her. He came before the Church; and when she was asked, 'Will you not accept the Church's interpretation of God for you?' she said, 'No; God must come first.'[1]

This is Shaw's opinion, which he gives to Warwick in the fourth scene of the play:

> . . . the protest of the individual soul against the interference of priest or peer between the private man and his God. I should call it Protestantism if I had to find a name for it.[2]

It is hard to understand quite why Shaw used this tag. According to Warwick's definition, Socrates was a Protestant, Jesus was a Protestant, and Luther the least great Protestant of them all, even though it is Luther who defined his theology in this way. The term means something other than what we understood as Protestant: Shaw really means Asserter, for Socrates, Jesus, and Joan – and no doubt other great 'outsiders' of history – do not protest. They have no need to protest. They are 'right', absolutely, incontrovertibly 'right',[3] and so suffer martyrdom in serene conviction of principles.[4]

In any event, Warwick goes to the core of Joan's Shavian tragedy: she is the genius, or saint, trapped by the accident of birth in a set of circumstances which both destroy and transfigure her. Both the

---

[1] 'Saint Joan', a B.B.C. radio talk, delivered on the five hundredth anniversary of the burning of Joan of Arc, 30 May 1931. In Dan H. Laurence, *Platform and Pulpit*, p. 210.

[2] *Saint Joan*, Sc. IV, p. 106.

[3] See Sc. V, p. 117: 'She is right and everyone else is wrong,' Charles complains.

[4] It is perhaps surprising that Shaw did not 'place' Joan in such a succession. 'Protestant' suggests a dislocation of historical perspective which is uncharacteristic of Shaw's high consciousness of history.

victim of and victor over the historical situation she is the prophet of individualism where conformity is the law, the lone spirit asserting its right to independent salvation where salvation was wholly dependent on the intercession of the Church, the spiritual, political, and military iconoclast where images were (as they always are) jealously guarded.

Though genius is not *ipso facto* against the established order of things, Joan's genius was such that it would clash with this order. She was a military genius, she was a political genius: she was these two things by reason of an intuitive force which she ascribed to God. She saved France from ignominy, gave a King his crown, and asserted the direct authority of heaven. She was a saviour and became inevitably an embarrassment to those she saved.

More than an embarrassment: she became a threat to the political and religious systems; her 'God' drove her on a course that imperilled temporal and spiritual authority. Here is Warwick's assessment:

> Her idea is that the kings should give their realms to God, and then reign as God's bailiffs. . . . It is a cunning device to supersede the aristocracy, and make the King sole and absolute autocrat. Instead of the King being merely the first among his peers, he becomes their master. That we cannot suffer: we call no man master. . . .[1]

And here is Cauchon:

> . . . The pope himself at his proudest dare not presume as this woman presumes. She acts as if she herself were The Church. . . . It is not the Mother of God now to whom we must look for intercession, but to Joan the Maid. What will the world be like when The Church's accumulated wisdom and knowledge and experience, its councils of learned, venerable pious men, are thrust into the kennel by every ignorant laborer or dairymaid whom the devil can puff up with the monstrous self-conceit of being directly inspired from heaven? It will be a world of blood, of fury, of devastation, of each man striving for his own hand: in the end a world wrecked back into barbarism.[2]

Cauchon sees the Maid threatening the Church in yet another way:

[1] *Saint Joan*, Sc. IV, p. 105.
[2] Ibid. pp. 102–3.

... To her the French-speaking people are what the Holy Scriptures describe as a nation. Call this side of her heresy Nationalism if you will: I can find you no better name for it. I can only tell you that it is essentially anti-Catholic and anti-Christian; for the Catholic Church knows only one realm, and that is the realm of Christ's kingdom. Divide that kingdom into nations, and you dethrone Christ. Dethrone Christ, and who will stand between our throats and the sword? The world will perish in a welter of war.[1]

There are other counts against Joan: in the end they amount to one, major charge – heresy.

Shaw is very careful to divest the word of sorcery, black magic, and other supernatural *bric-à-brac* of the unlettered mind; he is also very scrupulous – it is thought that he exceeds historical veracity in this respect – in playing Heaven's advocate for the judges at Joan's trial; and when, shortly before the trial scene, the Inquisitor speaks on heresy, it is defined quite simply as a threat to stability of institutions.[2] These are Cauchon's views over again, more gravely expressed, more soberly contained, more compassionately uttered. 'Brother Martin: if you had seen what I have seen of heresy, you would not think it a light thing even in its most apparently harmless and even lovable and pious origins. Heresy begins with people who are to all appearance better than their neighbors. A gentle and pious girl, or a young man who has obeyed the command of our Lord by giving all his riches to the poor, and putting on the garb of poverty, the life of austerity, and the rule of humility and charity, may be the founder of a heresy that will wreck both Church and Empire if not ruthlessly stamped out in time. . . .' There is no doubt that the Inquisitor is aware of the ironic paradox, that out of extreme orthodoxy unorthodoxy may grow, that righteousness and godliness may be the natural earth of corruption. A moment later he speaks of the 'saintly simpletons' who commit heresy: 'saintly' because they are near to God, 'simpletons' because they trespass upon that which their puny selves cannot comprehend: where their inspiration spreads like a blight among ordinary men and women, creating

---

[1] *Saint Joan*, pp. 106–7.
[2] Ensuing paragraphs refer to Sc. VI, pp. 127–9.

ruin. 'Heresy' – the Inquisitor goes on – 'Heresy at first seems innocent and even laudable; but it ends in such a monstrous horror of unnatural wickedness that the most tender-hearted among you, if you saw it at work as I have seen it, would clamor against the mercy of the Church in dealing with it.' Authority stands against anarchy; the natural order established by a centuries-long tradition of discipline – affirmed by the hierarchy of spiritual leaders and practised in the ritual of religious worship – is the bulwark against unrestrained licence and human depravity; the 'divine right' of order, degree, stability, has to be maintained against the 'diabolical wrong' of disorder. It *must* be maintained because all values, all truths, all life itself, would otherwise give way to chaos.

The Inquisitor begins to speak of Joan: 'You are all, I hope, merciful men: how else could you have devoted your lives to the service of our gentle Savior? You are going to see before you a young girl, pious and chaste; for I must tell you, gentlemen, that the things said of her by our English friends are supported by no evidence, whilst there is abundant testimony that her excesses have been excesses of religion and charity and not of worldliness and wantonness. . . . The devilish pride that has led her into her present peril has left no mark on her countenance. Strange as it may seem to you, it has even left no mark on her character outside those special matters in which she is proud; so that you will see a diabolical pride and a natural humility seated side by side in the selfsame soul.' It is clear: the judge is not disinterested, for the interests of Christianity are at stake, but he has no animus. He invokes mercy and 'our gentle Savior', not to depict himself as a hypocrite, but to lay down the canons of judgement; he describes Joan as 'pious and chaste' the better to define her sin; he admits the presence of 'natural humility' in the soul that houses 'diabolical pride'. 'Therefore', he continues, 'be on your guard'; and he adds, with the finality that his argument at this stage rightly and justly insists on: 'But if you hate cruelty – and if any man here does not hate it I command him on his soul's salvation to quit this holy court – I say, if you hate cruelty, remember that nothing is so cruel in its consequences as the toleration of heresy.'

This is one of the most remarkable speeches in Shaw's drama, long even by Shaw's capacious standards, and requiring an actor whose voice and ear can meet the tremendous demands of nuances of rhythm, gradations of tone, plastic suppleness of argument, and find emphasis in subtleties, passion in *pianissimo*, action in the mind. The speech continues: the mercy of the Church, the insensate cruelty of the superstitious and fearful mob, the Inquisitor's own compassion, and his profound conviction that the work he does is righteous, necessary, and merciful – these are brought into the argument, widening its frame of reference and quietly, insistently stressing its central issue, quietly, urgently culminating the inexorable logic of the stand that a conscientious and benevolent authority must appoint to itself. The Inquisitor concludes: 'Anger is a bad counsellor: cast out anger. Pity is sometimes worse: cast out pity. But do not cast out mercy. Remember only that justice comes first.'

Justice does come first for Joan, if again at the expense of strict historical veracity, certainly to the enrichment of Shaw's tragedy. She is given a fair trial, she recants, she lapses; the Spiritual authority sees her as an unregenerate heretic and hands her over to the Secular authority, which burns her. The Holy Roman Empire is saved, Christendom is saved: the 'gentle Savior' remains in triumph at the right hand of God.

Of course, there is a dreadful irony in this. Partly the irony in the historical process, which has reversed the judgement passed on Joan and thereby implied that Christendom was so far from saving as positively to be disgracing and practically to be wrecking itself. Partly the irony of a terrible act done in the name of the Prince of Peace. Mostly the irony in the spectacle of sincere, earnest men snatching at permanence in the midst of relentless change and adjudicating over the infinite with pitifully finite, human minds.

So the gods laugh, for they know that Joan's necessary death is a sacrifice to the infinite on the altar of the finite. Joan does belong to the infinite. It is one of Shaw's most splendid achievements that, whilst denying her all supernatural attributes and delineating her with a strictly realistic pen, he portrays the growth of a vivid and vital personality from country-girl to fulfilled saint, with the agony of disillusionment and martyrdom on her, realizing her oneness with the infinite.

Disarming candour, vigour, spontaneity – these are the characteristics of the girl whom the astounded and finally awe-stricken Robert de Baudricourt sends on to the Dauphin; these characteristics, and a piety which shines through her utterances and actions so that a blush of shame rises to the cheeks even of the cynical Archbishop of Rheims – these smite the envious, quarrelling court and win for Joan her command of the army. A 'miracle' this; then other 'miracles' crowding on one another in the Maid's year of glory, until the final 'miracle', the Dauphin crowned by Joan herself in Rheims Cathedral.

The final miracle, and by it Joan's tragedy is confirmed; as if to add irony to paradox, confirmed by Joan's friends. It is this scene, the fifth, which brings to a head what has obviously been brewing for a long time: the embarrassment and acute discomfort Joan causes her allies. Her candour they meet with equivocation, her boldness with rationalized discretion, her ideals for Charles, for France, for God with expediency. 'Why do all these courtiers and knights and churchmen hate me?' Joan cries in distress. 'Jack: the world is too wicked for me.' If wickedness is fear, smallness of mind, finiteness of vision, then the world was too wicked for Joan. Her awakening to the realities of her situation comes, we should remember, after that most brilliant dramatization, in Scene IV, of antagonisms and antipathies being welded together to seek common cause in her destruction. Now the assault is brought home to her. Charles whines and shuffles and whines; 'It all comes back to the same thing. She is right; and everyone else is wrong'; Dunois firmly and unambiguously rejects the possibility of future miracles from her: 'God is no man's daily drudge, and no maid's either . . . your little hour of miracles is over . . . God is on the side of the big battalions . . .'; the Archbishop remonstrates sonorously: '. . . you have stained yourself with the sin of pride . . . I am speaking in vain to a hardened heart. You reject our protection, and are determined to turn us all against you. In future, then, fend for yourself; and if you fail, God have mercy on your soul.'

Dunois says, acknowledging the Archbishop's warning: 'That is the truth, Joan. Heed it.'

The truth of mediocrity, of finite minds. Not Joan's truth, however, and she expresses her sense of human betrayal and affirms her identity with God:

> Where would you all have been now if I had heeded that sort of truth? There is no help, no counsel, in any of you. Yes: I am alone on earth: I have always been alone. My father told my brothers to drown me if I would not stay to mind his sheep while France was bleeding to death: France might perish if only our lambs were safe. I thought France would have friends at the court of the king of France; and I find only wolves fighting for pieces of her poor torn body. I thought God would have friends everywhere, because He is the friend of everyone; and in my innocence I believed that you who now cast me out would be like strong towers to keep harm from me. But I am wiser now; and nobody is any the worse for being wiser. Do not think you can frighten me by telling me that I am alone. France is alone; and God is alone; and what is my loneliness before the loneliness of my country and my God? I see now that the loneliness of God is His strength: what would He be if He listened to your jealous little counsels? Well, my loneliness shall be my strength too; it is better to be alone with God: His friendship will not fail me, nor His counsel, nor His love. In his strength I will dare, and dare, and dare, until I die. I will go out now to the common people, and let the love in their eyes comfort me for the hate in yours. You will all be glad to see me burnt; but if I go through the fire I shall go through it to their hearts for ever and ever. And so, God be with me![1]

The play is a complex study of the political and social reverberations that followed on Joan's advent, but the above passage is warrant for the bias I have given the discussion: *Saint Joan* is chiefly a religious play. Religious in the most profound sense, in its implicit acknowledgement of the force that can seize on certain individuals and carry them to spiritual heights ordinary people – people who do not possess inherent amplitude of heart and mind and soul – can simply not imagine. In this speech Joan awakens to full awareness of her destiny which, exalted and stirring though it is in the highest degree, and an affirmation to death and beyond of faith, is ineluctably tragic. Two mighty forces –

[1] *Saint Joan*, Sc. V, pp. 118–19.

the one the vested interests of a long-established civilization, the other a solitary, resplendent soul – are implacably opposed, and nothing can reconcile them.

So, when Joan is captured and brought to trial, it seems that everyone sighs with relief. She grows to the role divine grace has appointed her to – and grows to the role the drama has prescribed for her. It is Joan against the world: against the Church, which presides over her trial, against the temporal powers, which hover rapaciously in the background, against – finally – the multitude, which waits outside for the burning. She balances the conflict magnificently, not (it is worth remarking) by conforming to the pattern laid down by innumerable dramatic models and relying on elevated diction and sentiments, but by going almost to the other extreme and relying on her unaffected self. There is an exception, the speech when she lapses back to heresy, which we shall consider shortly. For the rest she remains true to the image we have formed of her and is candid, vigorous, and vital. Disconcertingly so, exhilaratingly so, for the only effective counter to the word-spinning and legalities and accusations that bear down on her is the answer which cuts direct and clear to the heart of the matter. The heart of the matter for Joan is always her God, and however unaffected and even pert she may be, the image which she carries in her heart and sustains her has the nobility of extreme simplicity.

But, as we all know, Joan does recant. The time comes when the pressure on her becomes too great and the sheer physical fear of death casts doubt on her convictions and makes uncertainties of her verities. Miserable, strife-torn she puts her X on the document of recantation. Then she hears sentence passed on her; then:

> JOAN: (*rising in consternation and terrible anger*) Perpetual imprisonment! Am I not then to be set free?
> LADVENU: (*mildly shocked*) Set free, child, after such wickedness as yours! What are you dreaming of?
> JOAN: Give me that writing. (*She rushes to the table; snatches up the paper; and tears it into fragments.*) Light your fire: do you think I dread it as much as the life of a rat in a hole? My voices were right.
> LADVENU: Joan! Joan!

JOAN: Yes: they told me you were fools (*the word gives great offence*), and that I was not to listen to your fine words nor trust to your charity. You promised me my life; but you lied (*indignant exclamations*). You think that life is nothing but not being stone dead. It is not the bread and water I fear: I can live on bread: when have I asked for more? It is no hardship to drink water if the water be clean. Bread has no sorrow for me, and water no affliction. But to shut me from the light of the sky and the sight of the fields and flowers; to chain my feet so that I can never again ride with the soldiers nor climb the hills; to make me breathe foul damp darkness, and keep me from everything that brings me back to the love of God when your wickedness and foolishness tempt me to hate Him: all this is worse than the furnace in the Bible that was heated seven times. I could do without my warhorse; I could drag about in a skirt; I could let the banners and the trumpets and the knights and soldiers pass me and leave me behind as they leave the other women, if only I could still hear the wind in the trees, the larks in the sunshine, the young lambs crying through the healthy frost, and the blessed blessed church bells that send my angel voices floating to me on the wind. But without these things I cannot live; and by your wanting to take them away from me, or from any human creature, I know that your counsel is of the devil, and mine is of God.[1]

Not all, but many of these lines are – as every commentator tells us – comprised of clichés; not all, but many of the lines are – as MacCarthy aptly puts it – not from Joan but from a suffragette – a 'cry from a garden city';[2] and not generally, but once or twice the rhythms lapse badly. Why at this most important (though not crucial) point has Shaw deserted the Joan of the play and superseded her by this poetaster? An answer lies partly in the fact that Shaw's gift of words did not include the poetically sublime, and when (as here) his aim is the suggestion of strong, potent immanent life it collapses into limp cliché. But the other part of the answer lies in the progression of thought in the passage.

[1] *Saint Joan*, Sc. VI, pp. 142–3.
[2] Desmond MacCarthy, *Shaw*, p. 173.

Joan's angry challenge is quite largely an implicit renunciation of the active, militant aspect of her mission and a hint that she would return to her village life. Hence the offending wind, larks, and lambs, which are intended to suggest her former occupation and her resignation to passive communion with God. There is a logic in the use of the images.[1]

But logic, for once, lets Shaw down, and in any event plays Joan false. The girl whose declared and committed purpose was to dare, and dare, and dare until she died may not consider renunciation. She may have done so in fact, but fact is not important here; she dare not do so in the drama. By the end of the speech the accustomed fire has flared, and Joan's final words luckily restore the picture:

> LADVENU: You wicked girl: if your counsel were of God would He not deliver you?
>
> JOAN: His ways are not your ways. He wills that I go through the fire to His bosom; for I am His child, and you are not fit that I shall live among you. That is my last word to you.[2]

That sentence: '... you are not fit that I shall live among you' consummates the tragedy of this genius. Hers is not indeed a tragedy that gives off the lightning flash of the Longinian sublime; it does, though, glow with a coldly burnished sheen.

*   *   *

What about the epilogue? Shaw's own defence is plausible rather than convincing: 'It was necessary by hook or crook to shew the canonized Joan as well as the incinerated one; for many a woman has got herself burnt by carelessly whisking a muslin skirt into the drawing room fireplace, but getting canonized is a different matter, and a more important one.'[3] A better argument for the epilogue is put forward by

---

[1] Actresses do not agree with this 'academic' point of view. Dame Sybil Thorndike (who created the part of Joan) speaks ardently of the magnificent speech cadences of the lines.

[2] *Saint Joan*, p. 143.

[3] Preface to *Saint Joan*, pp. 52–3.

Louis B. Martz: 'An epilogue is no part of the dramatic action: it is the author's chance to step forward, relaxed and garrulous, and to talk the play over with the audience. . . . Moreover, this kind of thing is not without precedent in performances of tragedy. The ancient Greeks appear to have liked exactly this kind of release in their festivals of tragedy, since they demanded that each dramatist, after presenting his three tragedies, should provide them with their satyr-play, usually of an uproarious and ribald variety, that had just been seen in tragic dignity. The Epilogue is Shaw's satyr-play. . . .'[1]

This argument may not silence critics who regard the Epilogue as a redundancy, but it has undoubted weight. Besides, the depiction of the canonized Joan is akin to the famous Shavian 'fourth act', which begins the drama when the story ends – in *Pygmalion*, for example, or *Mrs Warren's Profession*. Joan's drama does begin after her death: the drama of a world slowly awakening to her prophetic voice, yet, ironically, unwilling to be disturbed by her actual presence. The intimations in the Epilogue transcend the banality of 'life going on'; they touch the chord of spiritual energy, which vibrates through the centuries. This, surely, is piety.

III   'Back to Methuselah *is a world classic or it is nothing.*'[2]

Chesterton wrote in 1909, that Shaw had 'brought back into English drama that Shakespearian universality, which, if you like, you can call Shakespearian irrelevance.'[3] This was twelve years before Shaw's most ambitious attempt to achieve universality – in that 'Metabiological Pentateuch', *Back to Methuselah*. Would Chesterton have admitted the same praise for this work?

There is a great deal to admire in it; there is, despite Shaw's protesta-

---

[1] 'The Saint as Tragic Hero', *G. B. Shaw: A Collection of Critical Essays*, ed. by R. J. Kaufmann, p. 160.
[2] *Back to Methuselah*, Postscript, p. 271.
[3] Chesterton, *George Bernard Shaw*, p. 107.

tion that his powers were waning,[1] a fair amount of 'irrelevance', not to say irreverence; there is vivid characterization, energy, buoyancy; there is, reportedly a memorable theatrical experience for those who see it performed; and there are many profound moments.

Notwithstanding these considerations, to me the work as a whole must remain a failure. The audacity of the vast concept and the imaginative range Shaw does achieve should not and cannot be ignored; but equally the enormous, perhaps insuperable, difficulties of the undertaking and the imaginative lack Shaw reveals should and must be taken into account.

Back to Methuselah aims at being the new myth for twentieth-century man; that is, it aims at being our new bible written by a modern prophet. We should not scorn either the aim or the pretensions of the writer: very much lesser men have often tried to do the same. The fault is not here. The fault is quite simply that Shaw is not a myth-maker. He is a myth flouter, a myth mocker, a myth destroyer: his criteria are fact, sanity, intelligence. No myth ever arose from these. Shaw does not know – despite his colossal intelligence, it seems that it was something he could never know – that myth arose round images that waken in the blood. It is the articulation of experience that grows out of the unconscious genius of a people, the familiar of our living being.

The Life Force, it is acknowledged, is *the* familiar of our being: it *is* our being, in whatever name we might wish to bestow on it. But the name is not the thing and the dramatic exposition of the name is still less the thing. It is the metaphor or the symbol or the poetic image. What is Shaw's metaphor? Fact. What his symbol? Thought. What his poetic image? Prose.

Fact, thought, prose: these cannot add one cubit to one's longevity when eternity is the goal. They abort religion and instil scepticism. They eventually diminish the noble concept of life ever ascendant to a group of human insects squatting in a timeless void and talking, talking, talking. Talking entertainingly, wittily, provocatively – but in the end trivially.

Finally, then, we have no triumphant prophetic revelation. We have, it is true, several effectively solemn ritualist passages and a magnificent

[1] Preface to *Back to Methuselah*, p. lxxxvi.

rhetorical peroration from Lilith, but these have little overall effect. They can have no effect when the mighty answer of the play to the theory of mechanistic evolution is itself perversely mechanistic – intellectually mechanistic, as though Shaw, our *deus ex machina*, were thinking humanity through an evolutionary process that, so far from being the thrilling and spontaneous manifestation of the immanent Life Force, seems as soullessly predetermined, as calculated and ruthless, as any theory biological science might wish on mankind.

It is a little saddening that this universal man of modern drama should have consummated his religious message in a dramatic work of such limited intelligibility and relevance.

Chapter Eight

1929-1939: DISSOLUTION

'No, beloved: the riddle of how to choose a
ruler is still unanswered; and it is the riddle of
civilization.'[1]

2

We tend to speak of the 'wit' and the 'wisdom' of Bernard Shaw as
though they were separate entities. Perhaps they are very often, and it
is probably easy to enjoy the 'wit' and ignore the 'wisdom'. As a critic
has remarked, it was clever of Shaw to sugar his pill but even cleverer
of the public to lick the sugar off and leave the pill behind.[2] Yet it
may be urged that what the public does is not a necessary reflection on
the plays; what the public does is often an unflattering reflection on the
public. The fact is, up to *Saint Joan* the 'wit' and the 'wisdom' of Bernard Shaw are generally to be seen only in the amalgams of accomplished art: when Shaw is at his greatest, the play and the teaching have
no join.

But after *Saint Joan* the picture begins gradually to change. There is
still the wit and there is still the wisdom, both in seemingly inexhaustible abundance. There is also a cleavage between the two, a crack
zig-zagging across the mirror of Shaw's art, widening with the years.
Unity of form disintegrates before improvisation, chiselled classical
extravaganza deteriorates into rococo extravagance, the resonance of
the self-contained work is carelessly dissipated. Finally there is only
the thin echo of past mastery.

Yet it is this Shaw – 'Bernard Shaw at Eighty' – who in Edmund
Wilson's opinion deserved greater attention than was usually given
him[3] and it seems increasingly this Shaw who is attracting the public to

---

[1] *In Good King Charles's Golden Days*, Act II, p. 229.
[2] Egon Friedell. Cited by Bentley, *Bernard Shaw*, p. 188.
[3] See 'Bernard Shaw at Eighty', *The Triple Thinkers*, p. 180.

the theatre. Certainly the last plays, or most of the last plays, from *The Apple Cart* to *Geneva* revolve round theatrically arresting situations, though it must be said that far-fetched hypothesis rather than sober probability, or even possibility, are more than ever becoming the plot postulates. But the Shavian sop to entertainment is less than important as a reason why the plays are gaining a new lease on life and why they should not be summarily dismissed. The important reason is that taken together they offer to a degree perhaps unrivalled in any other body of contemporaneous work an interpretation of the western political dilemma.

That Shaw at seventy, and then at eighty, and then at ninety should have fixed his attention on this is proof enough of the resilience of his mind. It is often said that after the war he was caught out as a Victorian in a world which had violently put aside Victorian things and he became something of an anachronism, a relic of a past sensibility, uttering oracular statements on a situation which only faintly answered to his conception of it. There is a good deal of truth in this. The man who since 1885 had been in the vanguard of thought started slowing down, Socialist revolution began to gain on the Socialist revolutionist. We may permit ourselves to imagine Bernard Shaw at eighty smiling wanly when recollecting Tanner's maxim: 'Every man over forty is a scoundrel.'[1] At the same time, Shaw retained a vivid vital spark of under-fortyness in him. It was a habit of mind, a condition of life, an instinct of this moral relativist and creative evolutionist not to stand still but to exert all the sinews of his athletic intellectualism to stride forward with the times. A 'journalist' until his death at ninety-four, he preached the lesson from the newspaper headlines of the day, and left those of ten or twenty or forty years before, not to languish, but to inform the present with *their* cautionary lessons. Dramatically speaking, he was no Sophocles, politically he was often less than wise, but he accomplished a remarkable intellectual feat; for if the world between the wars was one where more than ever he found himself a stranger, it was also a world where he found ample, justified opportunity for his exhortations and criticism.

[1] 'Maxims for Revolutionists', *Man and Superman*, p. 224.

2

The Apple Cart, the first and the best of the political extravaganzas, gives us a more than ordinarily intelligent and competent person as the King (Magnus) and a more than ordinarily unintelligent and incompetent Cabinet of (Socialist) ministers in opposition to him. If the line-up of forces does scant justice to what we may hopefully assume is the fact of ministerial capacity, it nevertheless provides the opportunity for both high comedy and an unblushing betrayal of incompetence in those holding high office:

MAGNUS: You think this prosperity is safe?

NICOBAR: Safe!

PLINY: Oh come, sir! Really!

BALBUS: Safe! Look at my constituency: Northeast-by-north Birmingham, with its four square miles of confectionary works! Do you know that in the Christmas cracker trade Birmingham is the workshop of the world?

CRASSUS: Take Gateshead and Middlesborough alone! Do you know that there has not been a day's unemployment there for five years past, and that their daily output of chocolate creams totals up to twenty thousand tons?

MAGNUS: It is certainly a consoling thought that if we were peacefully blockaded by the League of Nations we could live for at least three weeks on our chocolate creams.[1]

Magnus's mild sarcasm does not put an end to the list: English industry is made more glorious by 'plenty of solid stuff' like the English golf club, the new crown Derby, racing motorboats and cars, the English polo pony. It is on such items that the prosperity of England – incidentally, an England of *circa* 1960 – is based; it is on such a rock that these zealous statesmen build their nation. In reply Magnus says simply and gravely:

I dread revolution. . . . The more I see of the sort of prosperity that comes of your leaving our vital industries to big business men as

[1] *The Apple Cart*, Act I, p. 216.

long as they keep your constituents quiet with high wages, the more I feel as if I were sitting on a volcano.[1]

The Cabinet has not sought audience with Magnus to sing the praises of the English chocolate cream; it has actually come to serve an ultimatum on Magnus – he must undertake to curb his natural inclination for active politics and resign himself to being a mere royal cipher, otherwise the Prime Minister will go to the country on a monarchy-democracy issue. This is the apparent reason for the meeting, but the issue is continuously put aside for matters like those indicated above. Nor are such matters peripheral. The comedy should not and does not hide the serious undertones in the chocolate cream and kindred metaphors. Big business has the 'democratic' politician – be he Liberal, Conservative, *or* Socialist – securely under its thumb. Big business, or as Shaw calls it in the play, Breakages, Limited.

Lysistrata, the Powermistress Royal, the one Cabinet minister with a sense of disinterested service, breaks out impetuously and feelingly against Breakages, Limited. Breakages, Limited, makes power cost twice as much as it should. It buys up and suppresses new inventions. It grows richer on every breakdown, every accident, every smash and crash. It wields enormous power which is directed only towards self-interest, waste, and inefficiency.

The Cabinet's joyous adumbration of the country's 'prosperity' and Lysistrata's denunciation of the power Breakages, Limited, has to smash her and her department, provide the serio-comic backdrop to the matter of the ultimatum: provide the backdrop which says as plainly as any words that the villain of the piece is not the Prime Minister or any of his ministers and not King Magnus, but the huge, impersonal Breakages, Limited.

Seen in this way, the ultimatum itself really becomes a great deal of talk about something else, for the democratically elected ministers of the Crown, whether they know it or not, like it or not, are really ministers of Breakages, Limited, put into office by Breakages, Limited, to serve the interests of Breakages, Limited. Magnus may be a threat to the vanities of his loyal ministers but he is in no sense a threat to

[1] *The Apple Cart*, p. 217.

democracy. He is a bulwark of democracy because he stands above its mistakes, because only he stands above Breakages, Limited, and can refuse to accept Balbus's brother-in-law Mike (a creature of Breakages, Limited) as a member of the Cabinet. But the Cabinet obstinately refuses to heed him, even when he delivers his fine oration on his position and status in the political arena:

. . . Our work is no longer even respected. It is looked down on by our men of genius as dirty work. What great actor would exchange his stage? what great barrister his court? what great preacher his pulpit? for the squalor of the political arena in which we have to struggle with foolish factions in parliament and with ignorant voters in the constituencies? The scientists will have nothing to do with us; for the atmosphere of politics is not the atmosphere of science. Even political science, the science by which civilization must live or die, is busy explaining the past whilst we have to grapple with the present: it leaves the ground before our feet in black darkness whilst it lights up every corner of the landscape behind us. All the talent and genius of the country is bought up by the flood of unearned money. On that poisoned wealth talent and genius live far more luxuriously in the service of the rich than we in the service of our country. Politics, once the centre of attraction for ability, public spirit, and ambition, has now become the refuge of a few fanciers of public speaking and party intrigue who find all the other avenues to distinction closed to them either by their lack of practical ability, their comparative poverty and lack of education, or, let me hasten to add, their hatred of oppression and injustice, and their contempt for the chicaneries and false pretence of commercialized professionalism. . . . Do not misunderstand me: I do not want the old governing class back. It governed so selfishly that the people would have perished if democracy had not swept it out of politics. But evil as it was in many ways, at least it stood above the tyranny of popular ignorance and popular poverty. Today only the king stands above that tyranny. You are dangerously subject to it. . . . I stand for the future and the past, for the posterity that has no vote and the tradition that never had any. I stand for the great abstractions: for conscience and virtue: for the eternal against the expedient; for the evolutionary appetite against the day's gluttony; for intellectual integrity, for humanity, for the rescue of industry from commercialism and of science from professionalism, for everything that you desire as sincerely as I, but which in you is held in leash by the Press, which can organize against you the ignorance and superstition, the timidity and credulity, the gullibility and prudery, the hating and hunting instinct of the voting mob, and cast you down from power if you utter a word to alarm or displease the adventurers who have the Press in their pockets. Between you and that tyranny stands the throne.[1]

As it happens, this evaluation of the democracy myth is not very new: Belloc, among others, had been saying the same things for a number of years: democracy, as it was being practised, was a travesty of the ideal, an open sesame to Balbus's jobbery, Crassus's incompetence, to the defilement of high hopes and disinterested service. In such a situation as Magnus outlines, those imperatives of government – stability, selflessness, a sense of responsibility – cannot be found as viable potentials in the common man, not because the common man is naturally evil, but because he is not strong enough to resist, control, and shape the very forces which have given him nominal leadership. The democratically elected leader is the victim of an inescapable, tragic situation. Where, then, is a nation to find its purpose?

In me, King Magnus says: 'I stand for the great abstractions: for conscience and virtue; for the eternal against the expedient . . .': in a monarchy, therefore?

The answer to this is yes, but it is a paradoxical yes. King Magnus wins against the Cabinet in the end by threatening to abdicate and stand for election to Parliament as a commoner. Proteus, the Prime Minister, knows at once that he will be defeated at the polls – for Magnus is an uncommonly able man. As Shaw explains in his preface: 'The change would rally the anti-democratic royalist vote against him [Proteus], and impose on him a rival in the person of the only public man whose ability he has to fear. The comedic paradox of the situation is that the King wins, not by exercising his royal authority, but by threatening to

[1] *The Apple Cart*, pp. 229–30.

resign it and go to the democratic poll.'[1] The paradox and the irony do
not stop here. If the King *were* to go to the democratic poll and win, it
will be for quite the wrong reasons that the popular vote – already
defined as an ignorant, superstitious thing – will put him in office.
Democracy will be well and truly hoist by its own petard. Is democracy,
therefore, utterly unreliable as a system? Emphatically not; it is a

> . . . very real thing, with much less humbug about it than many
> older institutions. But it means, not that the people govern, but
> that the responsibility and the veto now belong neither to kings
> nor demagogues as such, but to whoever is clever enough to get
> them.[2]

To which words from Magnus, Lysistrata asks: 'Yourself, sir, for
example?' and Magnus modestly says that he thinks he is in the running
– in the running, not as the representative of an institution, but as
himself, as a man.

Obviously the dilemma of government, though it is the most
honourably tackled by democracy, is not going to be solved by any
institution. It can only be solved by the man. By Caesar, by Magnus:
by the leader in whom the 'great abstractions' and a genius for practical
affairs combine to make the natural monarch. The ordinary politicians – the Proteuses of demogogy – are simply not strong enough for
the task.

An 'Interlude' divides the political debate into two. It depicts King
Magnus at 'half-time', so to speak, relaxing in the boudoir of his
mistress, Orinthia, and it seems to have nothing to do with the main
themes of the play. Yet it accomplishes several important things. The
portrait of Magnus is filled in and he faces the Cabinet in the second
act endowed with much greater amplitude of character than his
opponents. He has background; and the conflict becomes more than ever
one between the man Magnus and the creatures of the Cabinet. Another
thing is that the King in his play hour demonstrates very clearly that
the play hour is not the reality. Orinthia, tempestuous, possessive,
beautiful, challenges and tempts him on this very point:

[1] Preface to *The Apple Cart*, p. 167.
[2] *The Apple Cart*, Act I, p. 225.

Give me a goddess's work to do; and I will do it. I will even stoop to a queen's work if you will share the throne with me. But do not pretend that people become great by doing great things. They do great things because they are great, if the great things come along. But they are great just the same when the great things do not come along.[1]

This dangerous philosophy – that of the greatness of simply being as opposed to the greatness of doing – is thrown at Magnus in the name of 'Nature':

I am one of Nature's queen's. . . . If you do not [know it], you are not one of Nature's kings.[2]

But Magnus, whose *raison d'être* and greatness of being is ineradicably in doing, will allow her no more than an indulgent and amused hearing. She is his fairy tale, nothing more, and he leaves her shortly (after an indecorous but entirely puritanical wrestling match on the carpet) for his tea, his Queen Jemima, and his Cabinet. Orinthia refreshes him, no doubt, much as a brief escape into high romance would refresh anybody, but she is decidedly not for his workaday world.

Before Magnus faces his Cabinet to give his answer to its ultimatum, there is another 'interlude' which throws the entire constitutional crisis into relief against the international scene. Mr Vanhattan, the American ambassador, is granted an audience with the King and brings the joyous news that America has cancelled the Declaration of Independence and, like a prodigal son, decided to return to the British Empire. 'We may survive only as another star on your flag', Magnus says aghast.[3]

The history of the past twenty-five years should be sufficiently explicit warning against our being satisfied merely to laugh at the terms of Mr Vanhattan's announcement. American 'colonization', the extension of her 'sphere of influence' over the western world is the political fact of the era: not only the political but also the social and cultural.

---

[1] *The Apple Cart*, An Interlude, p. 242.
[2] Ibid. p. 244.
[3] Ibid. Act II, p. 258.

'Prophet' is a title that has been bestowed on Shaw: I am not at all certain if he did not himself assume it too glibly. None the less it is in such 'extravagances' as America's return to the fold that we may admit Shaw's possessing a discernment and a range of vision well beyond the ordinary. In sober dialogue like this as well:

> PROTEUS: By your Majesty's leave, we will take the question of the ultimatum first.
> MAGNUS: Do you think the ultimatum will matter much when the capital of the British Commonwealth is shifted to Washington?
> NICOBAR. We'll see it shifted to Melbourne or Montreal or Johannesburg first.
> MAGNUS: It would not stay there. It will stay at a real centre of gravity only.
> PROTEUS: We are agreed about that. If it shifts at all it will shift either west to Washington or east to Moscow.[1]

What in 1929 was topical provocativeness is today topical in quite another sense. We should not, of course, subside in reverential awe before such 'prophecies': they are not excessively profound, and anyway many people beside Shaw foresaw such things. All the same, they denote, as so much else does, Shaw's faculty for synthesis and his gift for presenting this in the metaphor of comedy.

When *The Apple Cart* was first produced there arose on the one hand a paean of praise and on the other vilification. Both reactions have been proved wrong. The first was simply an excess of sentimental admiration for The Grand Old Man of English Drama, the second was the delusion that the play blasphemed against democracy. *The Apple Cart* is certainly a good play, full of vitality, wit, and wisdom; the discussion emerges with the usual vigour and lucid complexity; King Magnus is one of Shaw's finest creations. Yet the dialogue lacks the density of earlier work; it sparkles vividly and the lines move with unabated rhythmic grace; but underneath this, those recurring ironies and paradoxes, which were the stuff of Shaw's art and are the stuff of life, seem to be melting away.

[1] Ibid. p. 260.

3

Too True to be Good, another political extravaganza, follows *The Apple Cart*. The new play begins in the bedroom of a young girl reduced to a state of chronic invalidism by a mollycoddling mother – much to the annoyance and distress of a 'Monster' measles microbe, who provides a kind of Aristophanic-Mary Baker Eddy-ish 'chorus' to the goings-on in the sickroom. This abode of death-in-life is eventually the scene of an attempted burglary carried out by the new, extremely pretty 'nurse' and her accomplice, a young man whom she summons through the window. The invalid, displaying astonishing strength in defending her jewels, foils the would-be burglars. However, they talk her round to joining them in the burglary and finally —

> The aspiring soul escapes from home, sweet home, which, as a well-known author has said, is the girl's prison and the woman's workhouse.[1]

Away the three go, assured of a great deal of money from the projected sale of the invalid's pearls, anticipating an enormous amount of 'fun'. The Monster, now completely cured of the measles, turns to the audience and says:

> The play is now virtually over; but the characters will discuss it at great length for two acts more. The exit doors are all in order. Goodnight.[2]

Sure enough, the 'play' *is* virtually over and the discussions in the second and third acts *are* very long: which begins to explain why *Too True to be Good* has never been popular. Moreover, it becomes diffuse. There is a great deal of profound discussion, a good bit of entertaining slapstick, several excellent character portraits, but as a whole the play does not cohere; it fails to focus on any distinct theme. Shaw in his preface explains that the 'main gist and moral of the play' is not that 'our social system is unjust to the poor, but that it is cruel

[1] *Too True to be Good*, Act I, p. 47.
[2] Ibid. p. 48.

to the rich. . . . My play is a story of three reckless young people who come into possession of, for the moment, unlimited riches, and set out to have a thoroughly good time with all the modern machinery of pleasure to aid them. The result is that they get nothing for their money but a multitude of worries and a maddening dissatisfaction.'[1] In fact, this old and somewhat stale Shavian paradox is evident only by inference, for if the three adventurers are certainly maddeningly dissatisfied, the social, as distinct from the personal, indictment is remote. Prefatorial Shaw is – as is not uncommon – less than helpful in explaining dramatist Shaw.

The play, as I say, has no focus; it seems aimless, unplanned, episodic. Yet it may be argued – and it is a point of view I shall adopt for a few minutes – that the very aimlessness and incoherence *is* Shaw's focus: it is the representation of aimless humanity, of the 'lost generation' after the war, engulfed in futility, squabbling fretfully on the brink of eternity (as the sets of a desert coast for the second and third acts indicate).

Aubrey, the erstwhile burglar, an exceedingly eloquent young man, who can preach anything, true or false, 'is the most hopeless sort of scoundrel',[2] but his scoundrelism has been largely forged for him by a father who tried to bring him up as a God-fearing atheist, a mother who tried to bring him up as a God-fearing conformist, and by the war which caught him when he was hardly more than a boy and impelled him to drop a bomb on a sleeping village —

> I cried all night after doing that. Later on I swooped into a street and sent machine gun bullets into a crowd of civilians: women, children, and all. I was past crying by that time. . . .[3]

Implausibly enough, Aubrey's father turns up as an 'Elder' living in a near-by grotto. His is the tragi-comedy of the Determinist caught out by Einstein; now finding the faith in science to be bankrupt, he declaims the nullity of things in long inauspiciously reverberant speeches. Meanwhile a Sergeant peruses John Bunyan and the Bible, and shows how

[1] Preface to *Too True to be Good*, p. 3.
[2] Ibid.
[3] *Too True to be Good*, Act III, p. 88.

orthodox religions have been thrown into confusion and contrariety of spirit by the state of the world.

> Well, London and Paris and Berlin and Rome and the rest of them will be burned with fire from heaven all right in the next war: that's certain. Theyre all Cities of Destruction. And our Government chaps are running about with a great burden of corpses and debts on their backs, crying 'What must we do to be saved?'[1]

Here are three legacies of history – three men who declare that history itself has been a series of appalling blunders: man's inheritance is dispossession of the earth and all things on it. 'What must we do to be saved?'

The two women, one the erstwhile Patient and the other the erstwhile nurse, now called Sweetie, give some sort of answer. Shaw's women usually do. His men talk a good deal but never actually do very much – nothing purposeful and positive. There are exceptions, of course, like Caesar and Undershaft and Magnus, all of whom serve the national, the global, the cosmic, interest. They are almost the heroic exceptions in a masculine world devoted to the interest of Self, here and now. On the other hand, Shaw's women, generally considered, naturally embody perpetuity. The biological fact is a beginning, by no means a necessary beginning, and by no means the end of the matter. History, if not Creative Evolution itself, quickens in their wombs; they aspire to and often realize communion with the Life Force. They are very often daughters of divine Grace – that is to say, Shaw's concept of divine Grace. It seems that Shaw saw the woman as holding out most hope for mankind. He was, as we know, a great champion of woman's rights, though not excessively in sympathy with the Suffragette movement. The emancipation he sought for the woman was subtler than that of mere suffrage, and in fact not one of his heroines is a political creature. In the long prospect of Shaw's women, starting with Candida and going onward through Lady Cicily Waynflete, Ann, Barbara, Liza, Lavinia, and Ellie, we may legitimately see Joan as something of an inevitability in his creative life, the heroic consummation of the unwomanly woman's ideal.

[1] *Too True to be Good*, p. 81.

Now, in *Too True to be Good*, the Patient and Sweetie, driven mad by doing nothing for several months on end, decide to do something. The Patient, though free and healthy, is utterly miserable: she sees herself and her two fellow adventurers as 'inefficient fertilizers', 'walking factories of bad manure', and so she departs for 'Beotia', that is, The Union of Federated Sensible Societies, that is Russia, where she will find some purpose for living. In a little postscript to the play, Shaw informs us that the Patient is his particular favourite;[1] no doubt she is, saddening though this may be, for the Beotia business is triviality in the posture of redemption.

Sweetie thinks quite otherwise about life. To be accurate, Sweetie does not think. While the Patient is – to put it as nicely as Aubrey puts it – governed by her 'higher centres', Sweetie is governed by her 'lower centres'. She is a vestal of sexual love, is as promiscuous as only a pretty woman can be when she wants to be, and as ardent in her attachments, however transient, as any male can desire. 'Since the war', Aubrey says, and for once we are entitled to believe him —

> Since the war the lower centres have become vocal. And the effect is that of an earthquake. For they speak truths that have never been spoken before – truths that the makers of our domestic institutions have tried to ignore.[2]

Truths they may be, but it is mildly surprising to find Shaw's characters enunciating them quite as they do. Not because these truths present a belated offering to the Freudian god, however. Shaw had no need to do this. 'I have said it all before him', he crowed when he came across Freud's writings;[3] and he *had* said a lot of it, if not all, before Freud, though far more 'delicately'. To Shaw, Freud's lack of 'delicacy' was a hideous defect,[4] emphatically not because sex was at the bottom of Freudian science, but because Freud advertised it in terms that did dirt on it quite as efficiently as social and religious taboos had done. Sex

[1] Postscript to *Too True to be Good*, p. 108.

[2] Ibid. Act II, p. 66.

[3] In Winsten's *Jesting Apostle*; quoted by B. B. Watson, *A Shavian Guide to the Intelligent Woman*, London, Chatto and Windus, 1964, p. 132.

[4] See 'Who I am and What I Think', *Sixteen Self Sketches*, p. 52.

was life, and Freud's utterances, as much as the usual repressiveness, were a blasphemy against life.

By jumping into bed with every desirable male (and, really, she is not a wanton), and by marrying the Sergeant with only the gratification of her 'lower centres' in view, Sweetie is true to both Freud and Shaw. More important, she is true to her instincts: there is no blasphemy against life in this unblushing succubus; on the contrary, there is worship, and, as I say, no cause for surprise.

What *is* surprising is the blatancy of the discussion about Sweetie's appetite, which is 'shouted all over the place' as though Shaw in old age had decided to give his metaphysic of sex a lick of bright new paint. There are a few more similar licks in *The Simpleton of the Unexpected Isles*.

T. E. Lawrence, who had become a friend of Shaw and Mrs Shaw, thought *Too True to be Good* one of Shaw's great works, a rival of even *Heartbreak House*.[1] Since Lawrence was the original of Private Meek, one of the undisputed successes of the play, an all too brief reminder of the incisive bathos that had once seemed the perennial inspiration of Shaw's comedy, there may be some cause for believing him prejudiced. The play is not a masterpiece: very far from it. However, it is more than it is generally given credit for being, has some little of what Lawrence saw in it, and may yet grow in stature and claim the last vindicatory word for itself. For the present, we may still legitimately expect greater coherence in the depiction even of incoherence, a firmer declaration of purpose in the midst of purposelessness. Prophecy must be more than trombones blaring in the void.

*　　　*　　　*

There are still several plays. As they succeed one another it becomes increasingly evident that Shaw's control over form is failing; the importance they may have becomes increasingly dependent on the quality of thought they display.

On the Rocks is the companion piece to *Too True to be Good*, another

[1] For Lawrence's comments on this play, see S. Weintraub, *Private Shaw and Public Shaw*, London, Cape, 1963, pp. 214–15.

political extravaganza, and perhaps the most bitter play that Shaw ever wrote. Beyond this impression it is not remarkable. Sir Arthur Chavender, the British Prime Minister, is Proteus of *The Apple Cart*, without benefit of Magnus, put to severe test of government. The result is predictable: he does not have the personal magnitude to haul the country off the rocks; his desperate bid for revolutionary legislation fizzles out as one by one his colleagues, prompted by this interest and that, generally by the interest of 'Blackguardocracy', desert him; he is left alone contemplating the stark truth of an old democrat's remark:

. . . all this country or any country has to stand between it and blue hell is the consciences of them that are capable of governing it.[1]

Unless, the play concludes by implying, a man of action, a very Hercules, comes to divert the Thames and thereby cleanses the stables of Albion, England is ripe for revolution. It is a dire enough warning; but the pity is that it is conveyed in a play that barely develops beyond the dialectic of *The Apple Cart*, is nowhere near the same play in point of characterization and subtlety, and is most unfair to the personalities it purports to reflect on the stage – MacDonald and his coalition government of the early 1930's.

In speech, preface, and impromptu utterance at this time, Shaw was, politically speaking, the nearest to despair and that fatal 'discouragement' that he ever came. Yet Inquisitions and liquidation and other 'remedies' to be found in his non-dramatic work do not carry great weight in his plays. Hard things are said against democracy, bitter indictments are piled up against the follies, the blunders, and the waste – the inconceivable waste – of contemporary political extemporization; but that understanding of, if not compassion for, human fallibility, which had always been the upshot of his dramatic dialectic, remains constant. And hope stays high. Even Sir Arthur Chavender can summon up a peaceful resignation to his impotence as a leader. Even an English revolution remains at most an unpleasant contingency.

The Simpleton of the Unexpected Isles is in keeping with his ideas at the time. It is a play about liquidation, not human though, but divine: it is about the Day of Judgement. The details of the plot are really too

[1] *On the Rocks*, Act II, p. 262.

trivial and the Shavian bombardment is really too stale to warrant description. The interesting thing is that the political – no, the human dilemma is solved, or partly solved, by selective liquidation: the House of Commons is cleared in an instant, the medical profession melts into thin air, and in the Unexpected Isles the offspring of a bizarre experiment in eugenics, four beautiful young creatures representing Love, Pride, Empire, and Bravery,[1] simply vanish. A chummy angel contributes some heavy 'fun' to the proceedings.

Shaw's Judgement Day – to the extent that his treatment of the theme can be taken at all seriously – is not a final 'solution': granted that the earth has been swept clean of offending members of the human race, but the survivors will still need their leaders. Who are they? Where are they to be found? *The Millionairess* is some sort of answer. *The Millionairess* is a remarkably lively answer, a gathering of energy for what in retrospect can be seen as Shaw's last really effective offering to the theatre. Epifania, the Millionairess, is a splendid young woman, chock-full of aggressive vitality, bursting to dominate the world she moves in. She is a natural boss and she proves it, not only by wearing down her opposition with a more or less incessant fusillade of verbal shot, but also, if need be, by employing her devastating ju-jitsu on obstructive males, and – this is important – by venturing out into the world with thirty-five shillings in her purse and within the space of six months:

> . . . I came to this hotel as a scullery maid: the most incompetent scullery maid that ever broke a dinner service. I am now its owner and there is no tuppence-hapeny an hour here.[2]

Epifania is specifically a money boss (though her whirlwind advance through sweatshops and hotel keeping may be seen to have general political reference), and as such she necessarily injures helpless and innocent people who stand in her way. Or are these injuries which she inflicts indictable? The Egyptian doctor, to win whose esteem she has sallied forth to sustain herself on thirty-five shillings, puts the question:

[1] *Heartbreak House* finds a tenuous echo, as it does several times in this series of political extravaganzas.
[2] *The Millionairess*, Act IV, p. 195.

The hotel looks well in photographs; and the wages you pay would be a fortune to a laborer on the Nile. But what of the old people whose natural home this place had become? the old man with his paralytic stroke? the old woman gone mad? the cast out creatures in the workhouse? Was not this preying on the poverty of the poor? Shall I, the servant of Allah, live on such gains? Shall I, the healer, the helper, the guardian of life and the counsellor of health, unite with the exploiter of misery?[1]

To this Epifania answers:

I have to take the world as I find it.[2]

She is patently a flawed boss, a powerhouse humming to no communal advantage, and the doctor gravely voices the Shavian retort:

I see that riches are a curse; poverty is a curse; only in the service of Allah is there justice, righteousness, and happiness.[3]

We have heard this before, the dynamic of capitalist enterprise balanced by a sense of moral responsibility – in *Major Barbara*. Here Epifania risks the wrath of Allah by leaving the world no better than she found it. 'I think', she says defiantly, 'Allah loves those who make money.' Not always; Allah will most certainly not love Alastair, Epifania's husband, who once made a lot of money by good luck and trickery; Allah will, however, be inclined to love Epifania, since the money she makes is token of her integrity and genius; he will certainly love her if conscience were welded to her genius, an event we are permitted to anticipate when she declares her unshakeable intention of divorcing Alastair and marrying the doctor. If the union between Egypt and England does not make the doctor a businessman and does not make Epifania a humanitarian, eugenics may combine the two qualities in their offspring. Shaw does not say this in the play, but it is an obvious inference.

There is a kind of progression in the plays of the 1930's, the conclusion in one leading Shaw to examine this conclusion in the next. At the

[1] Ibid.
[2] Ibid.
[3] Ibid.

same time they seem to revolve round a primary statement, that postulating the conjunction of power and conscience. *Geneva* takes up the problem and proposes the International Court of Justice as an active and respected guardian of the world's conscience. The play is badly flawed: structurally it is probably the weakest that Shaw wrote; a boldly imaginative idea sputters out in interminable, frequently foolish, harangues. For this reason I shall say nothing about it, except this – that every now and again the dialogue gathers to itself the eloquence, fervour, and selfless passion of a long and miraculous crusade – more, that it gathers to itself the incessant cry of history and contains the dilemma of political man in great and noble words. Thus the Secretary of the League of Nations, speaking in the shadow of a tyranny that mocks the Covenant of the League:

> You are all enemies of the human race. You are all armed to the teeth and full of patriotism. Your national heroes are all brigands and pirates. When it comes to the point you are all cut-throats. But Geneva will beat you yet. Not in my time perhaps. But the Geneva spirit is a fact; and a spirit is a fact that cannot be killed.[1]

And the Judge of the International Court:

> . . . None of you seem to have any idea of the sort of world you are living in. Into the void created by this ignorance has been heaped a groundwork of savage superstitions: human sacrifices, vengeance, wars of conquest and religion, falsehoods called history, and a glorification of vulgar erotics and pugnacity called romance which transforms people who are naturally as amiable, as teachable, as companionable as dogs, into the most ferocious and cruel of all the beasts. And this, they say, is human nature! But it is not natural at all: real human nature is in continual conflict with it; for amid all the clamor for more slaughter and the erection of monuments to the great slaughterers the cry for justice, for mercy, for fellowship, for peace, has never been completely silenced: even the worst villainies must pretend to be committed for its sake.[2]

[1] *Geneva*, Act III, pp. 76–7.
[2] Ibid. p. 81.

'As long as I live I must write.'[1] Shaw died when he was working on his fifty-third play. We could follow him beyond *Geneva* (the forty-eighth in his dramatic *corpus*) but there does not seem much point in doing so. The plays of his last years, especially in *Good King Charles's Golden Days*, would no doubt have made a resounding reputation for a lesser writer; for Shaw they represent a good deal of what was enduring and vital in him, but nothing new.

[1] Preface to *Buoyant Billions*, p. 3.

PART III:
ARTIST-PHILOSOPHER

Chapter Nine

ARTIST-PHILOSOPHER

*I '... I am by way of being a professional
thinker...'*[1]

'He who can, does. He who cannot, teaches',[2] the sardonic Tanner informs us. Shaw was not a doer. We should not, of course, under-
estimate his achievement as a principal committee-man of the early
Fabian Society: he deserves a page or two in the story of British Socialism. This is something, but not much, and little is added by his record,
admirable though it is, as a vestryman and then a borough councillor
of St Pancras. Shaw was not a doer, he was a teacher.

How successful has his teaching been? To answer this we must
impose an unnatural separation between manner and matter. The
manner (to confine ourselves for the present to Shaw's non-dramatic
works) is one of the splendours of English letters. The velocity of his
prose, his command over the techniques of language (though he
faltered now and again in his rhetorical moments), his fusion of Augustan grace and symmetry with colloquial forthrightness, his lucidity,
wit and power to entertain, are the characteristics of a style which even
his detractors agree belongs to a master of his craft. But style for its
own sake, like literature for its own sake, did not interest him. He said:
'I have never aimed at style in my life: style is a sort of melody that
comes into my sentences by itself. If a writer says what he has to say
as accurately and effectively as he can, his style will take care of itself...'
to which he confusingly adds: '... if he has a style.'[3] And he once re-
proved the critic, Dixon Scott, for making too much of 'style' in his –
Shaw's – writing:

It was very much as if I had told him the house was on fire, and he had

---

[1] *The Intelligent Woman's Guide*, p. 3.
[2] 'Maxims for Revolutionists', *Man and Superman*, p. 213.
[3] Preface to *Immaturity*, p. xxxix.

said, 'How admirably monosyllabic!' and left the nursery stairs burning unheeded. My impulse was to exclaim, 'Do you think you conceited young whelp, that I have taken all the trouble and developed all that literary craft to gratify your appetite for style? Get up at once and fetch a bucket of water. . . .'[1]

The manner, then, is superlative, but if we are to heed Shaw not to be singled out. He is quite right, of course. The buckets of water are what count – at least, they will count if there are any.

Writing in the *New Statesman* of July 1943, Joad challenged Shaw on this point. 'How much of your teaching has been learnt by the world to-day? And by "learnt" I don't only mean accepted in theory but acted on in practice.'[2] Shaw's letter of reply, already cited, is chirpily confident, but the evidence of the past twenty-five years does not endorse his mood.

The evidence of the past twenty-five years points of course to little other than social betterment in Britain. No one with the image of Jarrow before him could seriously deny this. But apart from the fact that this social betterment is only marginally Shavian (it cannot be anything else, not while 'Trade Union Capitalism' holds its present sway), there is also the fact that Shaw's contribution was that of one person among many. To the degree that we can define the far-off causes that brought MacDonald to his brief inglorious reign between the wars and Attlee to power after the last war, they were in the work done for Socialism by economists, social workers, politicians, and writers, from all walks of life, from all over England. It was not only Shaw, but Sidney and Beatrice Webb and other Fabians (and other non-Fabian Socialists), Keir Hardie, H. G. Wells – and a steadily growing army of believers, all of whom prepared the way for the economic and social revolution after 1945. This is very obvious, and it would be silly, if not impossible, to try to ascribe any concrete reform to Shaw alone.

He no doubt would want us to think otherwise. He could plausibly indicate, for example, the national health scheme in Britain and say that he had written in support of something like this in 1911, and in

---

[1] 'The Artstruck Englishman', *Pen Portraits and Reviews*, pp. 232–3.
[2] Quoted by Joad in his *Shaw*, pp. 137–44.

fact he did, although the Preface to *The Doctor's Dilemma* (and his other papers and polemics on the matter) was certainly not the only literature to promote this. He could point to the relaxed marriage laws and say that it was just like the English to take fifty years to put into effect 'solutions' he had found for them by 1910, and again he would be partly right. He could point to schools and to gaols and say much the same thing and yet again be partly right, for there is a distinctly Shavian finger in several revised institutional pies. All this is something, but still for a Shaw it is not much, and if we consider him alone in relation to the three big issues of his life – economics, politics, religion – we see that they have gone their way almost as though he had never existed.

We put the question to the savants – at any rate to those few who pause to consider Shaw – to the economist, the theologian, and others. (We shall ignore the literary critic for the time being.) Each answers in effect: 'Shaw? – I admire his cheek, but he knew next to nothing about my discipline.' Then the scientist adds, 'Yet there have been few more profound analysts of our society',[1] and the economist says, 'But it is probably as a mode of exposition, rather than as a systematic construction of novel economic doctrine, that Mr Shaw's economic writings ought properly to be judged. . . .'[2] The others may or may not modify their rebuttals but one thing remains plain. There is no real desire to endorse Shaw, still less to implement his teaching.

Perhaps we should not expect any endorsement. Shaw himself was a specialist anti-specialist; as such he frequently understood his subject of the moment less well than his confidence and fluency might lead one to believe. Beatrice Webb was suggesting the sober truth when she once told an audience: 'If you want a brilliant answer, ask Mr Shaw. If you want a plain statement of fact, ask me.'[3] Shaw is brilliant, yes, and supremely persuasive; he is also plausible. He is eloquent and awe-inspiringly dedicated; he is also sweeping. He is a purposeful and coherent thinker; he is also often wrong.

We do not need to be specialists to see this. Pursue him into the

---

[1] J. D. Bernal, 'Shaw the Scientist', *G.B.S.90, Aspects of Bernard Shaw's Life and Work*, p. 105.
[2] Maurice Dobb, 'Bernard Shaw and Economics', ibid., p. 137.
[3] Henderson, *G.B.S.: Man of the Century*, p. 841.

detail of many of his arguments and more than merely occasional opportunity for query, scepticism, or plain disbelief will present itself. There are contradictions; thus: the 'maxim' for 1903, 'Every man over forty is a scoundrel',[1] is superseded in 1923 by a new 'maxim', that only men who are twice or three times or four times more than forty can be relied on to govern themselves and the world.[2] There is oversimplification, as in the Preface to *Back to Methuselah* which, though admittedly a *tour de force* in its way, barely begins to comprehend the ramifications of modern biological theory. There is misrepresentation – or should one say highly interested representation? – in the delineation of Jesus in the Preface to *Androcles and the Lion*, which may be in some sort of keeping with modern humanist-Christian thought but is so lacking in perception of grace that orthodoxy has greater warrant than its own implied belittlement to feel shocked.[3] There is ignorance in the Preface to *Misalliance*, in which Shaw presents himself as an authority on the rearing of children; and further ignorance in some of the attacks on doctors, on scientists such as Pavlov, and on the practice of vivisection. There is the refusal of his messianic determinism to admit the enormous practical difficulties that would inevitably impede, and possibly obstruct, his schemes for economic and political reform; there is in this respect a perceptible tendency on his part to ignore or condone the bureaucratic coercion or meddling his schemes often implied. There is – but no need to continue; a person who wishes to quarrel with Shaw will find ample opportunity, opportunity if need be, and if minutae are beneath contempt, to quarrel with his views on the establishment in general.

Perhaps our wonder should be that within the framework of his general philosophy – whatever we may think of it – there should not be inconsistency so much as consistency. Shaw never really changed his views. He elaborated on them and they grew with the years into the most intricate edifices. He rarely corrected himself or qualified an expressed opinion, and since he often said silly things, he was apt to

[1] 'Maxims for Revolutionists', *Man and Superman*, p. 224.
[2] In *Back to Methuselah*.
[3] One may say substantially the same of *The Adventures of the Black Girl in Her Search for God*.

devise tortuous reasons for vindicating something that could more easily and more sensibly have been rejected as a mistake. The upshot in his sixty year-long career as a public man was inevitable: the most up-to-date man of the time slowly became a most out-of-date man as well.

This is why Shaw is in twilight at present. His teaching is at variance with most modern trends. He remained a Vitalist while the twentieth century grew more and more Mechanistic. He asserted a form of holism while intellectual life pursued fragmentation. He was a mystic among rationalists, a believer among sceptics. He founded his faith on hope while the fashionable attitudes were doubt, guilt, and despair. He was, quite simply, an outsider: in his own words, 'a sojourner on this planet rather than a native of it'.[1] It is this admission that uncovers the final paradox of Shaw: he was the specialist physician of the contemporary world prescribing medicines from a dispensary that seemed not to belong to the world at all.

The world can be wise in its way. The deadest thing is yesterday's idea. The deadest person is the man or woman who lives by yesterday's idea. Shaw's own perception of these truths explains his continuous campaigns to have the corpses of nineteenth-century thought buried. It is therefore undesirable to wish unnatural longevity on his ideas. The changing patterns of society have made many of them a part of history. They are fixed in the past and are dead.

Does this mean that one must judge his preaching and pamphleteering to have failed? The answer is yes – in the sense that all moral crusades of the past have 'failed'. Their champions fail to revolutionize the world and they are crucified, either actively or by indifference. And yet they are not dead. They cannot die whilst history informs and enriches the present. Shaw's message was like a peal of laughter in church: it appalled the nineteenth century and enraptured the twentieth century. To three generations he was the uncontested intellectual leader, 'gloriously irreverent, transparently sincere, divinely inspired, and prophetic';[2] and it can hardly be thought that all he urged came to nothing.

---

[1] Preface to *Immaturity*, p. xliii. The passage continues: 'Whether it be that I was born mad or a little too sane, my kingdom was not of this world: I was at home only in the realm of my imagination, and at my ease only with the mighty dead.'
[2] See *The Religious Speeches of Bernard Shaw*, ed. by W. S. Smith, p. 37.

Of course it did not. We cannot measure impalpables, yet we may say to the extent that his voice was the clearest, his message the most brilliantly enunciated and in the course of time the most widely known, he created the Socialist conscience of the twentieth century, which is to say that he created our conviction that privilege of any kind – economic social, or racial – was wrong. He so worked on and coloured the sensibility of his time that in the flux and fusion by which ideas are generated and manners are formed his ideas entered into the English, possibly the European, way of life. His mission transcends the moment with its ever-decaying particulars; his 'gospel' is ahead, and for this reason cannot be said to have failed. As a postulate of the 'Good' it cannot ever be thought to have 'failed' until the present imperatives of individual and social man have been replaced by others as yet undreamt of.

What are these imperatives and how does Shaw's concept of man measure up to them? In his usual serio-jocular view, Shaw once referred to himself as a 'professor of natural psychology'[1] and it is as such a professor and not as a Socialist or Creative Evolutionist that we may now briefly consider him.

We must live. This is the first law of nature and the first law in the Shavian canon – the first law and also the last, the absolute imperative of being. In our modern, ramified societies this means that we have to have money to keep us alive. Without it, we would perish, with too little we would not be able to fulfil our potential selves, but be stunted creatures, scarcely more than beasts in our endeavours simply to stay alive. The bearing these truths have on Shavian doctrine is too obvious to be explained. Then, we ensure our survival in procreation, which, as the second principle of *homo vitalis*, if not *sapiens*, is nearly as constant a subject in Shaw: it is the basis of a major work, *Man and Superman*, and the theme of any number of other writings. The drive to procreate leads us to the next aspect of this law, which is that we can best manage to live in the company of our fellows. We are gregarious creatures, and although the family as an institution was scarcely a 'natural' thing to Shaw (he had a good deal to say about the burden the family could impose on one), he always maintained the social fact. We exist to a

[1] Preface to *Major Barbara*, p. 226.

large extent in the eyes of others; we can only come to know ourselves in the company of others.

'Know yourself'. With this Socratic injunction we part company with monkeys and accept the condition of human intelligence. It is a condition which many people are perhaps disposed to waive, but not Shaw. 'Know yourself' may be taken as his motto. It was his unrelenting demand – that we should know ourselves as well as he, the professor of natural psychology, knew us, which meant that we should see the prime imperatives as recoiling on us, demanding integrity, responsibility, purpose; demanding that we actively pursue our birthrights of security and self-respect.

Intelligence imposes yet further, its own, conditions, those of the 'higher centres'. These transform what could be the vulgar curiosity of a monkey into a drive to explore the unknown. We go adventuring in mind or body quite simply because it is in our nature to do so, and Shaw's teaching never fails to acknowledge this. It never fails to be a fully creative adventure he calls on people to make, especially young people, in whom he generally founded his hope for the world. 'I'll dare, and dare, and dare, until I die', Joan cries, acknowledging those 'voices' which we more prosaically would call the inner compulsion of her being. Her example urges all of us to 'dare' the unknown with courage and the will to succeed. For those who prefer to relax with the imperfect 'present' Shaw has an emphatic disclaimer:

> Clive says why not live in the present? Because we don't, and won't, and can't. Because there is no such thing as the present: there is only the gate that we are always reaching and never passing through: the gate that leads from the past into the future. . . . The only sensations intense enough to be called precious or beautiful are the sensations of an irresistible movement to an all-important end.[1]

This quotation brings us to the fifth imperative, that we have something within us – and if we wish, we may describe it as 'soul' – which looks for satisfaction or fulfilment in what, for want of a better word, we may call the beautiful. This word can have many interpretations. It may connote aesthetic perfection, or 'holiness', or 'divine law', or

[1] 'On Clive Bell's Article', *Shaw on Theatre*, op. cit., p. 151.

'God'. It may be seen as justice and liberty and peace and the 'Good' – in those Forms which may be brought to realization through the harmonious interaction of our drive to live. It may be seen as 'life with a blessing' or as the 'Life Force'. Whatever the word, it will be all right provided the unity of being and our immortal longings are understood.

Shaw's philosophy rests squarely on these natural laws and it declares in the name of the fifth law the inviolability of them all. If in this total concept we see nothing of ineradicable evil, it is because to Shaw evil was not part and parcel of accommodated man. Properly accommodated man would banish evil from the face of the earth and live by and with the will to betterment. Hence the form his message usually took: to attack and attack any and everything that he thought misled, or paralysed, or suffocated that miraculous gift of the eternal Lilith – life.

II 'I dare not claim to be the best play-wright in the English language; but I believe myself to be one of the best ten, and may therefore perhaps be classed as one of the best hundred.'[1]

G.B.S. 90 covers aspects of Bernard Shaw's life and works – 'G.B.S. and the Victorians', 'Shaw the Scientist', 'Shaw as Theologian', and so on. It is an interesting and comprehensive collection, but there is one glaring omission. There is nothing on Shaw as a force in literature, nothing by any member of the literary establishment; and it is an open secret that Winsten, the compiler, was unable to get any celebrity to contribute anything. The reason for this is simple. English pundits had had their say on Shaw a long time before he turned ninety and their say was not the kind to repeat in a largely eulogistic volume. But for one slight, kindly pat on the back from Auden,[2] English poets and critics had – and by and large still have – turned a cold shoulder on Shaw. T. S.

---

[1] *Everybody's Political What's What?*, p. 47.
[2] 'The Fabian Figaro', *George Bernard Shaw: A Critical Survey*.

Eliot, for example, in his 'Dialogue on Dramatic Poetry', disposes of him with characteristic urbanity:

> Shaw *was* a poet – until he was born, and the poet in Shaw was still-born. Shaw had a great deal of poetry in him, but all stillborn.[1]

And F. R. Leavis, commenting, as far as I can ascertain, for the first and last time on a man he would, quite evidently, rather not comment on:

> . . . Shaw represents as well as any writer the disorder of modern life that it was Lawrence's genius to diagnose so unanswerably. . . .
> What repels Lawrence in Shaw is what Mr Rubinstein acclaims as the triumphs of reason. It is the automatism, the emptiness and the essential irreverence – all that makes Shaw boring and cheap. . . . And the criterion of intelligence we bring from Lawrence exposes Shaw's 'reason' as clever, conceited stupidity. The stupidity, the conceit and the irreverence are of a mind that has no vital relations with the body.[2]

These represent the extreme views, and there seems no point in echoing them, either from Lawrence himself or from lesser men, who only too blatantly are parroting their teachers.

Outside England, critics and fellow artists have responded more generously. Thomas Mann, though he was inclined to think that Shaw was not 'ever the man to take grave matters with their full gravity',[3] could evince due appreciation of his dramatic ability; and Sean O'Casey, proving that when one Irishman speaks about another Irishman the most exalted of comparisons will go, wrote:

> . . . Christ was something of a logician, and something of a poet, too; and so was Shaw. . . . Let those who write plays today throw a wider chest than Shaw's, in either poetry or prose – if they can![4]

[1] 'A Dialogue on Dramatic Poetry' in *Collected Essays*, London, Faber, 1928, p. 51.
[2] 'Shaw Against Lawrence', *The Spectator*, London, 1 April 1955.
[3] 'He was Mankind's Friend', *George Bernard Shaw: A Critical Survey*, p. 256.
[4] 'A Whisper About Bernard Shaw', *The Green Crow*, New York, Braziller, 1956, pp. 202–3.

Americans have probably been the most willing to see greatness in Shaw, in the theatre as much as in the study. Hundreds of academic theses which take him to pieces, scrutinize the bits, and label them attest to the widespread interest in him. There have been several outstanding critical works and at least two internationally respected critics and scholars, Jacques Barzun and Edmund Wilson, have contributed essays to the literature on Shaw. America, more than any other country, signifies that the 'official' British attitude is far from being unquestioned.

Whatever one's own opinion may be, the fact is that the general picture of Shaw criticism is not one of amiable agreement, even though he is now studied more widely than ever before. There are divergences of opinion, very definite ones, and as a Shavian I see the reasons for this as revolving round two not distinctly separate issues. The first is that raised by Leavis's comment and may be swiftly dealt with. Leavis does not know what he is talking about when he talks about Shaw; very many people do not know what they are talking about when they talk about Shaw: like Denis Donoghue and the writer for *The Times Literary Supplement*, cited in the Preface, they have not read him carefully, they have not understood him, they have not begun to fathom either his intentions or the special way which he carries them out.

The second issue is raised by Eliot's remark and has to do with the nature of 'poetry' – of literary art. Shaw is not admitted to the ranks of literature because he did not write 'poetry'. But what is poetry? How may we best define it? These questions will have to be settled before we can arrive at a final assessment of Shaw's drama; and it seems to me the best way of settling them is by putting Shaw on one side for a while and invoking in his place certain abstracts of the 'apostolic succession' of literature.

*   *   *

There are many approaches to the problem, perhaps as many as there are critics who wish to approach it. And there is no final answer; which is just as well, because that would imply a finiteness of possibilities in poetry (or creative literature) – a kind of law of poetry, which is a repellent but fortunately unlikely possibility.

We can only theorize about literature. Often a theory will become elevated to the status of doctrine; it gathers disciples to itself, all of whom seem happy to rush, if not to the stake, at least into print, in spirited, sometimes intemperate, advocacy of their faith. Conviction is an admirable characteristic, in literary theory no less than in other matters. To lack conviction would be to lack zest; worse, would be to give the appearance of lacking anything anyone might think worth listening to. But conviction can, and it sometimes does, lead to bigotry. I cannot imagine a more intolerable theory of poetics than one founded on that vice.

Shaw, by the way, was not a bigoted theorizer. He was very dogmatic about his views on literature, perhaps occasionally too vehemently dogmatic, but his wit and breadth of ready appreciation preclude a charge of bigotry. However, it was on the basis of didacticism in literature that he took his stand and so I approach the question – What is literature? – from, first, the direction diametrically opposed to Shaw's own, and, second, from Shaw's direction.

The first view is soon stated: all art is quite useless. It has no value worth speaking of, no value, that is, as a moral or social or political force. It exists for and in itself. It is remote, other worldly, and usually spelt with a capital 'A'. Wilde's name is often associated with this belief and we shall accordingly use him to further the argument. He said in *The Critic as Artist*:

It is through Art, and Art only, that we can realize our perfection; through Art and Art only that we can shield ourselves from the sordid perils of actual existence.[1]

I do not want to reject all that Wilde says here, and shall return to what I consider an important part of the doctrine – that there is a perfection to be realized. But the second part of the statement, that Art should shield us from the sordid perils of actual existence, seems to indicate a total unawareness of the material a writer uses. A writer uses words. Words are representational. They stand for things which

[1] In *The Works of Oscar Wilde*, ed. G. F. Maire, London, Collins, 1948, p. 977.

Q

find themselves repeated, by sound, colour, shape, movement, or mood in the experience of everyone not physically or mentally incapacitated. Words are like burrs, and to them will stick the strands of infinitely complex associations which reach beyond their immediate context; words are often the triggers to our deepest emotions, to our loves or hates, our ideals or prejudices, and they will – provided they are not utter nonsense – induce a response which reaches beyond a purely aesthetic experience. If we were to consider some of Wilde's own work – *The Sphinx*, for example – we would find it virtually impossible not to apply a moral yardstick. To my mind, *The Sphinx* is decadent; it does not shield me from the sordid perils of actual existence; it exposes me to the very real perils of non-existence, and by doing this it falls short, as it inevitably will, of the ideal of absolute uselessness and begins to operate in spheres outside the poem itself.

It seems clear that literature must be functional, if only minimally. It cannot be a graven image, a bejewelled idol enshrined within the temple of aesthetics, eternally, inscrutably, looking inwards on its own perfect uselessness. It must exist outside itself, and its terms of reference, if it is to have any profound and enduring interest for us, must be macrocosmic.

It follows that literature cannot be at all confined in its application. That it should be – that some subjects make for 'suitable' or 'good' literary treatment whilst others make for 'unsuitable' or 'bad' treatment – has ever been a standpoint of conservative criticism; but the attitude is not so marked today and we may now say that the whole world is there for the writer to use: everything that bears the imprint of man's activities is potential material. Politics, sociology, economics, ethics, religion, history, biology – these segments of life have their abstract disciplines; some lay claim to being sciences; but as parts of the influences and events which form the kaleidoscope of individual and corporate life, they fall within the compass of literature.

However, if we try to refine on the relationship between literature and other disciplines the matter becomes tricky. It is possible to over-refine, and so it is better to leave things where T. S. Eliot does when he says:

. . . poetry certainly has something to do with morals, and with religion, and even with politics perhaps, though we cannot say what.[1]

No, we cannot say what, not with any degree of confidence, at any rate; which does not mean that from the time of Plato down to the present many critics have not given the impression of being infallibly able to say what.

To Plato himself literature was literature only if it had a distinctly socio-political bias, a view, admittedly sketchy, that has been rewarded with the censure it deserves. But Platonic poetics dies hard and the twentieth century has produced broadly similar literary ideologies in which political doctrine turns literature into a travesty of itself, into propaganda. 'Every writer,' George Orwell wrote, 'especially every novelist, *has* a "message", whether he admits it or not, and the minutest details of his work are influenced by it. All art is propaganda.'[2]

'All art is propaganda.' We are approaching the problem from the opposite direction now; we have gone over to the other extreme, in which the quality of art would appear to be directly related to its expressly didactic intent, to its having everything to do with morals, religion, politics, and the rest; its measure of excellence would be in proportion to its ability to move us to become good patriots, or good Catholics, or good Protestants, or good anything the author, or his bosses, desires. Less ambitiously, but no less didactically, a writer may wish to do away with the slums, or the dole, or certain marriage laws, or – for that matter – the entire institution of marriage.

It seems to me that there are different levels of didacticism, one level being what we may call 'lower' or 'interested' didacticism. At this level the 'message' may well be enunciated, and invariably is enunciated in the name of the Good; but apart from the fact that the Good may well be, and often is, perverted to serve selfish ends, its Goodness is highly transient, a matter of significance for a decade or two, for a generation or two, and then fated to petrify. Didacticism involves ideas, and most

[1] Preface to the 1928 edition of *The Sacred Wood*, London, Methuen, 1948, p. x.
[2] 'Charles Dickens', *Critical Essays*, London, Secker and Warburg, 1951, p. 45.

social, or political, and even religious, ideas tend to lose their relevance. And continuing relevance is surely a criterion of literary art.

But we cannot throw all didacticism on to the scrap heap. Earlier on I mentioned the necessity of conviction in one's approach to literature; a writer's own conviction is no less necessary. Without it his work would be insipid, purposeless, devoid of that energy and urgency that is a hallmark of great literature. Conviction implies adherence, possibly as an article of what we may call faith, to certain ideas; more than this, conviction implies the writer's desire, not to convert his readers, but to open their eyes to hitherto unseen or inadequately understood possibilities of human relationships. Didacticism seems to me to be an inescapable attribute of great literature.

A didacticism that transcends topicality, a 'higher' or 'disinterested' didacticism, which adheres to seemingly immutable ideas. George Boas has remarked:

> ... the ideas in poetry are often stale and often false and no one older than sixteen would find it worth his while to read poetry merely for what it says.[1]

This is simply not true. There are poems, and they are great ones, which get by without any real profundity of idea, but there are not many such, and some of our greatest masterpieces, such as Shakespeare's later plays, owe their continuing vitality in substantial part to their intellectual content. 'No man', Coleridge wrote, and who today but a starry-eyed romantic would disagree? – 'No man was ever yet a great poet, without being at the same time a profound philosopher.'[2]

Now an invariable of great literature lies within a framework of ideas we may call humanistic. Literature is frankly anthropocentric in its view. Its focus is on man; and man's environment, both of the natural and supernatural worlds, is important only to the extent it intensifies this focus.

Humanism has its origin in the natural law, and it finds its readiest expression in the seven cardinal virtues. That is to say, it is pagan as

[1] *Philosophy of Poetry.* Quoted in Wellek and Warren's *Theory of Literature*, Harmondsworth, Penguin, 1964, p. 110.
[2] *Biographia Literaria*, London, Dent (Everyman), 1906, p. 156.

much as Christian. These virtues are the moral positives which organized societies in the West, partly since the time of the Greeks and especially since the Renaissance, have thought it right and proper to extol: they are necessarily the verities which literature must acknowledge; they are the very stuff of the 'higher didacticism', the bridge of intelligibility between writer and reader.

What are these verities? We all know them and they find frequent iteration in these pages. I repeat them here because it seems apposite to do so, in the words not of Shaw but of two other thinkers. To Bronowski and Mazlish the essence of the humanistic verities are, first,

> . . . the emphasis on the development of the human personality. The individual is prized for himself. His creative powers are seen as the core of his being. The unfettered development of individual personality is praised as the ideal, from the Renaissance artists, through the Elizabethans, and through Locke and Voltaire and Rousseau. . . .
>
> The second of the two great formative ideas is the idea of freedom. We see in fact that human fulfilment is unattainable without freedom, so that these two main ideas are linked together. . . .
>
> Yet . . . freedom is a supple and elusive idea, whose advocates can at times delude themselves that obedience to tyranny is a form of freedom. . . . Philosophically, there is indeed no unlimited freedom. But we have seen that there is one freedom which can be defined without fear of contradiction, and which can therefore be an end in itself. This is freedom of thought and speech: the right to dissent.[1]

These remarks are here being applied to the tradition of ideas in general; they can of course be applied to the tradition of ideas in literature.

I have studiously avoided bringing Shaw into the present discussion and now I wonder if there is any need to bring him in at all. In spite of his many sillinesses, particularly in regard to his political opinions, his general philosophy and his didactic drama are so conspicuously in accord with this tradition, that one imagines it to be obvious to

[1] J. Bronowski and Bruce Mazlish, *The Western Intellectual Tradition*, Harmondsworth, Penguin, 1964. See pp. 555–8.

everyone. Yet people fail to see it. They say, speaking of Shaw as a 'lower didactic': 'He always intrudes on his dramas and he always wins the debate.'[1] This does happen now and again, admittedly; it happens in *Back to Methuselah*, which is consequently one of his weakest dramatic works. But Shaw the Socialist, Shaw the moral revolutionist, Shaw – in brief – of platform, pulpit, and preface, is consistently left in the lurch by Shaw the artist. Shaw the artist, in point of fact, is scrupulously impartial, almost over-scrupulous at times, and the 'Shavian' characters regularly give a comparatively poor account of themselves whilst the 'anti-Shavian' ones are the strong, positive people. In point of further fact, there is very little outright 'winning' in the plays. They are concerned to depict through the confrontation of opposed attitudes and ideas the complexities of normally ill-considered or half-understood situations and to progress to a conclusion by means of the Hegelian dialectic. Thesis . . . antithesis . . . synthesis does not postulate the crushing victory of one set of ideas over another, as though the denouement were a melodrama in the intellectual mode, but moves to a resolution in which the idealistic irreconcilables reveal the imperatives of the 'higher didacticism'.

*   *   *

Another aspect of the matter must engage our attention now, and we shall again have to put Shaw on one side for a while.

Literature has its own mode of existence, not, as I have been suggesting, *for* itself, but certainly *in* itself. Failure to admit this can be seen as the fault of all overt didacticism trying to win the accolade of art. It is, for example, the fault of Matthew Arnold's theory of poetry and – since Arnold's influence has extended into the twentieth century – of a good deal of modern criticism. By assuming the oracle and foreseeing the day when poetry would replace philosophy and religion, Arnold failed to see the fact before his eyes – that literature is literature, philosophy is philosophy, and religion is religion.

Literature is literature by its being, as someone has put it, the concrete universal – a helpful phrase, if an oversimplification of the problem.

[1] See, for example, Bentley, *Bernard Shaw*, p. xvii.

The universals arise in part from the ideas I have been discussing. Concreteness arises from the representation of sensuous and emotional man. But literature – really great literature – is not merely the interplay of bodied ideas, the coldly mechanistic clash of particularized abstractions, which this dichotomy of concrete and universal might imply. Literature reveals no dichotomy: it acknowledges only the wholeness of experience and is characterized by – and gains its excitement from – the ironies, the paradoxes, the contradictions, which attest to this wholeness and confound the rationalist. Life is much more than mind can make it. And literature, which has its justification only in the fidelity with which it images and interprets all life, must image and interpret those experiences – sensuous, emotional, spiritual – which are inexpressible by formulae but are unquestionably part of our being. Arnold applauds Wordsworth for describing literature as 'the breath and finer spirit of all knowledge'.[1] How well placed the applause; for it is only through the study of literature that we can arrive at some knowledge, no matter how fleeting, of the subtle ramifications of life – of the triple unity of things as realized by what Flaubert has called the 'triple thinkers'. It is literature that has that ability in itself to body forth and illuminate, so that we may really know, the restless, urgent reality of the passions, the conflicts, the fears, the ideals, which divide or unite humanity.

Immediacy – this word explains the fascination and excitement of literature; it also hints at one of its vital paradoxes, for the dazzling immediacy of such a line as

Keep up your bright swords, for the dew will rust them

cannot be limited to its function in the passage, but reaches out in an ever-widening context, until the sonorous command, evocative at once of the bright sparkle of martial valour and of the desire for amity between foes, is seen to be universally significant.

It is the vivid immediacy of the poetic image which shows us the essential paltriness of homiletic or tendentious writing. If we admit a form of didacticism, it can be admitted only by inference; the 'message' (to attach a crude label to it) of hope, or the kinship of man, or

[1] Ibid.

whatever it might be, and however admirable it may be, is latent in the plot, never as a pat moral answer, for only a fool knows the pat moral answer, but as an integrated part of a conflict which exhibits the difficulty, if not impossibility, of pronouncing final judgement on human affairs.

The word 'conflict' brings us to the next point. It seems to me that the slightest-seeming poem as much as the most towering tragedy achieves its inner harmony by a balance of opposed tendencies. The metaphysical 'reality' of a finished work may be said to be in motionlessness and silence, yet a 'reality' such as this can only be achieved through the resolution of conflict. We, while reading a poem or a novel or a play, are made aware, first, of this conflict, this tension between unresolved elements, until by the consummation of the particular work, we experience a release (perhaps like the Aristotelian *catharsis*), which in turn brings us to the feeling of having perceived horizons hitherto undreamt of – horizons which may, in Wordsworth's phrase, enable us to realize that we are greater than we know.

So, literature is revelatory. But revelatory of what precisely I cannot say. I suggest, though, that literature is in part a revelation of its own perfection, of those purely aesthetic qualities which Wilde postulated as the only ideal in art. It seems to me, however, that literature is a revelation of very much more than this, of the soaring possibilities in man himself.

*   *   *

We may leave the matter here and return to Shaw, and ask: Is it by such terms as those of the foregoing definition that the English literary establishment has dismissed Shaw? It may think so. But it seems to me that it cannot be so by any honest application of our criteria. It seems to me that the establishment has failed to allow for a most important thing within any definition of literature – the variable of the artist's convention and personal idiom, the variable which I have tried to determine for Shaw in the present work.

We may agree that Shaw does not measure up to all the criteria mentioned above: he was not, as I have remarked, a poet of the flesh or of the visual sense; his concept of evil is suspect; the wells of his compassion are fathomable. Yet this is only to say that his drama does not have Shakespeare's range; it certainly does not say that his stature as a creative writer is negligible.

And it certainly does not – it cannot – invalidate the positive qualities of his plays – the conflicts, which flash and sparkle in a white heat of urgency, detonating words with prodigal zest and taking to themselves a vivid complexity, a crystalline density of meaning; the music of the lines, the song of the spoken word, terse and epigrammatic, yet also supple and graceful, heightening impressions with its melodies, realizing the harmony and unity of form with its resonances; and then the comedy. The comedy, no doubt, is the lasting impression.

Shaw once wrote: 'If you cannot get rid of the family skeleton, you may as well make it dance.'[1] His comedy is the dance of the skeletons. Of the family skeleton, and the political skeleton, and this skeleton and that, whisked out of musty cupboards throughout the length and breadth of the English-speaking world and set to dance the story of man's silliness before our gaze. The skeletons twist and turn, shake and gibber, and yet there is nothing macabre, nothing ghastly, in their dance. True enough, their grinning jaws and gaping sockets are full of tragic awareness. But over and above this, these rattling bones reveal to us that in the midst of death we are in life. These symbols of man's absurdity, lifting their ridiculous shanks for yet another solemn minuet, inspire a response of life, the *catharsis* of laughter. They may, in far distant time, be laughed off the face of the earth and Shaw's drama will have done its work. For the present the dance goes on and we are still laughing.

[1] Preface to *Immaturity*, p. xxiv.

SELECT BIBLIOGRAPHY

A

BERNARD SHAW

When bibliographical details are not supplied, it should be assumed that the work is available in the Standard Edition of the works of Shaw, London, Constable, 1931 – continuing to 1950.

I. *NOVELS*

1879–1883 *Immaturity*
The Irrational Knot
Love Among the Artists
Cashel Byron's Profession
The Unsocial Socialist

II. *THE COMPLETE PLAYS*

Chronology and numerical sequence according to C. B. Purdom, *A Guide to the Plays of Bernard Shaw*. London, Methuen, 1963.

1. 1885–1892 *Widowers' Houses; A Play*
2. 1893 *The Philanderer; A Topical Comedy*
3. 1893 *Mrs Warren's Profession; A Play*
4. 1894 *Arms and the Man; An Anti-Romantic Comedy*
5. 1894 *Candida; A Mystery*
6. 1895 *The Man of Destiny; A Fictitious Paragraph of History*
7. 1895–1897 *You Never Can Tell: A Comedy*
8. 1896–1897 *The Devil's Disciple; A Melodrama*
9. 1898 *Caesar and Cleopatra; A History*
10. 1899 *Captain Brassbound's Conversion; An Adventure*

11. 1901 *The Admirable Bashville: or Constancy Un-rewarded*

12. 1901–1903 *Man and Superman; A Comedy and a Philosophy*

13. 1904 *John Bull's Other Island*

14. 1904 *How He Lied to Her Husband*

15. 1905 *Major Barbara*

16. 1905 *Passion, Poison and Petrification: or The Fatal Gazogene*

17. 1906 *The Doctor's Dilemma; A Tragedy*

18. 1907 *The Interlude at the Playhouse* (Not included in the Standard Edition. Reprinted in *The Shaw Review*, III, 2 May 1960 (New York), as 'Bernard Shaw and the Interlude at the Playhouse' by Myron Matlaw.)

19. 1908 *Getting Married; A Disquisitory Play*

20. 1909 *Press Cuttings; A Topical Sketch*

21. 1909 *The Shewing-Up of Blanco Posnet; A Sermon in Crude Melodrama*

22. 1909 *The Fascinating Foundling; A Disgrace to the Author*

23. 1909 *The Glimpse of Reality; A Tragedietta*

24. 1910 *Misalliance*

25. 1910 *The Dark Lady of the Sonnets*

26. 1911 *Fanny's First Play; An Easy Play for a Little Theatre*

27. 1911–1912 *Androcles and the Lion; A Fable Play*

28. 1912 *Overruled*

29. 1912 *Pygmalion; A Romance in Five Acts*

30. 1913 *Great Catherine: Whom Glory Still Adores*

31. 1914 *The Music Cure; A Piece of Utter Nonsense*

32. 1915 *O'Flaherty, V. C.; A Recruiting Pamphlet*

33. 1916 *Augustus does his Bit; A True-to-Life Farce*

34. 1916 *The Inca of Perusalem; An Almost Historical Comedietta*

35. 1917 *Annajanska: The Bolshevik Empress; A Revolutionary Romancelet*

36.	1913–1916	*Heartbreak House; A Fantasia in the Russian Manner on English Themes*
37.	1918–1921	*Back to Methuselah; A Metabiological Pentateuch*
38.	Circa 1920	*Jitta's Atonement*
39.	1923	*Saint Joan; A Chronicle Play in Six Scenes and an Epilogue*
40.	1929	*The Apple Cart; A Political Extravaganza*
41.	1931	*Too True to be Good; A Political Extravaganza*
42.	1933	*Village Wooing; A Comediettina for Two Voices*
43.	1933	*On the Rocks; A Political Comedy*
44.	1934	*The Simpleton of the Unexpected Isles; A Vision of Judgement*
45.	1933	*The Six of Calais; A Medieval War Story*
46.	1935–1936	*The Millionairess; A Comedy in Four Acts*
47.	1937	*Cymbeline Re-finished*
48.	1938	*Geneva; Another Political Extravaganza*
49.	1939	*In Good King Charles's Golden Days; A True History that Never Happened*
50.	1947	*Buoyant Billions; A Comedy of No Manners*
51.	1949	*Shakes versus Shav; A Puppet Play*
52.	1948	*Farfetched Fables*
53.	1950	*Why She Would Not; A Comedietta* (Unfinished. Not in print. A typewritten version in the British Museum.)

III. *LETTERS*

BAX, Clifford, ed. *Florence Farr, Bernard Shaw, W. B. Yeats: Letters.* London, Home and Van Thal, 1946.

DENT, Alan, ed. *Bernard Shaw and Mrs Patrick Campbell: Their Correspondence.* London, Gollancz, 1852.

LAURENCE, Dan H., ed. *Bernard Shaw: Collected Letters, 1874–1897.* London, Max Reinhardt, 1965.

PURDOM, C. B., ed. *Bernard Shaw's Letter to Granville Barker.* London, Phoenix House, 1956.

ST. JOHN, Christopher, ed. *Ellen Terry and Bernard Shaw: A Correspondence.* London, Reinhardt and Evans, 1949.

WEST, E. J., ed. *Advice to a Young Critic and Other Letters.* New York, Crown, 1955.

IV. *OTHER NOTABLE WORKS*

The following list represents essays, prefaces, speeches, and articles which I have found most instructive and interesting. The list is by no means definitive: such a list would have to include hundreds of items; such a list, in fact, has yet to be drawn up.

My sources have been largely, although not entirely, the Standard Edition of the works of Shaw, and three posthumous collections of his speeches and essays. These three are:

LAURENCE, Dan H., ed. *Platform and Pulpit: Bernard Shaw.* London, Rupert Hart-Davis, 1962.

SMITH, William Sylvester, ed. *The Religious Speeches of Bernard Shaw.* Pennsylvania, Pennsylvania State University Press, 1963.

WEST, E. J., ed. *Shaw on Theatre.* London, MacGibbon and Kee, 1958.

There are other collections, but I found these three the most useful.

1888	'The Transition to Social Democracy'. (*Essays in Fabian Socialism.* Standard Edition.)
1889	'The Economic Basis of Socialism'. (*Essays in Fabian Socialism.* Standard Edition.)
1888–1890	Music Criticism for *The Star*, reprinted as *London Music in 1888–89 as Heard by Corno di Bassetto* (Standard Edition.)
1890–1894	Music Criticism for *The World*, reprinted as *Music in London 1890–94*; 3 vols. (Standard Edition.)
1891	'The Quintessence of Ibsenism'. (*Major Critical Essays.* Standard Edition.)
1891	'The Impossibilities of Anarchism'. (*Essays in Fabian Socialism.* Standard Edition.)

1894	'Socialism and Superior Brains'. (*Essays in Fabian Socialism.* Standard Edition.)
1894	'A Dramatic Realist to his Critics'. (E. J. West: *Shaw on Theatre.*)
1895	'The Problem Play – A Symposium: Should social problems be freely dealt with in the Drama?' (E. J. West: *Shaw on Theatre.*)
1895	'The Sanity of Art'. (*Major Critical Essays.* Standard Edition.)
1895–1896	Drama criticism for *The Saturday Review*, reprinted as *Our Theatres in the Nineties*; 3 vols. (Standard Edition.)
1896	*On Going to Church.* (Shavian Tract No. 5, The Shaw Society, London, 1957.)
1896	'Socialism for Millionaires'. (*Essays in Fabian Socialism.* Standard Edition.)
1897	*The Illusions of Socialism.* (Shavian Tract No. 4, The Shaw Society, London, 1956.)
1898	'The Perfect Wagnerite'. (*Major Critical Essays.* Standard Edition.)
1900	'The Dynamitards of Science'. (Dan H. Laurence: *Platform and Pulpit.*)
1901	'Who I am, and what I think'. (*Sixteen Self-Sketches.* Standard Edition.)
1904	'The Commonsense of Municipal Trading'. (*Essays in Fabian Socialism.* Standard Edition.)
1906	'The Religion of the British Empire'. (Warren Sylvester Smith: *The Religious Speeches of Bernard Shaw.*)
1907	'The Court Theatre'. (Dan H. Laurence: *Platform and Pulpit.*)
1909	Preface to *Three Plays by Brieux*. (*The Complete Prefaces of Bernard Shaw.* London, Hamlyn, 1965.)
1909	'Chesterton on Shaw'. (*Pen Portraits and Reviews.* Standard Edition.)

1911	'The Religion of the Future'. (Warren Sylvester Smith: *The Religious Speeches of Bernard Shaw*.)
1912	'Modern Religion I'. (Warren Sylvester Smith: *The Religious Speeches of Bernard Shaw*.)
1913	*The Case for Equality*. (Shavian Tract No. 6, The Shaw Society, London, 1958.)
1914	Preface to *Killing for Sport*. (*The Complete Prefaces of Bernard Shaw*. London, Hamlyn, 1965.)
1914–1915	'Commonsense about the War'. (*What I Really Wrote about the War*. Standard Edition.)
1917–1918	'What is to be Done with the Doctors?' (*Doctors' Delusions, Crude Criminology, Sham Education*, Standard Edition.)
1919	'Ruskin's Politics'. (Dan H. Laurence: *Platform and Pulpit*.)
1919	'Modern Religion'. (Warren Sylvester Smith: *The Religious Speeches of Bernard Shaw;* also Dan H. Laurence: *Platform and Pulpit*.)
1921	'Tolstoy: Tragedian or Comedian?' (*Pen Portraits and Reviews*. Standard Edition.)
1921–1922	'Imprisonment'. The preface to Sidney and Beatrice Webb's *Prisons Under Local Government*. (*Doctors' Delusions, Crude Criminology, Sham Education*. Standard Edition.)
1927	'How William Archer Impressed Bernard Shaw'. (*Pen Portraits and Reviews*. Standard Edition.)
1928	*The Intelligent Woman's Guide to Socialism and Capitalism*. (Standard Edition.)
1929	*Socialism: Principles and Outlook*. (Shavian Tract No. 4, The Shaw Society, London, 1956.)
1929	'The Need for Expert Opinion in Sexual Reform'. (Dan H. Laurence: *Platform and Pulpit*.)
1932	'In Praise of Guy Fawkes'. (Dan H. Laurence: *Platform and Pulpit*.)

1932	'The Adventures of the Black Girl in Her Search for God'. (*The Black Girl and Her Search for God and Some Lesser Tales.* Standard Edition.)
1935	Preface to *London Music in 1888–89.* (Standard Edition.)
1944	*Everybody's Political What's What?* (Standard Edition.)
1950	'The Play of Ideas'. (*The New Statesman and Nation*, 39, 6 May 1950; also E. J. West: *Shaw on Theatre.*)

In addition to the foregoing there are the prefaces to the novels and plays, all printed in the Standard Edition. To my mind, the most outstanding (and sometimes the most contentious) of these prefaces are:

1898	'Mainly about Myself'. (The preface to *Plays Unpleasant.*)
1898	Preface to *Plays Pleasant.*
1900	Preface to *Three Plays for Puritans.*
1902	Preface to *Mrs Warren's Profession.*
1903	'Epistle Dedicatory: to Arthur Bingham Walkley'. (The preface to *Man and Superman.*)
1906	Preface to *Major Barbara.*
1910	Preface to *The Shewing-up of Blanco Posnet.*
1910	'Parents and Children'. (The preface to *Misalliance.*)
1911	'Preface on Doctors'. (The preface to *The Doctor's Dilemma.*)
1915	'Preface on the Prospects of Christianity'. (The preface to *Androcles and the Lion.*)
1921	'Preface: the Infidel Half Century'. (The preface to *Back to Methuselah.*)
1921	Preface to *Immaturity.*
1924	Preface to *Saint Joan.*
1930	Preface to *The Apple Cart.*
1933	Preface to *On the Rocks.*

R

1935   'Preface on Bosses.' (The preface to *The Millionairess.*)

B

CONCERNING BERNARD SHAW

The literature on Shaw is considerable and is being added to daily. My lists represent only a fraction of the body of critical and biographical comment available.

I. *BOOKS*

BENTLEY, Eric. *Bernard Shaw: A Reconsideration*. New York, New Directions, 1947.

BROWN, Ivor. *Shaw in his Time*. London, Nelson, 1965.

CHESTERTON, Gilbert Keith. *George Bernard Shaw*. London, Guild Books, The Bodley Head, 1949.

DUFFIN, Henry Charles. *The Quintessence of Bernard Shaw*. London, Allen and Unwin, 1920.

ERVINE, St John. *Bernard Shaw: His Life, Work and Friends*. London, Constable, 1956.

HARRIS, Frank. *Frank Harris on Bernard Shaw: an unauthorised biography based on firsthand information with a postscript by Mr Shaw*. London, Gollancz, 1931.

HENDERSON, Archibald. *Bernard Shaw: Man of the Century*. New York, Appleton-Century-Crofts, 1956.

IRVINE, William. *The Universe of G.B.S*. New York, Whittesley House, 1949.

JOAD, C. E. M. *Shaw*. London, Gollancz, 1949.

KAYE, J. B. *Bernard Shaw and the Nineteenth-Century Tradition*. Oklahoma, University of Oklahoma Press, 1958.

MacCARTHY, Desmond. *Shaw*. London, MacGibbon and Kee, 1951.

MAYNE, Fred. *The Wit and Satire of Bernard Shaw*. London, Edward Arnold, 1967.

MEISEL, M. *Shaw and the Nineteenth-Century Theater*. London, Oxford University Press, 1963.

PATCH, Blanche. *Thirty Years with G.B.S.* London, Gollancz, 1951.

PEARSON, Hesketh. *Bernard Shaw: His Life and Personality*. London, Collins, 1942.

——————. *G. B. S.: A Postscript*. London, Collins, 1951.

PURDOM, C. B. *A Guide to the Plays of Bernard Shaw*. London, Methuen, 1963.

STRAUSS, E. *Bernard Shaw: Art and Socialism*. London, Gollancz, 1942.

WARD, A. C. *Bernard Shaw*. London, Longmans, Green, 1951.

WATSON, Barbara Bellow. *A Shavian Guide to the Intelligent Woman*. London, Chatto and Windus, 1964.

WEINTRAUB, Stanley. *Private Shaw and Public Shaw*. London, Jonathan Cape, 1963.

WINSTEN, S. *Days with Bernard Shaw*. London, Hutchinson, n.d.

II. *ARTICLES AND ESSAYS*

As far as I can find out, there are three collections of essays on Shaw. These are:

KAUFMANN, R. J. ed. *G. B. Shaw: A Collection of Critical Essays*. Englewood Cliffs, New Jersey, Prentice-Hall, 1965.

KRONENBERGER, Louis, ed. *George Bernard Shaw: A Critical Survey*. Cleveland and New York, The World, 1953.

WINSTEN, S., ed. *G.B.S. 90: Aspects of Bernard Shaw's Life and Work*. London, Hutchinson, 1946.

The following select list is derived largely from these books:

AUDEN, Wystan Hugh. 'The Fabian Figaro', in *George Bernard Shaw: A Critical Survey*, ed. L. Kronenberger.

BARBER, George S. 'Shaw's Contribution to Music Criticism', in *Publications of the Modern Language Association*, Vol. LXXII, 1957.

BELGION, Montgomery. 'According to Mr Bernard Shaw', in *Our Present Philosophy of Life*. London, Faber, 1929.

BARNES, T. R. 'Shaw and the London Theatre', in *The Modern*

Age, Vol. 7; *The Pelican Guide to English Literature*. Harmondsworth, Penguin Books, 1961.

BARZUN, Jacques. 'Bernard Shaw in Twilight', in *George Bernard Shaw: A Critical Survey*, ed. L. Kronenberger.

——————. 'Shaw and Rousseau: No Paradox', *The Shaw Bulletin* (now *The Shaw Review*), New York, Vol. I, 8 May, 1955.

BENTLEY, Eric. 'The Making of a Dramatist (1892–1903)', in *G. B. Shaw: A Collection of Critical Essays* ed. R. J. Kaufmann.

——————. 'Bernard Shaw', in *The Playwright as Thinker: A Study of Drama in Modern Times*. New York, Meridian Books, 1957.

BERNAL, J. D. 'Shaw the Scientist', in *G.B.S.90: Aspects of Bernard Shaw's Life and Work*, ed. S. Winsten.

BRECHT, Bertold. 'Ovation for Shaw' in *G. B. Shaw: A Collection of Critical Essays*, ed. R. J. Kaufmann.

COUCHMAN, Gordon W. 'Here was a Caesar: Shaw's Comedy Today', in *Publications of the Modern Language Association*, Vol. LXXII, 1957.

DEMAREY, John G. 'Bernard Shaw and C. E. M. Joad: The Adventures of Two Puritans in their Search for God', in *Publications of the Modern Language Association*, Vol. LXXVIII, 1963.

DOBB, Maurice. 'Bernard Shaw and Economics', in *G.B.S.90: Aspects of Bernard Shaw's Life and Work*, ed. S. Winsten.

DUERKSON, Roland A. 'Shelley and Shaw', in *Publications of the Modern Language Association*, Vol. LXXVIII, 1963.

DUFFIN, Henry Charles. *Creative Evolution*. Shavian Tract No. 1, The Shaw Society, London, 1950.

FISKE, Irving. 'Bernard Shaw and William Blake', in *G. B. Shaw: A Collection of Critical Essays*, ed. R. J. Kaufmann; also available as *Bernard Shaw's Debt to William Blake*, Shavina Tract No. 2, The Shaw Society, London, 1951.

GASSNER, John. 'Shaw on Ibsen and the Drama of Ideas', in *Ideas in the Drama: Papers from the English Institute*, ed. John Gassner. New York, Columbia University Press, 1965.

GEDULD, H. M. 'Bernard Shaw and Adolf Hitler'. *The Shaw Review*, New York, Vol. IV, 1 January 1961.

HENN, T. R. 'The Shavian Machine', in *G. B. Shaw: A Collection of Critical Essays*, ed. R. J. Kaufmann.

HOWE, P. P. 'Shaw's Economics', in *George Bernard Shaw: A Critical Survey*, ed. L. Kronenberger.

HUIZINGA, Johan. 'Bernard Shaw's Saint', in *Men and Ideas: History, the Middle Ages, the Renaissance*. London, Eyre and Spottiswoode, 1960.

HUNEKER, James. 'The Quintessence of Shaw', in *George Bernard Shaw: A Critical Survey*, ed. L. Kronenberger.

INGE, W. R. 'Shaw as a Theologian', in *G.B.S.90: Aspects of Bernard Shaw's Life and Work*, ed. S. Winsten.

JONES, Henry Arthur. 'Bernard Shaw as a Thinker', *The English Review*. London, Vols. 36–37, Jan.–June and July–Dec., 1923.

KNIGHT, G. Wilson. 'Shaw's Integral Theatre', in *G. B. Shaw: A Collection of Critical Essays*, ed. R. J. Kaufmann.

LEAVIS, F. R. 'Shaw against Lawrence', *The Spectator*, London, No. 6614, 1 April 1955.

'LIFE and Letters', in *The Times Literary Supplement*, London, 16 June 1966.

McCARTHY, Mary. 'Shaw and Chekhov', in *Mary McCarthy's Theatre Chronicles, 1937–1962*, New York, Noonday, 1963.

————————. 'Shaw off Broadway', in *Mary McCarthy's Theatre Chronicles, 1937–1962*, New York, Noonday, 1963.

McDOWELL, F. P. W. 'Technique, Symbol and Theme in Heartbreak House', in *Publications of the Modern Language Association*, Vol. LXVIII, 1953.

MANN, Thomas. '"He was mankind's friend"', in *George Bernard Shaw: A Critical Survey*, ed. L. Kronenberger.

MARTZ, Louis L. 'The Saint as Tragic Hero', in *G. B. Shaw: A Collection of Critical Essays*, ed. R. J. Kaufmann.

MORGAN, Margery M. 'Back to Methuselah: The Poet and the City', in *G. B. Shaw: A Collection of Critical Essays*, ed. R. J. Kaufmann.

NETHERCOT, Arthur H. 'Bernard Shaw, Philosopher', in *Publications of the Modern Language Association*, Vol. LXIX, 1954.

O'CASEY, Sean. 'A Whisper about Bernard Shaw', in *The Green Crow*, New York, Braziller, 1956.

——————. 'Bernard Shaw: An Appreciation of a Fighting Idealist', in *The Green Crow*, New York, Braziller, 1956.

O'DONNELL, Norbert F. 'Shaw, Bunyan, and Puritanism', in *Publications of the Modern Language Association*, Vol. LXXII, 1957.

PALMER, John. 'George Bernard Shaw: Harlequin or Patriot?', in *George Bernard Shaw: A Critical Survey*, ed. L. Kronenberger.

ROPPEN, Georg. *Evolution and Poetic Belief: A Study in Some Victorian and Modern Writers*. Oslo, Oslo University Press, 1956.

SCOTT, Dixon. 'The Innocence of Bernard Shaw', in *George Bernard Shaw: A Critical Survey*, ed. L. Kronenberger.

STEWART, J. I. M. 'Shaw', in *Eight Modern Writers*; *The Oxford History of English Literature*, ed. F. P. Wilson and Bonamy Dobrée, Vol. XII. London, Oxford University Press, 1963.

USSHER, Arland. 'Bernard Shaw: Emperor and Clown', in *Three Great Irishmen: Shaw, Yeats, Joyce*. London, Gollancz, 1952.

WILSON, Edmund. 'Bernard Shaw at Eighty', in *The Triple Thinkers*. London, Lehmann, 1952; also in *George Bernard Shaw: A Critical Survey*, ed. L. Kronenberger.

WILLIAM, Raymond. 'Bernard Shaw', in *Drama from Ibsen to Eliot*. Harmondsworth, Penguin Books, 1964.

*　　　*　　　*

In addition, there are several journals devoted exclusively to Shaw. Among these are:

THE SHAW REVIEW, Pennsylvania State University, U.S.A.

THE SHAVIAN, The Journal of the Shaw Society, London.

III. *OTHER WORKS*

The following titles represent works with a general or an occasional bearing on Shaw and Shavianism.

ARCHER, William. *The Old Drama and the New*. London, Heinemann, 1923.

BALL, Sidney. 'The Moral Aspects of Socialism', in *Socialism and Individualism*; Fabian Socialist Series, No. 3. London, Fifield, 1909.

BEER, M. *A History of British Socialism*, Vol. 2. London, Allen and Unwin, 1953.

BEERBOHM, Max. *Around Theatres*. London, Rupert Hart-Davis, 1953.

DUNBAR, Janet. *Mrs G.B.S.: A Biographical Portrait of Charlotte Shaw*. London, Harrap, 1963.

JACKSON, Holbrook. *The Eighteen Nineties*. Harmondsworth, Penguin Books, 1939.

PEASE, E. R. *The History of the Fabian Society*. London, Cass, 1963.

ROWELL, George. *The Victorian Theatre: A Survey*. London, Oxford University Press, 1956.

——————. *Introduction to Nineteenth Century Plays*. World Classics. London, Oxford University Press, 1953.

STYAN, J. L. *The Elements of Drama*. Cambridge, Cambridge University Press, 1960.

TERRY, Ellen. *The Story of My Life*. London, Hutchinson, 1908.

WEBB, Sidney. 'The Difficulties of Individualism', in *Socialism;* Fabian Socialist Series, No. 3, London, Fifield, 1909.

INDEX

Works by Shaw in small capitals; works by other authors in italics.

Duncan Macleod.

BERNARD SHAW

Playwright and Preacher